HD
8085
.P53
S65
1990

By the same author:

(with Richard Wojtowicz) *Blacks Who Stole Themselves: Advertisements for Runaways in the Pennsylvania Gazette, 1728–1790*. Philadelphia: University of Pennsylvania Press, 1989.

The "Lower Sort"

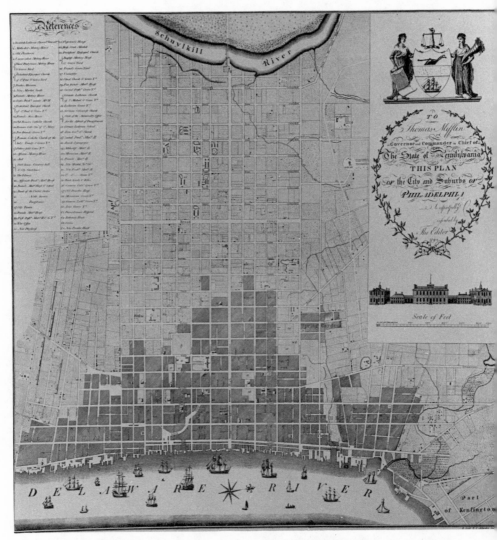

"Plan of the City and Suburbs of Philadelphia," 1794. The shaded area indicates densely settled neighborhoods. Adjacent to the Delaware River at the city's southern end is the suburb of Southwark, and the Northern Liberties parallel the river to the north. Engraving by R. Scot and S. Allardice, 1794. Photograph courtesy of Robert Blair St. George and the Historical Society of Pennsylvania.

The "Lower Sort"

PHILADELPHIA'S LABORING
PEOPLE, 1750–1800

BILLY G. SMITH

Cornell University Press

ITHACA AND LONDON

First published 1990 by Cornell University Press.

International Standard Book Number 0-8014-2242-6
Library of Congress Catalog Card Number 89-46174
Printed in the United States of America
Librarians: Library of Congress cataloging information
appears on the last page of the book.

⊛The paper used in this publication meets the minimum requirements of the American National Standard for Permanence of Paper for Printed Library Materials Z39.48—1984.

For Michelle

Contents

Illustrations and Tables

TABLES

Preface

IN 1767 A RESIDENT of Philadelphia, describing the plight of a soldier, remarked that "no Observation is more common, and at the same time more true, than That one half of the world are ignorant [of] how the other half lives."[1] This book examines how the other half in America's largest port city lived during the second five decades of the eighteenth century. It belongs among the work of many historians who, especially during the past two decades, have shifted their focus in order to rewrite American history "from the bottom up."

For a great many years scholars have depended primarily on the records of elite individuals and groups to interpret the American past. The result, as W. E. B. Dubois noted nearly forty years ago, is that "we have the record of kings and gentlemen ad nauseum and in stupid detail; but of the common run of human beings, and particularly of the half or wholly submerged working group, the world has saved all too little of authentic record and tried to forget or ignore even the little saved."[2] Of course, not all scholars ignore common people, nor is the history of presidents and elites without considerable merit. But at their worst, historians sometimes have acted, to paraphrase Leo Tolstoy, like deaf people, answering questions about the rich and famous which nobody ever posed.

The recent outpouring of studies about the "inarticulate" (people who left few traces in historical records) has begun to redress the problem. Common people are no less worthy of historical research—and at least are equally

---

1. "Effects," *Pennsylvania Gazette* (Philadelphia), Feb. 12, 1767.
2. "Introduction," in Herbert Aptheker, ed., *A Documentary History of the Negro People in the United States* (New York, 1951), i.

deserving if only because of sheer number—than groups who wielded greater political, social, or economic power. In that sense alone this book, counterpoised against numerous investigations of Philadelphia's lawyers, merchants, and politicians, contributes to a more balanced historical view of the city and its people.

But this book represents more than a quest for simple equality in rewriting the past. The story of urban laboring people is intrinsically valuable not only because of the part they played in the human drama but also because they performed a major role on the historical stage. They helped shape the evolution of their society by acquiescing (or not acquiescing), resisting (or not resisting), and fighting (or not fighting) in the struggle to control their destinies. Laboring Philadelphians may not have been the "engineers" of economic development, as Thomas M. Doerflinger has dubbed the city's merchants, but they produced and transported goods and performed services without which the economy could not have functioned and the tragicomedy could not have continued. Poor men and women were not merely actors directed by political and economic leaders: they engaged in a dynamic tension with those above them, and they participated in the important events of the era. In large part, their society assumed its form from that tension and their participation.

"Anybody can make history," Oscar Wilde wrote, but "only a great man can write it."[3] Except for the sexist language, most historians might find the sentiment amusingly agreeable. However, Wilde had it wrong on at least one count: no person writes history by herself; all historians draw on scholars and friends for support. In the course of spending what sometimes seems to have been most of my adult life researching and writing this book, I have received considerable assistance, which I am pleased to acknowledge. Gary B. Nash, initially my teacher and now my friend, generously shared his ideas and research since the inception of the project. Lois Green Carr, P. M. G. Harris, and Lorena S. Walsh instructed me in the art and mystery of analyzing primary documents. Philip Morgan and several anonymous readers offered invaluable criticism of the entire manuscript. John K. Alexander, Lois Green Carr, Paul G. E. Clemens, Michaele Cohen, Constance Coiner, David E. Dauer, P. M. G. Harris, Stephen Innis, Susan E. Klepp, Michelle Maskiell, Adrienne Mayor, William Mulligan, Glenn Porter, Steven Rosswurm, Sharon Salinger, Cindy Shelton, Jean R. Soderlund, Carole Srole, Lorena S. Walsh, Marianne Wokeck, and Michael Zuckerman commented on various chapters. Richard Beeman, Richard Dunn, and Michael Hindery provided essential support at vital points in my work. I also benefited greatly from

3. Quoted in *Journal of Women's History*, 1 (1989), i.

wide-ranging discussions with numerous individuals connected with the seminars of both the Philadelphia Center for Early American Studies and the Transformation of Philadelphia Project, the latter inspired primarily by Michael Zuckerman. Susan E. Klepp and Jean R. Soderlund generously shared their research, and Robert St. George kindly provided several illustrations. Linda Stanley helped make the Historical Society of Pennsylvania an enjoyable and enormously rewarding place to work. My parents, Jack and Betty, and my brother, Jack, encouraged me throughout the project. My wife, Michelle Maskiell, to whom this book is dedicated, assisted in ways far beyond intellectual discussions. Her innumerable irreverent suggestions about what to do with this book prevented me from taking the project more seriously than any endeavor in life deserves.

Financial aid from several institutions enabled me to visit numerous archives and gave me time for writing. I thank the Eluetherian Mills–Hagley Foundation, the Philadelphia Center for Early American Studies, the American Council of Learned Societies, the American Philosophical Society, the Mellon Fellowship Program at the University of Pennsylvania, the Research/Creativity Program at Montana State University, and Montanans on a New Trac for Science. Grants from the latter program allowed me to employ a team of work-study students, including Patrick Caulfield, Peter Daniels, Debbie Kennedy, Jamie Powell, Staci DiMaggio, and Jodee Kuske, to process and computerize data.

Chapter 2 is a much recast version of "Death and Life in a Colonial Immigrant City: A Demographic Analysis of Philadelphia," *Journal of Economic History,* 37 (1977), 863–889. An earlier version of chapter 4 appeared as "The Material Lives of Laboring Philadelphians, 1750–1800," *William and Mary Quarterly,* 3d Ser., 38 (1981), 163–202.

BILLY G. SMITH

Bozeman, Montana

Abbreviations

APS	American Philosophical Society, Philadelphia
GSP	Genealogical Society of Pennsylvania, Hall of the Historical Society of Pennsylvania, Philadelphia
HSP	Historical Society of Pennsylvania, Philadelphia
JEH	*Journal of Economic History*
LC	Library of Congress, Washington, D.C.
NA	National Archives, Washington, D.C.
PCA	Philadelphia City Archives, City Hall Annex
PH	*Pennsylvania History*
PHMC	Pennsylvania Historical and Museum Commission, Harrisburg, Pennsylvania
PMHB	*Pennsylvania Magazine of History and Biography*
RW	Registrar of Wills, City Hall Annex, Philadelphia
WMQ	*William and Mary Quarterly*

The "Lower Sort"

Introduction

THE FOLLOWING CHAPTERS present a history both of Philadelphia and of its lower-class residents. Various features of the city are documented, and the urban center becomes visible through the eyes of laboring people. The demographic and economic characteristics of the "lower sort" (as they were called by their contemporaries) and the manner by which various forces constrained their lives likewise are examined. This book deals primarily, although not exclusively, with the outward structure and experiential aspects of their lives, addressing such questions as *how many* of them were born, moved, and died; *how much* they earned, saved, and spent for essentials; and *what was* the nature of their health, shelter, and families.

Some of this analysis, with its emphasis on the objective rather than the subjective reality of the lower classes, departs from other recent attempts by historians to explain the meaning of life and events as they were understood by the historical actors themselves.[1] My approach resulted, in part, from the

---

1. Among important efforts to interpret the meaning of events to urban laboring people during the eighteenth century are Alfred F. Young, "George Robert Twelves Hewes: A Boston Shoemaker and the Memory of the American Revolution," *WMQ*, 3d Ser., 38 (1981), 561–623; Steven Rosswurm, *Arms, Country, and Class: The Philadelphia Militia and "Lower Sort" during the American Revolution, 1775–1783* (New Brunswick, N.J., 1987); Sharon V. Salinger, *"To Serve Well and Faithfully": Labor and Indentured Servants in Pennsylvania, 1682–1800* (Cambridge, England, 1987); Cynthia J. Shelton, *The Mills of Manayunk: Industrialization and Social Conflict in the Philadelphia Region, 1787–1837* (Baltimore, Md., 1986); Marcus Rediker, *Between the Devil and the Deep Blue Sea: Merchant Seamen, Pirates, and the Anglo-American Maritime World, 1700–1750* (Cambridge, England, 1987); John K. Alexander, *Render Them Submissive: Responses to Poverty in Philadelphia, 1760–1800* (Amherst, Mass., 1980); William A. Williams, "Samuel Adams: Calvinist, Mercantilist, Revolutionary," *Studies on the Left*, 1 (1960), 47–57; Pauline Maier, "Coming to Terms with Samuel Adams," *American Historical Review*, 81 (1976), 12–37; Eric Foner, *Tom Paine and Revolutionary America* (New York, 1976). Jesse

nature of available sources, especially the paucity of personal papers that would reveal how the "inarticulate" interpreted reality. Moreover, agreeing with Marx and Engels that "where speculation ends—in real life—there real, positive science begins,"[2] I adopted a social scientific approach, attempting systematically to measure vital details of lower-class existence about which scholars have too often been forced to rely on inference and supposition. Wherever possible, I also drew heavily on nonstatistical, qualitative records to supplement, enhance, and corroborate the quantitative analysis and to convey the subjective reality of laboring people. The major thrust of the analysis is to establish elementary facts, based on the hardest possible data, often measured quantitatively, about the life experiences of the lower classes. Such an approach, I hope, will enable us eventually to grasp the meaning laboring people attributed to their lives and the ways in which they were able to create their own history.

Eighteenth-century urban laboring people left few personal records in the form of correspondence, diaries, or journals, but they did leave a trail that can be tracked through public and a few private documents. This book relies on such sources as church records; bills of mortality; tax and assessment rolls; censuses; city directories; wills; inventories of estate; petitions for divorce, pardons, and pensions; dockets from the hospital, almshouse, and prison; merchants' and artisans' papers; maritime records of the port; ships' crew lists; oaths of allegiance; newspaper stories and advertisements; and indenture and apprentice rolls.

In general, I assumed that, where feasible and appropriate, it was better to calculate as precisely as possible various characteristics of the lives of laboring Philadelphians than to rely primarily on scattered and sometimes contradictory impressionistic evidence. Thus I sought the types of records which could be analyzed systematically. As a result, methodological concerns occasionally assume some importance within the text. But I have attempted to avoid the format of some early quantitative historical studies that all too often shared a trait in common with pornographic magazines: the text served merely to connect the illustrations. Since most readers find this format tedious, I have relegated a great deal of the data and technical discussions to footnotes and extensive appendixes. Scholars who, like Disraeli, believe that there are lies, damn lies, and statistics, should be able to evaluate the legitimacy of the approaches and the validity of the conclusions through those sources.

Lemisch and James A. Henretta made significant contributions to this type of analysis in Lemisch, "Jack Tar in the Streets: Merchant Seamen in the Politics of Revolutionary America," *WMQ*, 3d Ser., 25 (1968), 371–407; Lemisch, "Listening to the 'Inarticulate': William Widger's Dream and the Loyalties of American Revolutionary Seamen in British Prisons," *Journal of Social History*, 4 (1971), 333–356; and Henretta, "Families and Farms: *Mentalité* in Pre-Industrial America," *WMQ*, 3d Ser., 35 (1978), 7.

2. Karl Marx and Friedrich Engels, *The German Ideology* (New York, 1963), 15.

This book does not examine extensively the political beliefs and activities of urban laboring people, in part because I believe that even during an age of revolution politics was not *the* paramount concern of the great majority of the lower sort. This is not to argue that the American Revolution and the formation of a new nation were unimportant or that the working populace did not influence the swirl of events; their political behavior and ideologies have been well documented elsewhere.[3] Instead, this book considers the ways in which the war disrupted the economy, absorbed low-income men into the army, and transformed the lives of many urban residents. It also attempts to place these events in perspective. The European conflicts of the 1790s and the Seven Years' War, for example, may have altered the immediate circumstances of laboring Philadelphians in a nearly equally significant fashion. And when compared with many nonpolitical events—such as the periodic outbreaks of smallpox or the introduction of yellow-fever-carrying mosquitoes into the city—the death, destruction, and dislocation caused by the American Revolution diminishes somewhat in importance.

The following pages document the nuances and variations in the daily lives of the lower classes but do not attempt to explain their causes with one or two organizing principles. Human life is too complex to be so neatly arranged. Instead, incidents such as wars, epidemics, poor harvests, and bad weather combined with such general phenomena as the shifting trans-Atlantic migratory stream, nascent industrialization in England, and the

3. Gary B. Nash, *The Urban Crucible: Social Change, Political Consciousness, and the Origins of the American Revolution* (Cambridge, Mass., 1979); Richard Ryerson, *The Revolution Is Now Begun: The Radical Committees of Philadelphia, 1765–1776* (Philadelphia, 1978); Edward Countryman, "Consolidating Power in Revolutionary America: The Case of New York, 1775–1783," *Journal of Interdisciplinary History*, 6 (1976), 645–678; Countryman, "The Problem of the Early American Crowd," *Journal of American Studies*, 7 (1973), 77–90; John K. Alexander, "The Fort Wilson Incident of 1779: A Case Study of the Revolutionary Crowd," *WMQ*, 3d Ser., 31 (1974), 589–612; Dirk Hoerder, *Crowd Action in Revolutionary Massachusetts, 1765–1780* (New York, 1977); Pauline Maier, "Popular Uprisings and Civil Authority in Eighteenth Century America," *WMQ*, 3d Ser., 27 (1970), 3–35; Maier, "The Charleston Mob and the Evolution of Popular Politics in Revolutionary South Carolina, 1765–1784," *Perspectives in American History*, 4 (1970), 173–196; Staughton Lynd, "The Mechanics in New York Politics, 1774–1788," *Labor History*, 5 (1964), 225–246; Roger Champagne, "Liberty Boys and the Mechanics in New York City, 1764–1774," *Labor History*, 8 (1967), 123–135; Charles S. Olton, *Artisans for Independence: Philadelphia Mechanics and the American Revolution* (Syracuse, N.Y., 1975); Olton, "Philadelphia's Mechanics in the First Decade of Revolution, 1765–1775," *Journal of American History*, 59 (1972–1973), 311–326; Richard Walsh, *Charleston's Sons of Liberty: A Study of the Artisans, 1763–1789* (Columbia, S.C., 1959). Important studies of the post-Revolutionary era include Alfred F. Young, "The Mechanics and the Jeffersonians: New York, 1788–1801," *Labor History*, 5 (1964), 247–276; Young, *The Democratic Republicans of New York: The Origins, 1763–1797* (Chapel Hill, N.C., 1967); Howard Rock, *Artisans of the New Republic: The Tradesmen of New York in the Age of Jefferson* (New York, 1979); Charles Steffen, "Changes in the Organization of Artisan Production in Baltimore, 1790 to 1820," *WMQ*, 3d Ser., 36 (1979), 101–117; Graham Russell Hodges, *New York City Cartmen, 1667–1850* (New York, 1986); Richard G. Miller, *Philadelphia—The Federalist City: A Study of Urban Politics, 1789–1801* (Port Washington, N.Y., 1976); and Sean Wilentz, *Chants Democratic: New York City & the Rise of the American Working Class, 1788–1850* (New York, 1984).

transformation of labor relations in America's mid-Atlantic region to account for the nature and changes in the lives of Philadelphia's laboring people.

Who were eighteenth-century urban laboring people? Historians have employed various terms to describe the "laboring class" or "laboring classes": laborers, unskilled workers, lower class, lower sort, commonality, populace, artisans, mechanics, tradesmen, the crowd, ordinary people, indentured servants, slaves, masters, journeymen, apprentices, and a host of occupational identifiers such as cordwainer, carpenter, and baker (to name but a few of the hundreds of jobs that existed in America's port towns).[4] "Laboring class" and "laboring classes" thus are broad terms embracing all people who worked with their hands. Given the state of the preindustrial economy and technological development, the terms cover a large majority of the residents of any eighteenth-century city.

The laboring classes were differentiated between skilled and unskilled people, among as well as within crafts, and between free and unfree workers. Unskilled people, often designated as "laborers," included porters, woodcutters, sawyers, scavengers, chimney sweeps, washerwomen, and waterside and construction workers who stowed and unloaded ship cargoes, assisted in building structures and vessels, excavated cellars, drained swamps, hauled materials, and the like. Merchant seamen (not including mates or ship captains), the most numerous occupational group in any major port, often possessed considerable skills, but they generally are categorized with unskilled workers because their income and social standing were similar. Laborers and merchant seamen belonged predominantly to the lower ranks of the laboring classes since their material standards, status, and occupational and economic mobility were the most restricted of all laboring people.

4. Historians have defined the urban lower sort imprecisely, partly because eighteenth-century terms were imprecise. Staughton Lynd, for example, used the term "mechanics" as it was employed in the eighteenth century, to refer to "all groups below merchants and lawyers," including "anyone who worked with his hands"; in "Mechanics in New York Politics." Herbert Morais equated "craftsmen" and "lower class," in "Artisan Democracy and the American Revolution," *Science and Society*, 6 (1942), 227–241. Eric Foner has described several divisions within Philadelphia's middle and lower orders, in *Tom Paine*. James H. Hutson mistakenly identified a highly skilled artisan group of ship carpenters as part of the lower sort in "An Investigation of the Inarticulate: Philadelphia's White Oaks," *WMQ*, 3d Ser., 28 (1971), 3–25. See also Jesse Lemisch and John K. Alexander, "The White Oaks, Jack Tar, and the Concept of the 'Inarticulate,'" ibid., 29 (1972), 109–134; Simeon J. Crowther, "A Note on the Economic Position of Philadelphia's White Oaks," ibid., 134–136; and Hutson, "Rebuttal," ibid., 136–142. For further discussion about the meaning of these terms, see Philip Foner, *Labor and the American Revolution* (Westport, Conn., 1976), 3–5; Hermann Wellenreuther, "Labor in the Era of the American Revolution: A Discussion of Recent Concepts and Theories," *Labor History*, 22 (1981), 576–579; Gary B. Nash, Billy G. Smith, and Dirk Hoerder, "Laboring Americans and the American Revolution," ibid., 24 (1983), 415–418; and Staughton Lynd and Alfred Young, "The Mechanics in New York City Politics, 1774–1801," ibid., 5 (1964), 217.

Artisans occupied all ranks of society, although they were concentrated in its middle layers. While nine out of ten laborers and seven out of ten seamen in Philadelphia paid the minimum tax in 1772, for example, only one out of every three artisans was assessed that rate.[5] Craftsmen were spread along the entire spectrum of wealth in their possession of property, ranging from impecunious apprentice tailors to wealthy master carpenters. The lower end of the scale, where tailors, shoemakers, and coopers congregated, had much in common with merchant seamen and laborers, sharing low wages, uncertain prospects of advancement, and, usually, a position of propertylessness that also meant disfranchisement. In the higher brackets, where some tanners, bakers, sugarboilers, brewers, and construction tradesmen were located, artisans blended into the ranks of shopkeepers, proprietors, and even urban developers. But in terms of status, artisans rarely achieved the upper levels of the social hierarchy. While goldsmiths commanded considerably more respect than coopers, their wealth did not entitle them to the deference expected by most clergymen, merchants, and lawyers.

Internal gradations marked the various crafts as well. Each craft consisted of three tiers: masters, who were experienced artisans, usually worked for themselves and either owned their places of business or operated out of their homes; journeymen, who hired out to masters but generally possessed their own tools; and young apprentices, who learned the "art and mystery" of the craft under contractual arrangements with masters, men who frequently served as surrogate fathers. Theoretically, artisans moved from one position to another, spending seven years as apprentices and perhaps an equal number as journeymen. In reality, the transition from journeyman to master, at least among "lesser" Philadelphia artisans, appears not to have been so easily accomplished.

Outside of these layers of skilled and unskilled workers stood unfree laboring people: indentured servants, who were bound to individual masters for specific periods of time and were restricted in their civil rights; and slaves, who were owned perpetually by others and whose unfree position was hereditary. Slaves and servants were either skilled or unskilled. The number of both dwindled considerably after the Revolution. Despite being legally bound, they were important participants in the life of the community.

The focus of the following chapters is the lower ranks of the free elements of the laboring classes. Specifically, laborers and merchant seamen as well as two "lesser" groups of artisans—shoemakers and tailors—form the primary basis of analysis. These laboring people clustered near but not at the very bottom of the social and economic hierarchy. Although at times falling onto public and private relief rolls, they generally lived an independent economic

5. 1772 Provincial Tax List, PCA.

existence. This independence differentiated them from the city's most marginal inhabitants, the dependent poor who continually relied on aid from others for their subsistence. In addition, the variety of economic activities in which these four occupational groups participated makes their experiences representative of many among the lower echelons of urban society. Finally, as four of the largest occupational groups in the city, laborers, merchant seamen, cordwainers, and tailors accounted for a substantial segment of the working populace, comprising at least one-third and more often near one-half of Philadelphia's free males during the second half of the century.[6]

The initial three chapters depict overall conditions in Philadelphia. To convey the sights, smells, and "feel" of the city, the opening chapter follows two working people as they walk the streets searching for employment and carrying out some of their routine daily tasks. Most among the urban lower classes faced uncertain futures; indeed, life itself was peculiarly vulnerable, threatened continually by various ailments, diseases, and accidents. Chapter 2 considers the demographic realities, including the joys and sorrows of birth, marriage, and death, encountered by all the city's inhabitants, with a special emphasis on the conditions of the lower sort. Chapter 3 analyzes the structure and development of the city's economy, and the growth of inequality in the Pennsylvania capital, and places its laboring residents within that context.

The succeeding pages shift the focus exclusively to the particular circumstances of the lower sort themselves. Chapter 4 measures the everyday struggle encountered by laborers, mariners, cordwainers, and tailors to provide the basic necessities of life, and chapter 5 chronicles the careers of men in those occupations, evaluating their chances to improve their lot. Chapter 6 considers the social and economic background of Philadelphia's poor, tracing their migratory patterns to the city as they searched for better conditions, a competent livelihood, or a place of refuge. The physical conditions they found, especially the housing, are also discussed, as are the strategies adopted by the poverty-stricken to cope with their situation. Chapter 7 describes the family lives of white and black laboring Philadelphians, detailing the structure of their households and the nature of the relationships among family members. The concluding chapter comments retrospectively on a few of the book's themes.

6. These groups are discussed in more detail in chapter 3 and in Appendix C.

Chapter One

Walking the Streets

The city of Philadelphia is perhaps one of the wonders of the world.
— Lord Adam Gordon, 1765

I cannot see that extraordinary beauty [of Philadelphia] . . . that is so much boasted of.
— Dr. Robert Honyman, 1775

THE CLEAR, CRISP MORNING could have done little to lift the spirits of Peter and Hannah Carle when they rolled out of bed and built a small fire to take the chill off the room.[1] The day before, on November 12, 1799, they had buried their thirteen-month-old daughter Johanna Marie. That this was a common, almost expected event, with one out of every four or five Philadelphia children dying by this age, must have afforded small comfort to the Carles. The years between one and three were hazardous for most infants. As babies were weaned from mother's milk to sometimes contaminated foods, they lost the mild resistance to certain diseases acquired through nursing and their susceptibility to a variety of life-threatening ailments consequently increased. Only newborns perished during their first few days of life at a higher rate. When worms infested Johanna Marie, she, like so many other

---

1. The respective walks taken by Peter Carle and Susannah Cook as depicted in this chapter are hypothetical, although they may well have performed these activities at some point during their residence in the city. The vignettes about Carle, Cook, and the people who lived along their routes and the descriptions of the city's streets are real. These are constructed from a large number of records using the techniques of "limited prosopography." As described in Appendix A, I amassed information on more than fifty thousand people who lived in Philadelphia during the second half of the eighteenth century. Only the sources of information about specific people or events are cited in the notes to this chapter. Most comments about the social, economic, and demographic conditions of Philadelphia are based on arguments and evidence presented in later chapters; generalizations are substantiated by notes in this chapter only if they are not fully considered later in the book. I have intentionally used assertive language to describe Carle's and Cook's activities in order to avoid burdensome prose.

babies, proved too weak to withstand both the parasites and the medicinal poisons designed to destroy them.[2]

Arranging for the funeral had been a trial. Peter and Hannah wanted their daughter interred in the cemetery of Gloria Dei, the city's oldest church and the one where they worshiped. But the service and plot cost five dollars—the equivalent of nearly a week's wages for Peter—and the Carles were destitute. The city's economy, booming since the early 1790s, foundered in 1799, and Peter had located only sporadic employment during the previous few months. Without sufficient money for the funeral, Hannah and Peter might have been forced to bury their daughter cheaply in the unconsecrated ground of Potter's Field. Fortunately, their plea that they were "very poor" moved the rector to perform the service and to inter Johanna in Gloria Dei's cemetery for a price they could afford.

Many other Philadelphians also experienced grief, having lost loved ones to recent yellow fever epidemics. The disease had struck in the late summers and autumns throughout most of the decade, sending many people to their graves and increasing the emotional and monetary burdens of the survivors (except, presumably, the grave diggers). For years, wealthy citizens had fled to their country homes each summer to escape the heat and the seasonal agues. The 1799 epidemic chased away more inhabitants than usual, scared off farmers and ship captains from bringing in trade goods, closed down businesses, and left many residents to grapple with financial difficulties and another bout with the "pale-faced messenger." Ironically, the most despised group in the city, free blacks, enjoyed limited immunity to the disease and actively assisted their white neighbors during this crisis.[3]

Government officials likewise responded to "the distressed situation of many of the inhabitants of the City." In late September the Guardians of the Poor had borrowed ten thousand dollars to purchase and distribute supplies to the needy. Indeed, on the day preceding their daughter's burial the Carles sought such relief. Having passed the committee's inspection and obtained a

2. The almshouse clerk often noted weather conditions in the Daily Occurrences Docket, Guardians of the Poor, PCA, hereafter cited as Daily Occurrences. Information about the Carles is from Burial Records, Old Swedes Church, Gloria Dei, Nov. 12, 1799, GSP, hereafter cited as Burial Records, Old Swedes Church; and Cornelius William Stafford, *The Philadelphia Directory for 1800* (Philadelphia, 1800). (Page numbers are not indicated when directories are cited since they list names alphabetically.)

3. Firsthand accounts of the yellow fever epidemics of the 1790s are provided in the Diary of Edward Garrigues, Aug. 26, 1798 (quotation), HSP; Elizabeth Cope Harrison, ed., *Philadelphia Merchant: The Diary of Thomas P. Cope, 1800–1851* (South Bend, Ind., 1978), 41; and John Harvey Powell, *Bring Out Your Dead: The Great Plague of Yellow Fever in Philadelphia in 1793* (Philadelphia, 1949). Richard Allen, a leader of the black community, offered the assistance of the city's blacks in each issue of the *Aurora* (Philadelphia) between Nov. 7 and Nov. 13, the week preceding Peter Carle's walk.

certificate from a "respectable citizen" attesting to their plight, Peter and Hannah were eligible to receive bread and other foodstuffs each Monday afternoon throughout the fall.[4]

The Carles had arrived in Philadelphia four years earlier from Amsterdam, where both had been born and raised. Like so many others during the eighteenth century, they were caught by forces that both pushed them out of their native land and pulled them to the New World. Immigrants landed in large numbers in the Quaker City, the primary American port of entry during this period. Although most quickly passed through to the countryside, enough of them settled in the city to help make it the continent's largest metropolitan center, containing nearly seventy thousand souls by 1800. The tide of European migrants, mostly Germans and Scotch Irish, crested during the quarter of a century before the Revolution and then quickly subsided during the war itself. The Carles belonged to a new, smaller wave of migrants that flowed through the city during the 1790s as the Irish, French, and itinerants from other parts of America—especially newly freed blacks—washed ashore in the temporary capital of the United States. The result was a city marked by remarkable ethnic and racial variety, swimming with natives from northern Europe, Africa, the West Indies, and various parts of North America.

Like many immigrants, Peter Carle earned his livelihood with his muscles. As a laborer, an occupation he shared with roughly one of every twelve of the city's free males, Carle belonged to the lower classes or, in the words of contemporaries, the "lower sort." His income, neighborhood, and housing likewise defined his position within the society. Peter and Hannah lived on Christian Street, more than a mile from the heart of the city, in Southwark, a suburb occupied predominantly by laboring people (see map). Since all but the wealthiest Philadelphians relied on walking as their primary form of transportation, the main market and prime residential and business districts were located in the center of town. Like many laboring folk, the Carles paid about six dollars a month to rent a frame two-story home, measuring about two hundred square feet per floor. During tight fiscal times, they shared their dwelling with another family or leased space to boarders for whom Hannah cooked and cleaned.

As the cold weather killed the mosquitoes that carried yellow fever, the city once again quickened with life, buoying the spirits of the survivors. "When I see our fellow citizens once more returned to their long deserted homes, and again with cheerful countenances pursuing their various occupations with

4. *True American* (Philadelphia), Sept. 28 and 30, Nov. 8, 1799. The Nov. 9 issue indicated that "charity sermons" had also been preached in many churches to raise funds for the poor.

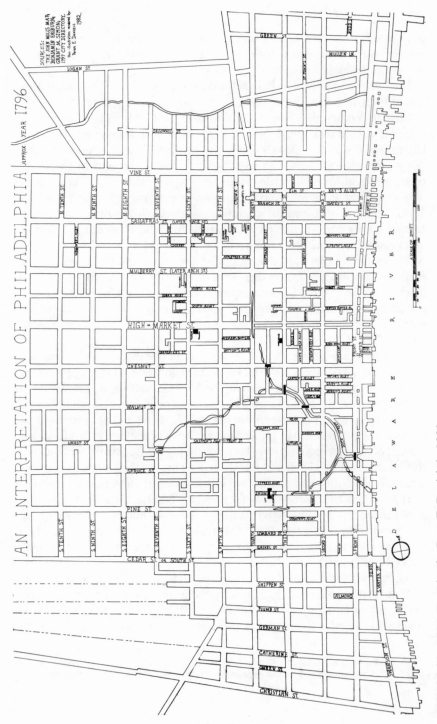

Philadelphia, 1796. Drawing by Peter E. Daniels in 1982.

redoubled intensity," one newspaper contributor rejoiced, "my heart exalts at the pleasing prospect before us, and reason whispers 'all will yet be well with Philadelphia.'"[5]

Peter Carle set off early that Wednesday, November 13, morning in search of a job. This chapter follows Carle's footsteps, and later those of the widow washerwoman Susannah Cook, on a hypothetical walking tour of the city. Their journeys enable us to observe the daily activities of the residents, peek inside their homes, inspect their living standards, detect some of their failures and successes, scrutinize their neighborhoods, examine their work and careers, glimpse the interaction of their community and family members, note the operation of their economy, probe into their social structure, and shop at their markets. The trips necessarily will provide a somewhat haphazard sense of the sights, sounds, and smells of the city, but the process will thereby more closely resemble the way in which they were actually experienced than the manner in which they would conventionally be arranged by scholars.

Advertisements for ship carpenters had appeared in recent newspapers, but because Carle sought a less-skilled position as a stevedore moving goods on and off ships, he walked east toward the Delaware River, turned left onto Front Street, then continued north for several miles, stopping periodically at the wharves to inquire about employment. A great many Philadelphians had prospered during the recent flush times, and, within several blocks, Peter passed the homes of successful artisans and ship captains. Anthony Pearson, a bricklayer, had owned three two-story brick houses near the corner of Front and Catherine Streets. When he died the previous year, Pearson left his property to his wife, Rebecca, and, at her death, the homes were to be equally divided among their son (also a bricklayer) and two daughters. From Carle's perspective, Pearson's house was well furnished, including five beds (two with curtains), a chest of drawers, a mirror, various chairs, and a dining and two smaller tables. Rebecca and her daughters cooked with two iron pots, a brass kettle, several warming and frying pans, and a coffee mill, and they used a shovel, tongs, and a pair of bellows to keep the fire going. Books, a tea table, and a clock "Wound Every 24 Hours" were among Pearson's luxury items.[6]

5. Ibid., Nov. 13, 1799.

6. The *Aurora* (Philadelphia), Nov. 11, 1799, contained several job advertisements for skilled workers. The list of Anthony Pearson's possessions, including the description of his clock, appears in the Philadelphia County Probate Records, Wills and Inventories of Estate, 1798, no. 495, RW, hereafter cited as Probate Records; Cornelius William Stafford, *The Philadelphia Directory for 1797* (Philadelphia, 1797); and Stafford, *Philadelphia Directory for 1800*. The changing nature of "luxury" items in early America is discussed in Lorena S. Walsh et al., "Forum: Toward a History of the Standard of Living in British North America," *WMQ*, 3d Ser., 45 (1988), 116–170.

Francis and Libby Feariss, a block farther north along Peter Carle's path, enjoyed greater affluence than the Pearsons. The master of a ship, Francis belonged to the richest quarter of the city's taxpayers. The Fearisses had spent more than five hundred dollars—two years' wages for a laborer like Carle—elegantly furnishing their home. They owned separate beds for themselves and each of their five children, a sure sign of wealth, and their sleeping chambers contained a dressing table, chairs, desks, two bureaus, six mirrors, and numerous carpets. Their dining facilities included four dinner and two breakfast tables, a carved tea table, various sets of tablecloths and napkins, and thirty windsor and mahogany chairs. Servants warmed the spacious quarters with two stoves and three fireplaces and prepared food in an amply supplied kitchen. The Fearisses also displayed silver plate worth a hundred and sixty dollars. Francis dressed to his social position, owning clothes valued at fifty dollars in addition to a silver watch. When Francis died at the turn of the century, the family pastor from the nearby Associate Presbyterian Church helped Libby divide the estate equally among herself and her three children. Francis's wealth and influence no doubt enhanced the career opportunities of his son and namesake, Francis, Jr. Interest on his father's investments paid for his education and helped him open a merchant house in the early nineteenth century.[7]

Several blocks north of the Fearisses resided Joseph Blewer, a young ship captain. Blewer could not match the wealth of Francis Feariss, Sr., nor is it likely that he ever would, even at the peak of his earning power. At this point in his life he could afford to rent only a small structure behind a grocer's store on Front Street. But he was fortunate to have a father who likewise had commanded sailing vessels and whose contacts helped his son acquire the training necessary for his present position. Young Blewer could expect to enjoy moderate economic success in future years.[8]

John Cribbin, who lived around the corner from Blewer, probably was aware that the skills men did or did not acquire in their youth generally determined the course of their lives. At age twenty-seven, John sailed the seas as a common sailor and, like most of his fellow seamen, did not acquire the necessary skills to become a ship's mate or master. His modest earnings meant that in 1799 his family's financial resources stretched thin. John and his wife, Elizabeth, consequently could do little to ensure a comfortable

7. Probate Records, 1799, no. 169; Clement Biddle, *The Philadelphia Directory* (Philadelphia, 1791), hereafter cited as Biddle, [1791] *Directory*; 1789 Provincial Tax List, PCA, hereafter cited as Provincial Tax List; Stafford, *Philadelphia Directory for 1797*; Anon., *Philadelphia Directory for 1816* (Philadelphia, 1816).

8. Blewer's father, also named Joseph, left a will recorded in 1789 in Will Book U, pp. 344–346, Wills, Philadelphia County Probate Records, 1683–1901, RW, hereafter cited as Wills; Stafford, *Philadelphia Directory for 1797*.

The pye from Bake-house she had brought / But let it fall for want of thought | The ACCIDENT in LOMBARD-STREET / PHILAD.ª 1787 | And laughing Sweeps collect around / The pye that's scatter'd on the ground Nº ?

Plate 1. "The Accident in Lombard Street," 1787. This etching depicts a residential neighborhood, looking west from the corner of Third Street and Lombard Street. Etching by Charles Willson Peale (1787). Courtesy of the Henry Francis du Pont Winterthur Museum. Funds for purchase were a gift of the Caroline Clendenin Ryan Foundation, Inc.

future for their five children. Thus, they apprenticed their eldest son, Jacob, to shoemaking, one of the "lesser" crafts, at the age of twelve. Had he not been murdered in his early twenties, Jacob most likely would have remained a cordwainer, experiencing some degree of pecuniary insecurity throughout much of his life. John died in the almshouse infirmary in the early 1820s, a victim of pneumonia.[9]

Episodes from the lives of several inhabitants of this neighborhood illustrate some aspects of the family relationships of laboring people. Samuel

9. Burial Records, Old Swedes Church, Mar. 5, 1824 and 1825; Birth Records, Old Swedes Church, Gloria Dei, Mar. 15, 1800; Feb. 10, 1802; Jan. 15, 1804; June 2, 1806, GSP; Stafford, *Philadelphia Directory for 1797.* Susan E. Klepp kindly provided information about the Cribbins.

Linten, a bricklayer, lived next door to Joseph Blewer. Two years earlier Samuel's son, Jacob, had married Margaret Shepard, whose widowed mother also resided in the city. But the bride may not have worn white: Jacob and Margaret had cohabitated for several years, already producing two sons.[10] This situation, far from rare, suggests that parents often did not control their children's sexual and marital choices.

Domestic violence marred the lives of many. Several months before Carle's present walk the constables had arrived at a dwelling nearby to arrest mariner John Green for beating his wife, Sarah.[11] Another neighbor, John O'Brian, had appeared three times in court, charged with assault on his wife and daughter. When the young daughter eventually died from her injuries, the judge incarcerated John for a month, fined him a small amount, branded an "M" (for "murderer") on his thumb, and required him to post a security deposit against his good behavior in the future.[12]

The Andrews lived at the intersection of Water and Pine streets, along Carle's route to the docks. A woman in her early twenties, Sarah had married Jacob, a successful tailor her father's age, in 1796, shortly thereafter giving birth to a daughter. But their marriage floundered, in part because Jacob had found it difficult to be monogamous. According to Sarah's divorce suit brought several years later, Jacob "has been unfaithful to his Marriage Vow having been guilty of Adultry by connecting himself criminally with other Women."[13] Pennsylvania was one of the few states that liberalized divorce laws after the Revolution, and even though divorces still were difficult and expensive to obtain, Philadelphians (especially women) increasingly took advantage of the new laws.[14]

Latitia and Asa Elkinton lived several blocks north. Asa, a tailor, was born in New Jersey in 1765, and Latitia a year later. They did not marry until their

10. Marriage Records, Old Swedes Church, Gloria Dei, Sept. 25, 1796, GSP; Stafford, *Philadelphia Directory for 1797*. The white wedding dress as a symbol of virginity became popular in the mid-eighteenth century; Phillis Cunnington and Catherine Lucas, *Costume for Births, Marriages & Deaths* (London, 1972), 60–61.

11. Prisoners for Trial Docket, Philadelphia County Prison, 1798, p. 60, PCA, hereafter cited as Prisoners for Trial Docket; Stafford, *Philadelphia Directory for 1797*.

12. Prisoners for Trial Docket, 1791, pp. 12, 13; Stafford, *Philadelphia Directory for 1797*. The Prisoners for Trial Docket contains numerous cases of assault against family members.

13. Records of the Supreme Court, Divorce Papers, September, 1801, Record Group 33, PHMC, hereafter cited as Divorce Papers; U.S. Census Office, *Return of the Whole Number of Persons within the Several Districts of the United States: Second Census* (Washington, D.C., 1800), hereafter cited as *Second Census*; Biddle, [1791] *Directory*; Stafford, *Philadelphia Directory for 1797*.

14. Thomas R. Meehan, "'Not Made Out of Levity': Evolution of Divorce in Early Pennsylvania," *PMHB*, 92 (1968), 441–464; Linda K. Kerber, *Women of the Republic: Intellect and Ideology in Revolutionary America* (Chapel Hill, N.C., 1980), 181. While a much larger number filed suit, approximately three dozen Philadelphians obtained a divorce during the last fifteen years of the century. This information is available in Divorce Papers, *passim*.

late twenties, about five years past the average for laboring people. Like most of their neighbors, they quickly had children: Latitia bore three sons and a daughter during the first dozen years of their marriage. Of these offspring, Charles died at age nineteen and Caleb at eleven months, not unusual in an environment where half of the children did not reach their twenty-first birthday. Although childbirth generally posed only slight danger to most Philadelphia women, the birth of the Elkintons' last child took Latitia's life.[15] At age forty, she died five years short of the median age of death for adults. Remarriage is common in many preindustrial societies in which life spans are relatively short and one spouse often perishes well before the other. Asa followed this pattern, marrying Lucy Davis, herself widowed eighteen months earlier. Asa died at the age of fifty-nine; only one-quarter of the city's residents lived longer lives.[16]

Immediately after passing Spruce Street, Carle crossed the drawbridge over Dock Creek. At the east end of the bridge along the Delaware River, the wives of fisherman gathered to peddle their husbands' catches, while oystermen wheeled their barrows of inexpensive delicacies through the streets, crying out their wares. One popular story, though undoubtedly exaggerated, related that a "countryman" paid an oysterman fifty cents for as many of the raw shellfish as he could eat.

> The oysterman, believing he should have the advantage, exposed his store with alacrity, but he saw his mistake, for after opening three hundred, which the countryman greedily swallowed, he would have returned the money to get clear, but the fellow insisted on having more & was only dissuaded from it by the intercession of some standersby, who compassionated the poor oysterman.[17]

After crossing Dock Creek, Peter entered one of the city's prime business districts. The dozens of ships docked at the wharves lining Water Street formed the backbone of Philadelphia's economy. During the previous five decades the city had developed into the nation's premier commercial center and one of the wealthiest urban areas in the world. As the agricultural produce of Pennsylvania, New Jersey, Delaware, and Maryland passed through the port to Europe and the West Indies, manufactured goods

15. The mortality statistics collected by the Philadelphia Board of Health from 1807 through 1826 indicate that only 1.2 percent of women between the ages of twenty and forty died during childbirth. Gouverneur Emerson, "Medical Statistics: Being A Series of Tables, Showing the Mortality in Philadelphia and Its Causes," Philadelphia Board of Health, Table 5, APS.

16. The story of the Elkintons is reconstructed from information contained in the Birth, Marriage, and Burial Records, Quaker Church, GSP, data generously supplied by Susan E. Klepp. The median age of death of Philadelphians is based on an analysis of the ages of the decedents reported by the City Board of Health from 1807 through 1810. These records are located in the PCA.

17. Harrison, *Philadelphia Merchant*, 41.

Plate 2. "The Arch Street Ferry," as it appeared in 1800, suggests the commercial activity of the waterfront. The foreground depicts coopers finishing barrels and laborers and draymen unloading ship's cargo. Peter Carle's walk would have taken him by this point. From W. Birch and Son, *The City of Philadelphia . . . As It Appeared in 1800.* Courtesy of the Historical Society of Pennsylvania.

arrived from England to be dispersed throughout the city and its hinterlands. Producing, transporting, and retailing these commodities created a complex economy involving the efforts of thousands of individuals. Mariners sailed ships, stevedores moved cargoes, and cart men and casual laborers transferred merchandise between boats and storage facilities. Waggoners, farmers, and flatboat operators carried flour, bread, and other foodstuffs into the city and returned to the countryside ladened with shoes, textiles, and other processed goods. Meanwhile, subsidiary sectors developed and provided jobs to workers in the construction of houses and boats, encouraged artisans to fashion wares for local consumption, and stimulated the service roles played by men and women who kept boardinghouses, inns, and taverns. All the while, merchants, shopkeepers, clerks, and other tradesmen directed and organized the entire system.

Carle's best opportunity to locate employment lay along the wharves jutting out into the Delaware River for a span of five blocks, a "busy place full of work and movement," as one visitor described it.[18] Convinced that this year's outbreak of yellow fever finally had been brought under control, thirty captains had steered their vessels into port during the previous two days and another half dozen were to land that day.[19] In the morning's twilight Carle gathered with scores of other men near the piers, seeking a job unloading West Indian sugar, South American coffee, or English cloth. The work entailed hoisting two-hundred-pound barrels out of the ship's hold, rolling them onto a cart or dray, transporting them to a warehouse or store, and then once again hoisting or rolling them upstairs to a loft or downstairs to a basement. As laborers toiled from dawn to dusk, they appreciated the short, though cold, November days, which lasted only eleven or twelve hours. The rhythm of their work was irregular: after spurts of extreme exertion, men rested, talked, and several times each morning and afternoon renewed their spirits with rum. Still, their activities were physically grueling, literally back-breaking, and sometimes dangerous. Many laboring men suffered injuries each year when barrels fell, wagons overturned, and ropes broke, while others gradually wore down under the hard physical labor and the exposure to the elements.[20]

Merchants likewise congregated along the wharves to take advantage of the commercial opportunities available; more than forty countinghouses stood between the drawbridge and the next street, Walnut. Stephen Girard, soon to be the richest man in America, recently had constructed a four-story brick home and several stores in this section of town.[21] Investing in ships and their cargoes to build his initial fortune, Girard later expanded into banking, housing construction, land speculation, and a host of other enterprises. Like many other merchants, tradesmen, and craftsmen, Girard turned a small profit by offering other men vocational training. Thus, in 1790 Girard

18. Kenneth Roberts and Anna M. Roberts, eds., *Moreau de St. Mery's American Journey* [1793–1798] (Garden City, N.Y., 1947), 259.

19. *True American* (Philadelphia), Nov. 12, 13, and 14, 1800. The newspaper reports of ship arrivals indicate the detrimental effect of yellow fever on the city's economy. Only 14 vessels docked during September when the disease raged out of control. During the next two months, 62 and 113 ships, respectively, arrived as the epidemic subsided.

20. Scores of injured workers entered the almshouse, as recorded in Daily Occurrences.

21. The composition of this area is evident in Edmund Hogan, *The Prospect of Philadelphia and Check on the Next Directory* (Philadelphia, 1795), hereafter cited as Hogan, [1795] *Directory*. While most of the directories are organized alphabetically by the householder's last name, this directory reports householders by residence, in a street-by-street fashion.

acquired the indenture of eighteen-year-old Dennis Civercoks from the Overseers of the Poor. Civercoks received food, lodging, instruction as a seaman, and a small sum of money at the end of his three-year apprenticeship.[22] A similar system provided training for girls. In 1797 the Guardians of Orphan Children indentured Tabitha Green to Nathan Field, Girard's neighbor, to serve as his maid for six years. Field promised Tabitha her daily maintenance, an elementary education in reading, writing, and needlework, and thirty dollars in cash when she reached her eighteenth birthday.[23]

Girard, Field, and other merchants directed the city's economy. None had contributed more to Philadelphia's economic development (or to financing the American Revolution) than Robert Morris. Comparing the experiences of Robert Morris, Dennis Civercoks, and Tabitha Green again reveals the value of early training to later success and the extent to which the instruction of young people depended on the status of their parents. The education of Morris differed significantly from that Civercoks and Green. Morris's father, a successful tobacco importer in Maryland, apprenticed his son to a prominent Philadelphia merchant in 1749. Five years later Robert became a partner in the company and, during the ensuing decades, helped build it into one of the most successful countinghouses in the colonies. The success of Willing, Morris, and Company symbolized the prosperity enjoyed by many of the city's merchants during the second half of the eighteenth century. Morris's personal fortune peaked after the Revolution, but, having overexpanded his financial empire, he was caught in the region's economic downturn at the century's close. When he fell into debt for more than twenty million dollars, Morris landed in debtor's prison in 1798, experiencing firsthand the insecurity that characterized the lives of many Philadelphians.[24]

At the time of Carle's search for work, three black families and their boarders were crowded into a few wooden structures behind Girard's and Field's businesses. Nearly one of every ten Philadelphians was black, most of them free. Their numbers had grown rapidly during the previous decade as manumitted slaves, runaways, and others who had achieved their liberty during and after the Revolution flocked to northern cities to find employ-

22. Information on Girard is available in Edgar P. Richardson, "The Athens of America, 1800–1825," in Russell F. Weigley, ed., *Philadelphia: A 300-Year History* (New York, 1982), 215, 256; and in Stafford, *Philadelphia Directory for 1797*. The record of the apprenticeship of Civercoks is contained in Indentures, 1790, Guardians of the Poor, PCA, hereafter cited as Indentures.

23. Stafford, *Philadelphia Directory for 1797*; Hogan, [1795] *Directory*; Indenture Papers and Bonds, 1797, Overseers of the Poor, PCA.

24. On Robert Morris, see Ellis Paxson Oberholtzer, *Robert Morris: Patriot and Financier* (New York, 1903); David Freeman Hawke, *Honorable Treason* (New York, 1976), 159–160; John and Katherine Bakeless, *Signers of the Declaration* (Boston, 1969), 125–136; and Harrison, *Philadelphia Merchant*, 37.

ment and to build lives in a community with others of their race.25 While African-Americans could avoid the racial isolation of rural areas, they could not escape the racism that permeated American society and kept them on the bottom rungs of the social and economic ladders, laboring in the most menial jobs. When Carle passed the two-story frame house of Samuel Saviel, his wife, and six children, their home for the past dozen years, the annual rent was seventy-five dollars. Saviel had worked as a lime salesman, fruit dealer, huckster, and carter for the past three decades. Tinee Cranshaw and her children lived in a similar structure next door; she sold lime and fruit for her livelihood, as had her husband Caesar before his death during the 1793 yellow fever epidemic. That Joseph Santone, a French "gentleman" in the house beside Cranshaw's, owned one of the fifty-five slaves left in the city was most likely a sore point for these black families.26

David Duncan headed a household of ten blacks in a three-story rental unit next to those of Saviel and Cranshaw. Duncan worked both as a peddler and as a sailor, the latter being the most common occupation available to black males. David had married Phoebe Seymour, a huckster, two years earlier and with his two children moved in with her. In 1800 David pooled his funds with Robert Turner, a black laborer, to buy a plot of land near Turner's residence on the northwest outskirts of the city. Several months later, setting out on an ocean voyage from which he would never return, Duncan made out his will to ensure that his property would be dispersed after his death according to his wishes. He left his entire estate to Phoebe, entrusting her to maintain and educate his children, and named as executors his wife and his friend John Exeter, a black carter. Thomas Shoemaker, a white merchant who owned a countinghouse across the street from the Duncans, appraised the estate, affording us a rare glimpse of the material home life of one of the city's more successful black families. The value of their furnishings totaled slightly more than a hundred dollars, the equivalent of a mariner's salary for four months. In the kitchen on the first floor, Phoebe cooked meals and fed

25. Gary B. Nash, *Forging Freedom: The Formation of Philadelphia's Black Community, 1720–1840* (Cambridge, Mass., 1988), 134–171; and Billy G. Smith and Richard Wojtowicz, *Blacks Who Stole Themselves: Advertisements for Runaways in the Pennsylvania Gazette, 1728–1790* (Philadelphia, 1989).

26. These vignettes are reconstructed from the following sources: Francis White, *The Philadelphia Directory* (Philadelphia, 1785), hereafter cited as White, [1785] *Directory*; Biddle, [1791] *Directory*; Hogan, [1795] *Directory*; Stafford, *Philadelphia Directory for 1797*; Anon., *Philadelphia Directory for 1816*; U.S. Bureau of the Census, *Heads of Families of the First Census of the United States Taken in the Year 1790: Pennsylvania* (Washington, D.C., 1908), hereafter cited as *First Census*; U.S. Direct Tax of 1798, Philadelphia: High Street Ward, 4, Form A, NA; and 1796 and 1798 Provincial Tax Lists. A great many street vendors in Philadelphia, as in New York City, were black, as discussed by Graham Russell Hodges, *New York City Cartmen, 1667–1850* (New York, 1986), 78n.

her family and lodgers. The Duncans spent most of their time in the room on the second story, where they kept a bureau, two mirrors, a small table, six chairs, and a settee. Phoebe and David slept in one of the beds in this room, while their children occupied the other. A set of china, a few wine glasses, a liquor case, and some books were the more elegant items owned by the Duncans. Two or three boarders, or perhaps another family, occupied the third floor of the house. After David's death, Phoebe continued to peddle petty merchandise and to rent space to lodgers. Meanwhile, Jude Duncan, another huckster and probable relative of her husband, moved in next door.[27]

In addition to merchants, tailors also clustered in this central section of town along the river, selling their services to the city's most prominent citizens. Three dozen tailors lived in the two blocks of Water Street running between Walnut and High. On a scale of income and prestige, tailors not only fell well below most merchants but also ranked among the poorer citizens in town, many grappling with financial problems familiar to laborers such as Peter Carle. To save money, tailor John and Mary Ashton and their infant daughter doubled up with cooper Donald Mulhallon and five other members of his family in a house along the wharves. That the Ashtons produced ten children during the next sixteen years must have kept Mary exhausted and their budget tight.[28] John Campbell, residing across the street from the Ashtons near the corner of Water and Walnut streets, languished in poverty during the closing years of the century, seeking refuge in the alms-house three or four times when illness left him unable to work.[29]

Of course, not all tailors faced such difficult circumstances. A block north of Campbell lived Elizabeth Graisbury, a tailor's widow. For the previous four decades, Elizabeth and Joseph had resided in their home, enjoying moderate prosperity. In 1756 Joseph belonged to the wealthiest half of Philadelphia's taxpayers, a position he maintained until his death forty years later. Outfitting the city's richest men in the latest fashions, Joseph earned an average of $480 annually during the 1760s and early 1770s, three or four times more than a common laborer. The work of several indentured servants and slaves contributed to his income and helped him purchase his home. Joseph's prosperity may have peaked during the Revolution, when he be-

27. Probate Records, 1800, no. 41; Hogan, [1795] *Directory*; Stafford, *Philadelphia Directory for 1797*; Cornelius William Stafford, *The Philadelphia Directory for 1801* (Philadelphia, 1801); *Second Census*; U.S. Census for 1810, Pennsylvania: City of Philadelphia, NA, hereafter cited as 1810 Census.

28. Data on the Ashtons are contained in the Birth, Marriage, and Burial Records, Christ Church, GSP. Susan E. Klepp provided me with this information. See also Hogan, [1795] *Directory*; Stafford, *Philadelphia Directory for 1797*; and *Second Census*.

29. Daily Occurrences, Apr. 6, May 31, Aug. 19, 1796, Apr. 9, 1800; Biddle, [1791] *Directory*; Stafford, *Philadelphia Directory for 1800*.

came a grocer and thus was responsible for retailing rather than producing goods. However, he returned to his position as a master tailor at the war's end. During their marriage, Elizabeth bore at least seven children, two of whom died prior to their father's death. But Joseph lived long enough to see his older daughters marry well, settle near his home, and have children of their own.

Although Joseph had been one of the city's most affluent tailors, Elizabeth, like the widows of nearly all mechanics, could not subsist solely on his estate. She had inherited most of the property, including the "use and Income of the house and lot" and a slave girl, Flora, with which to bring up their two minor children, and she may have received financial help from her sons-in-law as well. Still, she took in boarders. When shoemaker John Grant proved to be a shady character, often in trouble with the law, he was replaced by a series of other tenants: William Young and Leonard Shallcross, both cordwainers, and Samuel Tatem, another tailor.[30]

When Peter Carle failed to find employment along the docks, he continued north into a neighborhood that harbored a good many of Philadelphia's "underclass": criminals, alcoholics, vagrants, prostitutes, itinerants, escaped servants and slaves, the insane and incapacitated, and men, women, and children who were generally down and out. All together, they probably accounted for one of every ten people in the city, many of them living in the blocks north of Arch Street between the Delaware River and Third Street. Once known as "Helltown," this section had grown less distinctive by 1799 than it had once been. Its character had begun to change during the previous decade when merchants like Stephen Girard and wealthy French migrants who fled the revolutions in the West Indies and in France started to build offices in the area. This transformation was part of the continuing commercial process that stimulated increasing commercial specialization of neighborhoods in the center city and created a well-defined business district along the wharves by the end of the century.[31]

30. The Graisburys' lives are reconstructed from Will Book X, pp. 506–507, Wills; the 1756 tax list published by Hannah Benner Roach, comp., "Taxables in the City of Philadelphia, 1756," *Pennsylvania Genealogical Magazine*, 22 (1961), 3–41; 1772, 1780, 1789, and 1791–1800 Provincial Tax Lists; Philadelphia City Constables' Returns for 1775, PCA; *First Census*; *Second Census*; White, [1785] *Directory*; Biddle, [1791] *Directory*; Hogan, [1795] *Directory*; Stafford, *Philadelphia Directory for 1797*; Stafford, *Philadelphia Directory for 1800*; Anon., *Philadelphia Directory for 1816*. John Grant appears in Prisoners for Trial Docket, 1799, p. 21, and 1802, p. 28.

31. Elizabeth Gray Kogen Spera analyzes this process in "Building for Business: The Impact of Commerce on the City Plan and Architecture of the City of Philadelphia 1750–1800" (Ph.D. diss., University of Pennsylvania, 1980), 22, 30, 82, 93; see also Thomas Samuel Gentry, Jr., "Specialized Residential and Business Districts: Philadelphia in an Age of Change 1785–1800" (Master's thesis, Montana State University, 1988). For similar transformations in New York City, see Betsy Blackmar, "Re-walking the 'Walking City': Housing and Property Relations in New York City, 1780–1840," *Radical History Review*, 21 (1980), 131–150.

In 1790, before these alterations had occurred, the "Three Jolly Irishmen" at the corner of Race and Water streets epitomized this section of town. It had earned the reputation as one of the toughest taverns in Philadelphia, no small accomplishment in a city containing hundreds of licensed and unlicensed drinking establishments—approximately one for every twenty-five adult males. These ordinaries served as centers of neighborhood life, where men gathered not merely to consume rum and beer but also to gamble on cards, dice, cockfights, bull-baiting, and boxing matches; to view leopards, camels, trained pigs, and waxwork shows; to buy such drugs as "Jesuits Bark, Opium, and Spanish Flies"; to find employment on ships or at the dockyards; and to socialize and discuss recent events. Working people throughout the city raucously celebrated the first of May each year by drinking hard and eating "picnic dinners" in their favorite taverns.[32]

During the early years of the decade, John Roberts and his two "adopted wives," Elizabeth McSwain and Mary Carrol, used Mary Norris's lodging house, a block south of the "Three Jolly Irishmen," as their headquarters. Roberts, better known as Cock Robin to his compatriots and the town constables, engaged in a variety of illegal activities, mostly petty thefts. During the winter of 1790, he and Mary Carrol kept a "rendezvous" at Mrs. Norris's house where, according to the almshouse clerk, "the Paupers from this place and others [could be] Debauched in every way." Apparently not entirely sharing the clerk's revulsion, many poorhouse inmates sold their clothes and other small possessions to pay for participation in the debauching activities. When in dire need of money in March of that year, Elizabeth McSwain employed this popular strategy. She gained admittance to the almshouse, received clothing to cover her nearly naked state, stole garments from the other inmates, then absconded to sell "her gown, Petticoat, Shift, Shoes, and Hose with her Apron all for 6 shillings and which was all spent to Release Cock Robin from Jail." The proceeds also provided rum with which to toast her success.[33]

In a city filled with transient mariners and other young men and where women were restricted in their employment opportunities, prostitution flourished. The night watchmen often picked up streetwalkers such as Biddy Cummings, Margaret Jeffreys, Mary Young ("a Stout Young woman"), and

32. Joseph J. Kelly, Jr., *Life and Times in Colonial Philadelphia* (Harrisburg, Pa., 1973), 160–161; W. J. Rorabaugh, *The Alcoholic Republic: An American Tradition* (New York, 1979); Robert E. Graham, "Philadelphia Inns and Taverns: 1774–1780," MS, APS; Roberts and Roberts, *St. Mery's American Journey*, 318, 328–329, 336. The city's taverns are identifiable in most city directories. The tavernkeeper of the Indian King advertised drugs for sale in the *Pennsylvania Gazette* (Philadelphia), Aug. 28, 1776 (quotation). See also the descriptions of taverns in New York City in Hodges, *New York City Cartmen*, 47.

33. Daily Occurrences, Mar. 1, 5, 13, Apr. 16 (quotations), 1790; Vagrancy Docket, June 21, July 31, Nov. 12, 1790, PCA, hereafter cited as Vagrancy Docket; Biddle, [1791] *Directory*.

Sarah Evans as they plied their trade in this neighborhood, charging a dollar or two to each of their customers.[34] When apprehended, they faced thirty days in the city's workhouse. After her apprenticeship as a maid for Dr. Glentworth on Race Street, just half a block east of the "Three Jolly Irishmen," Biddy Cummings joined a number of other "seasonal customers" who made their winter quarters in the almshouse. As frequently occurred, in December 1789, "cold Boreas" blew Cummings into the institution with complaints of sore legs and feet. Not surprisingly, she healed in early spring and, along with Elizabeth McSwain, scaled the wall and ran away. During the next year, the constables apprehended Cummings for vagrancy, disturbing the peace, and prostitution. Margaret Jeffreys likewise frequently landed in jail for similar illicit activities during these years. By 1795, at the age of twenty-nine, she had managed to establish her own "bawdy house," but her success drew only a term in the workhouse. A host of her convictions for theft appear in the prison dockets during the closing years of the century. Sarah Evans, a widow, did not enjoy much luck avoiding watchmen. Between 1791 and 1795 they arrested her at least fifteen times for vagrancy, disorderly conduct, keeping bad company, and being a drunk and "Lewd Girl." Her brothel in the northwest section of town apparently did not draw many customers, since she resorted to the almshouse in the winter of 1795. The next March she eloped, "a young venereal Hussy," the clerk noted, "off to Innoculate, but not for the pox."[35]

Apprentices, servants, and slaves gravitated to this section of town for their evening pleasures, often against their master's wishes. Female servants, according to one visitor, "love to dress up for their evening promenade, which lasts from nine until eleven and, it's said, leads them to places where they traffic in their charms."[36] Periodic newspaper stories warned their owners of these activities:

At the late city sessions a negro was tried and convicted for keeping a disorderly house; it appeared upon this occasion that the offender kept a place of resort for all the loose and idle characters of the city, whether whites, blacks or mulattoes; and that frequently in the night gentlemens servants would arrive there, mounted on their masters horses (for which the landlord had provided a stable in the neighborhood) and indulge in riotous mirth and dancing till the dawn,

---

34. These activities are described in Roberts and Roberts, *St. Mery's American Journey*, 311–313. A great number of prostitutes appear in both the Daily Occurrences and the Vagrancy Docket.

35. Daily Occurrences, Dec. 5, 1789; Feb. 17, Mar. 1, 1790; Mar. 13, 1796 (quotation); Vagrancy Docket, 1790–1797; Prisoners for Trial Docket, 1790–1792, 1798–1800; Sentence Docket, 1798–1802, Philadelphia County Prison, PCA; Biddle, [1791] *Directory*; Hogan, [1795] *Directory*.

36. Roberts and Roberts, *St. Mery's American Journey*, 297.

when they posted again to their respective homes. These facts are laid before the public . . . as a hint to masters to watch the conduct of their servants, who may, in there nocturnal excurtions, commit a greater outrage upon their property than the midnight robber.[37]

Even George Washington found he could not keep his servants orderly, sober, and confined to their own beds, and in 1794 he briefly committed Wilhelmina Tyser and Martin Cline to the workhouse as punishment for their misbehavior. Like many other laboring people, Tyser and Cline seem not to have deferred to their social betters. As one admiring traveler observed immediately after the Revolution, "people think, act, and speak here precisely as it prompts them; the poorest day-laborer on the bank of the Delaware holds it his right to advance his opinion, in religious as well as political matters, with as much freedom as the gentleman or the scholar." Another visitor found that the city's "workmen are proud and unbearably haughty."[38]

If this neighborhood attracted some people for its excitement, it drew others because of their desperation. Sarah Ferguson, a seventeen-year-old woman afflicted with venereal disease, was apprehended in this area of the city. She had arrived in Philadelphia from Ireland "when she was a suckling." But since her parents "never bound her out or took any care of her indenturing," for several years after their death, according to the almshouse clerk, "she has been a lost wanderer thro' the streets, having no place to lay her head, by which means she has been exposed to every vile temptation."[39] Elizabeth Deford suffered not only from venereal disease but also from the "almost deprivation of the use of [her] limbs by being exposed to a Street lodging in the night, not having the wherewith to lay her head." She did not long survive the hardship.[40] John Griffin, an immigrant from Ireland who had worked as a laborer in the city for twenty-seven years, was carried into the almshouse in 1801. By the clerk's account, Griffin "has had no nourishment for this week past, slept at night in any hole or corner he could creep to, [was] sent here in a Cart, he not being able to walk, and being very dirty and swarming with bodily vermin."[41]

Many of the "strolling poor"—people knocking about from place to place in America in search of a livelihood or a refuge—congregated in these

37. *Pennsylvania Gazette* (Philadelphia), Aug. 8, 1787.

38. Johann David Schoepf, *Travels in the Confederation* [1783–1784], ed. and trans. Alfred J. Morrison (New York, 1968; orig. 1911), 99; Roberts and Roberts, *St. Mery's American Journey*, 334. Washington's servants appear in the Vagrancy Docket, July 2, Aug. 6, 1794.

39. Daily Occurrences, July 9, 1800.

40. Daily Occurrences, Aug. 28, 1800; Index of Admissions and Discharges (to the Almshouse), 1785–1827, Guardians of the Poor, PCA, hereafter cited as Admissions and Discharges.

41. Daily Occurrences, June 6, 1801.

blocks. Mary Malouney and Elizabeth Jones arrived from Albany, New York, in early 1796 "with the intention of begging." After several weeks spent soliciting alms, they were incarcerated and held until spring, "at which season," the constables believed, "they can doubtless get employment in the Country."[42] John Hazless landed in Boston from England in 1766, lived in that city and Cambridge for the next five years, and then became a "wanderer," never spending over a year in any location for the following three decades, until he finally settled in Philadelphia at the end of the century.[43] Mary Uncleson's itinerant behavior was not at all unusual for those engaged in "subsistence migration." After arriving in Philadelphia, she

> remained in the city 3 months, then removed with her husband to Lancaster where they remained 6 months; returned to Philadelphia and lived in different houses 4 to 5 years; to Pittsburgh, then to Shinneystown for one year; to Chester County for several years; returned to Philadelphia and rented a house for $9 per Quarter for one year and nine months; to another house for 6 months, then to a small frame for 6 months but paid no rent, since when she has not kept a house nor has she been hired at service with any one person for a year since she gave up housekeeping [after her husband's death].[44]

On the day of Peter Carle's job hunt, a reward was posted for the return of Isaac, a young slave who had escaped from his Bucks County master. "Free in address" to the point of "boarding on impertinence," and attired in "common labouring dress consisting of a light coloured cloth coatee, light vest, and linsey trousers," Isaac was "of course expected" to flee to Philadelphia. Like many other runaways, black and white, Isaac might well have sought safety in the anonymity of this section of town.[45]

Compounding the misery in this neighborhood were the recurring yellow fever epidemics of the 1790s, which took the lives of many residents too poor to flee to safety outside the city. The small red flags that, by order of the Board of Health, adorned the doors of houses with infected inhabitants proliferated in Moravian Alley and Fetter Lane during the 1793 outbreak. While 5 percent of the city's inhabitants perished in that year, 33 percent of the residents of the alley and 50 percent of those in the lane succumbed to the

42. Vagrancy Docket, Feb. 25, 1796.
43. Daily Occurrences, Jan. 2, 1801.
44. Examination of Paupers, 1826–1831, p. 32, Guardians of the Poor, PCA. Robert E. Cray, Jr., discusses the high rate of geographic mobility by the poor in the New York region in *Paupers and Poor Relief in New York City and Its Rural Environs, 1700–1830* (Philadelphia, 1988), 159–166.
45. *Claypoole's American Daily Advertiser* (Philadelphia), Nov. 13, 1799. Various escapees who fled to the city are discussed in Richard Wojtowicz and Billy G. Smith, "Advertisements for Runaway Slaves, Indentured Servants, and Apprentices in the *Pennsylvania Gazette*, 1795–1796," *PH*, 54 (1987), 34–71.

disease.[46] Jacob Flake, a tailor living at the end of Moravian Alley, lost six children to the pestilence as "whole families," according to one account, sank "into one silent, undistinguished grave." Along with the destitute, the *filles de joie* were particularly susceptible to the epidemics because the "wretched debilitated state of their constitutions rendered them an easy prey to this dreadful disorder, which very soon terminated their miserable career."[47]

Discouraged in his job search, Peter Carle stopped at Roger Tage's tavern, an inn at Water Street and Vine, straddling the official boundary separating the city from its northern suburbs.[48] James Cooper, Jr., a nearby resident, may have frequented this establishment, perhaps embellishing war stories about his nephew Tacey, who had lived briefly with Cooper during the Revolution. Many males had adventures similar to Tacey's and repeatedly relived them in their conversations. Born in Scotland in 1764, Tacey remembered:

> At the age of eight, [I] was put on board the British Ship Three Brothers, Gillas Master, carrying 34 Guns, and sent to the East Indies and was gone three years, and was then ordered to the American Coast. . . . I made my escape to the American Army . . . from there was sent to Philadelphia where I found an Uncle James Cooper and other kin with whom I remained until I entered the service.

Tacey served in the American navy for eighteen months, engaging in numerous battles and assisting in the capture of several British vessels. After the war, he returned to Philadelphia, knocked about as a sailor for several years, then headed west to the newly opened lands in Kentucky. Subsequently, he received a pension of a hundred dollars annually for his military service.[49]

Leaving the tavern and heading toward home, Carle noticed a commotion in the streets. At noon, according to one newspaper story, three "miserable wretches" were brought to the city in the sloop *Ganges* and then marched in chains to the prison, "exciting the attention of a vast concourse of people."[50] Several weeks earlier these sailors had conspired to murder the officers of the *Elizabeth* during its voyage to the West Indies and to seize control of the schooner. After killing the supercargo with an ax and pushing the mate overboard, they faltered when faced by the ship's master. A few days later,

46. Hogan, [1795] *Directory*, 42–43; *First Census*.

47. Mathew Carey, *A Short Account of the Malignant Fever, Lately Prevalent in Philadelphia* (New York, 1970; Philadelphia, 1794), 27; also see Elizabeth Drinker's account in Elizabeth Evans, ed., *Weathering the Storm: Women of the American Revolution* (New York, 1975), 179.

48. Stafford, *Philadelphia Directory for 1797*; Stafford, *Philadelphia Directory for 1801*.

49. Application for Revolutionary War Pensions, S12602, NA; Biddle, [1791] *Directory*; Hogan, [1795] *Directory*; Stafford, *Philadelphia Directory for 1797*; Stafford, *Philadelphia Directory for 1801*.

50. *Claypoole's American Daily Advertiser* (Philadelphia), Nov. 14, 1799. See also *True American* (Philadelphia), Nov. 13, 1799.

after promising cooperation and being allowed freely to roam the vessel, the captain caught the mutineers off guard, locked them in the hold, and single-handedly sailed the schooner to safety. Officials generally expected rebellious behavior by seamen, although mutinies were rare. Mariners were regarded as an unruly class of men who could be properly controlled only by investing the ship's master with godlike powers over his employees.[51] These three sailors had challenged that authority, although their failure to destroy it completely proved to be their undoing. Still, the extreme nature of the challenge itself, as well as the spectacle of chained prisoners, obviously appealed to large crowds of spectators.

Setting out on an afternoon shopping trip, Susannah Cook also was attracted by the midday tumult. Cook lived close to the center of the city, near the corner of Third and Walnut. She washed clothes for her livelihood, a job she had performed to supplement her family's income, at least since her husband's death six years earlier. John had been a successful hairdresser, able during the early 1780s to purchase a house in one of the more affluent areas of the city, where Susannah now lived. By 1790 the Cooks had three children. But yellow fever killed John and one of the boys in 1793, leaving Susannah a middle-aged widow with two children to support. Like the widows of most laboring men, Susannah had few marketable skills, little capital, and limited employment opportunities. She consequently performed the laborious tasks of a washerwoman, earning about three dollars a week, half the wages of an unskilled male laborer. To balance her budget, Cook also ran a boardinghouse, leasing space to cordwainer William Aitkin and two tailors after her spouse's death.[52]

Susannah was somewhat out of place among the nearby householders, most of whom belonged to the middling or better sort of citizens. In her immediate neighborhood, the half block of Third Street between Walnut and Dock streets, lived a physician, a lawyer, a cabinetmaker, a merchant

51. The Admiralty Court judges in Philadelphia extended great authority to masters, as is evident in William P. Farrand, ed., *Admiralty Decisions in the District Court of the United States, for the Pennsylvania District, by the Hon. Richard Peters . . .* (Philadelphia, 1807). The comments and decisions of the judges are in closer agreement with Marcus Rediker's analysis of relations on board ships than with that of N.A.M. Rodger; see Rediker, *Between the Devil and the Deep Blue Sea: Merchant Seamen, Pirates, and the Anglo-American Maritime World, 1700–1750* (Cambridge, England, 1987), and Rodger, *The Wooden World: An Anatomy of the Georgian Navy* (Annapolis, Md., 1986).

52. Information about the Cooks has been collected from White, [1785] *Directory*; Biddle, [1791] *Directory*; Hogan, [1795] *Directory*; Stafford, *Philadelphia Directory for 1797*; Stafford, *Philadelphia Directory for 1800*; *First Census*; and *Second Census*. Of course, not all widows faced such difficult financial problems, as discussed by Lisa Wilson Waciega, "A 'Man of Business': The Widow of Means in Southeastern Pennsylvania, 1750–1850," *WMQ*, 3d Ser., 44 (1987), 40–64.

tailor, two gentlewomen, two grocers, and two master shoemakers. The quality of housing in this neighborhood reflected the predominance of middling and wealthier inhabitants. At nine hundred dollars, Cook's home was the least valuable in the immediate vicinity and one of the few wooden structures in the downtown area. In 1799, Cook, along with her two children and three boarders, crowded into a two-story house, twelve feet wide and twenty-seven feet long. She and the children occupied one floor and the boarders another. Since no separate kitchen existed, Susannah cooked food for her family and tenants in the indoor fireplace, warming the house during these crisp autumn days but making it unbearably hot in the humid summer months. Most of Cook's neighbors lived in somewhat better circumstances. William Master and cabinetmaker Benjamin Lyndall rented identical, adjacent two-story brick houses, measuring twelve feet by twenty feet, for each of their families. Across the street from Cook, grocer William Letchworth, his wife, and six children leased a slightly larger two-story brick residence. Gentlewoman Elizabeth Griffith owned a three-story brick structure, 24 feet by 34 feet, with a separately constructed kitchen, all valued at $4,500, in which she and her servant lived. Dr. James Dunlap and merchant tailor Thomas Harrison occupied similar homes, each with kitchens and smokehouses built behind their dwellings.[53]

Still, even the most spacious houses in Cook's block did not match the palatial mansions symbolic of the exorbitant fortunes recently acquired by some Philadelphians. Just one block south of Cook, William Bingham, a merchant, land speculator, and United States senator, invested part of his wealth in a three-story brick house extended on both sides by two wings, the entire structure measuring one hundred feet wide and sixty feet long. It stood well back from Third Street and was surrounded by a fence to maintain Bingham's privacy. His home's interior included a library, study, banquet room, ballroom, and card room. The land behind the house contained a garden formally laid out in the English style, a small orchard, a greenhouse with five hundred different types of plants, and an icehouse, milk house, and stables. Charles Bullfinch, a noted Boston architect, compared Bingham's mansion to those "in the most luxurious part of Europe. Elegance of construction, white marble staircase, valuable paintings, the richest furniture and the utmost magnificence of decoration makes it a palace in my opinion far too rich for any man in this country."[54]

53. Cook's neighborhood has been reconstructed from Hogan, [1795] *Directory*; Stafford, *Philadelphia Directory for 1797*; Stafford, *Philadelphia Directory for 1800*; 1798 Provincial Tax List; *Second Census*; and U.S. Direct Tax of 1798, Philadelphia: Walnut Ward, 4, Form A, NA.

54. Hogan, [1795] *Directory*; Anon., *The New Trade Directory for Philadelphia, Anno 1800* (Philadelphia, 1800). Bullfinch is quoted in Kelley, *Life and Times*, 70. Bingham's mansion is described by Hogan and Kelley and in Richard G. Miller, "The Federal City, 1783–1800," in Weigley, *Philadelphia*, 177–178.

Plate 3. "View in Third Street, from Spruce Street Philadelphia," 1800. William Bingham's mansion, constructed between 1786 and 1788, is in the foreground, located one block south of Susannah Cook's home. From W. Birch and Son, *The City of Philadelphia . . . As It Appeared in 1800.* Courtesy of the Historical Society of Pennsylvania.

Susannah Cook completed her fifteenth year of residence in her home in 1799. She knew her neighbors well since turnover in this block was minimal, another indication that this was among the city's better residential areas. Except for James Dunlap, who moved into a newly constructed house next door to Cook in 1798, all of the eleven householders in the vicinity had lived there for at least five years. Six of them had been there for a decade, and three since the end of the War for Independence. In addition, nearly all of the householders were long-time residents of the city. Nine had called Philadelphia home for at least a decade, and two for more than twenty years. In a city filled with migrants, where instability marked most poor neighborhoods, Cook's block was neither in flux nor inhabited by many recent arrivals.[55]

Regardless of the stability of Cook's immediate environs, the blocks lying north and south had changed significantly during the recent past, a reflection of the growing specialization and differentiation of specific regions of the city during the second half of the eighteenth century. Originally, Dock Creek had attracted tanyards and currier shops, businesses that required access to water to produce their goods. Since Independence, however, financial establishments such as the Bank of the United States and the Department of the Treasury had located their offices in this area, driving many of the resident manufactures to other parts of the city. By the century's end, these blocks enveloped the country's prime financial district and included the homes of some of Philadelphia's wealthiest citizens.[56]

The winds wafted the stench from the nearby sewer, the outdoor "necessaries," and the garbage in the streets along with thousands of insects into Cook's home. "Innumerable flies," complained one visitor, "constantly light on face and hands, stinging everywhere and turning everything black because of the filth they leave wherever they light." Many people kept their windows tightly shut even during the heat of the day in order "to render the myriads of flies and mosquitoes inactive."[57]

As Susannah Cook walked to market on that November day in 1799, the cool weather dampened the pungent odors and the insect activity. To reach the center of the main market, she headed north on Third Street and then made her way through a maze of alleyways. Within several hundred feet she crossed a bridge over Dock Creek, a stream meandering from the Delaware River through the heart of the city, ending in swamps on its western edge. For decades tanyards had dumped animal carcasses and other waste products into its waters, which, along with garbage and excrement that flowed into the creek, created a stagnant sludge. On summer days the openings in the sewer "exhale the most noxious effluvia," according to one contemporary, "for, dead animals and every kind of nausea are thrown into them, and there remain till they become putrified." Besides being an irritant to sensibilities, Dock Creek posed serious health hazards not fully appreciated by Philadelphians. It polluted the drinking water with bacteria responsible for some of the dysentery (called the "bloody flux" by contemporaries) endemic to the

55. White, [1785] *Directory*; Biddle, [1791] *Directory*; Hogan, [1795] *Directory*; Stafford, *Philadelphia Directory for 1797*; Stafford, *Philadelphia Directory for 1800*; *First Census*; and 1772, 1780, and 1789 Provincial Tax Lists.

56. Spera, "Building for Business," 68, 105–119; Gentry, "Specialized Residential and Business Districts," 17–32.

57. Roberts and Roberts, *St. Mery's American Journey*, 324; Charles William Janson, *The Stranger in America, 1793–1806*, ed. Carl S. Driver (New York, 1971), 188. See also Schoepf, *Travels in the Confederation*, 60.

Plate 4. "Bank of the United States, with a View of Third Street, Philadelphia," 1798. The center of the city's financial district, the Bank stood a block north of Susannah Cook's residence. One visitor praised the structure as "a supurb edifice of the Corinthian order, with a majestic portico of six fluted columns of stone" (Charles William Janson, *The Stranger in America, 1793–1806,* ed. Carl S. Driver [New York, 1971], 192). From W. Birch and Son, *The City of Philadelphia . . . As It Appeared in 1800.* Courtesy of the Historical Society of Pennsylvania.

city. In addition, the mosquitoes that bred there accounted for the most serious yellow fever epidemics ever to plague an American city.[58]

Shortly after entering Carter's Alley, Cook passed the boardinghouse kept

58. Quote from *Philadelphia Monthly Magazine,* Aug. 1798, 69. For descriptions of Dock Creek, see Alexander Graydon, *Memoirs of a Life Chiefly Passed in Pennsylvania* (Harrisburg, Pa., 1811), 34, 43; Thomas Wilson, *The Picture of Philadelphia for 1824, containing the "Picture of Philadelphia, for 1811, by James Mease, M.D."* with All Its Improvements Since That Period (Philadelphia, 1823), 39; and Susan Edith Klepp, "Philadelphia in Transition: A Demographic History of the City and Its Occupational Groups, 1720–1830" (Ph.D. diss., University of Pennsylvania, 1980), 231–232.

by Elizabeth Cathers. Like so many other Philadelphians throughout the years, Cathers had taken an apprentice, ten-year-old Mary Duffey, to help with her work. The Guardians of the Poor had bound out Duffey, as often done with orphans and with children of those who needed assistance, sometimes against the will of the parents. Virtually all girls, whether put to service by their own parents or by the Guardians, learned the "art and mystery of housewifery." Because domestic skills were accorded scant financial rewards, this vocational system limited the future options of most females. On reaching adulthood Mary Duffey's personal desire for marriage would be strengthened by pragmatic considerations. While single or if widowed, she might well confront many of the same dilemmas encountered by Susannah Cook in attempting to support herself and her family. Duffey did not complete her eight-year indenture with Cathers. Her mistress physically abused her a number times, finally prompting the Guardians to cancel the contract.[59]

Jean Baptiste Lemaire also resided in Carter's Alley. Of French origin, he numbered among the most recent wave of migrants who fled the slave rebellion in Santo Domingo (then known as Saint Domingue). Lemaire worked as a fencing master, teaching the sport to his fellow expatriates as well as to the native elite. Such specialized services appeared with great frequency during the 1790s to satisfy the growing demands of the rich for jewels, children's toys, fancy coaches, and lessons in the fine arts of dancing and the French language.[60] Increasing consumption of these luxuries by wealthy French émigrés and American merchants complemented the grand mansions constructed by men such as William Bingham.

Turning north into Goforth Alley, Cook strolled by two of the least valuable houses in the downtown area. Mr. Sebastian, a black man employed as a whitewasher, rented a two-story frame structure, 12 feet by 21 feet, located on a lot of the same dimensions. Tax assessors appraised the house at 500 dollars, one of area's lowest values.[61] Next door John Ward, who worked alternately as a sailor and a shoemaker, leased a dilapidated but slightly larger brick home with one outbuilding, the entire property worth 750 dollars. The past year had been difficult for Ward and his family. In early March his wife had delivered a stillborn boy, and, more recently, the seasonal lull in ship traffic prevented him from securing a berth at sea.[62]

After walking through White Horse Alley, Cook emerged at the center of the city's main market, one of the most impressive on the continent. Three

59. Daily Occurrences, Aug. 23, 1800.
60. Stafford, *Philadelphia Directory for 1797*; and 1798 Provincial Tax List.
61. Hogan, [1795] *Directory*; and U.S. Direct Tax of 1798, Philadelphia: Walnut Ward, 4, Form A, NA.
62. U.S. Direct Tax of 1798, Philadelphia: Walnut Ward, 4, Form A, NA; Stafford, *Philadelphia Directory for 1800*; and Burial Records, Old Swedes Church, Mar. 4, 1799.

Plate 5. "High Street, with the First Presbyterian Church," 1799. This view depicts the central market house, looking toward the east. On her walk, Susannah Cook would have entered the market from White Horse Alley, adjacent to the church. From W. Birch and Son, *The City of Philadelphia . . . As It Appeared in 1800*. Courtesy of the Historical Society of Pennsylvania.

brick halls, open on the sides but covered on top, each a block long, stood in the middle of High Street, stretching between Front and Fourth. Merchants and grocers rented permanent stalls for twenty-four dollars per year in Jersey Market, the easternmost of the three and the choicest spot for sellers. Butchers leased similar but less expensive space in Middle and New Shambles, the western two markets. Vegetable and fruit dealers paid ten dollars per year to set up wooden stands interspersed between the market houses, while sawyers sold firewood at the eastern end of the three halls.[63]

63. Hogan, [1795] *Directory*; James Mease, *The Picture of Philadelphia . . .* (New York, 1970; Philadelphia, 1811), 117–119; and Carl Bridenbaugh, *Cities in Revolt: Urban Life in America, 1743–1776* (New York, 1955), 81–82, 278.

Plate 6. "High Street Market, Philadelphia," 1799. This depiction of the interior of one of the three stalls conforms to a traveler's description of the market as "a covered building, 420 of my steps, in length, exclusive of the intersections of streets, and I calculated my step to be a yard; but only five feet in breadth, including the butchers' benches and blocks" (Charles William Janson, *The Stranger in America, 1793–1806,* ed. Carl S. Driver [New York, 1971], 185). From W. Birch and Son, *The City of Philadelphia . . . As It Appeared in 1800.* Courtesy of the Historical Society of Pennsylvania.

Each Wednesday and Saturday more than 250 vendors sold, according to one observer, "an extraordinary store of provisions" ranging from foodstuffs to manufactured goods.[64] "For beef, veal and mutton," one French visitor noted, "the big market of Philadelphia is only second to that of London-hall, and for fish it only yields to that of New York."[65] "Besides the customary

64. Schoepf, *Travels in the Confederation,* 112.
65. Roberts and Roberts, *St. Mery's American Journey,* 316.

sorts of meat," a German traveler wrote, "Europeans find in season several dishes new to them, such as raccoons, opossums, fish-otters, bear-bacon, and bear's foot &c, as well as many indigenous birds and fishes."[66] These provisions generally had an "attractive" and "appetizing" appearance by contemporary standards, although meat slaughtered on demand, dripping with blood, covered by flies, and occasionally rancid was acceptable within that evaluation.[67] Seasonal rhythms determined the availability of foods just as they affected so many other aspects of life in the city. "After the season for fowls," for example, "come the fisheries of the spring," while "in the beginning and middle of summer it is difficult to procure fresh provisions of any kind."[68]

The market served a variety of communal purposes besides the exchange of merchandise. On the evenings before market days, the city's church bells attracted "people from a distance, especially the Germans . . . into Philadelphia in great covered wagons, loaded with all manner of provender, bringing with them rations for themselves and feed for their horses—for they sleep in their wagons."[69] As these vehicles rumbled down the western end of High Street, boats stocked with fruits, vegetables, and firewood landed at the wharves at the street's eastern edge. Meanwhile, "Negroes and sometimes white people" carried in squirrels, rabbits, and raccoons.[70] These were nights of celebration, with country and city folk alike participating in dances held in the market halls. They were busy times for prostitutes and constables as well. Margaret Britton, for instance, was apprehended for "skulking about Country Waggons in High Street at a late Hour of the Night, and acknowledges that she wished to have carnal Intercourse with them to get money."[71]

On market days "people swarm to the Market House thicker than Flies to a Hogshead from which Sugar has been started."[72] "Everything is full of life," according to one visitor who never grew tired of "watching this multitude of men and women all moving about and going in every direction."[73] The marketplace of Philadelphia, as much as any other market in the Western world, attracted people of various nationalities and races, speaking a host of

66. Schoepf, *Travels in the Confederation*, 112.
67. "During the summer the flies must be continually driven away" from the meat at the stalls, according to St. Mery, in Roberts and Roberts, *St. Mery's American Journey*, 316. Meat and milk spoiled very quickly on hot summer days; Janson, *Stranger in America*, 187.
68. Janson, *Stranger in America*, 187.
69. Schoepf, *Travels in the Confederation*, 112.
70. Janson, *Stranger in America*, 185.
71. Vagrancy Docket, Jan. 16, 1794.
72. Harrold E. Gillingham, ed., "Dr. Solomon Drowne," *PMHB*, 48 (1924), 236.
73. Schoepf, *Travels in the Confederation*, 112. See also J. P. Briscot De Warville, *New Travels in the United States of America, 1788*, ed. and trans. Durand Escheverria and Mara Soceanu (Cambridge, Mass., 1964), 199.

dialects and languages. Besides the intermingling of all sorts of humanity, part of the excitement, at least until the 1780s, entailed public floggings and the exhibition of criminals in stocks in the middle of the market.[74]

Having reached the market after two o'clock, when stalls began to close, Cook bargained for leftover or damaged foods and thereby trimmed her household budget. In the market's center, where Susannah arrived, stood the stalls of butchers, most of them of German descent. The slaughter of summer-fattened animals during autumn meant that meat prices generally held firm at this time of year. Cook haggled for pork at five or six cents a pound or for beef at a penny more, though she shunned fruits and vegetables as being too costly. Walking eastward to the staples section, Susannah purchased the cheapest type of flour available for about four cents a pound. Because she could afford a treat on this visit, Cook spent five cents for a quarter-pound of butter.[75]

After completing her purchases, Susannah started home, stopping along the way at Sarah Bristol's bakery in Letitia Court. Until recent years officials had set the cost of bread sold by bakers, operating on the long-standing assumption that a "just price" for essentials should be maintained to protect the consumer while allowing the producer a "fair" profit. Since the Revolution, however, an ethic emphasizing less governmental regulation of the economy had gained strength, resulting in the abandonment of the assize of bread during the mid-1790s. Instead of buying bread, Cook paid to have her own homemade loaves baked. Many of the city's poor either did not have baking facilities or else calculated that fuel for a fire built solely to heat their ovens would cost more than the penny or two needed to have their bread baked for them.[76]

Besides Sarah Bristol, Elizabeth Roberts and Patience Stoy also lived in Letitia Court; all had lost their husbands to yellow fever in 1793. The way these widows supported themselves illustrates the importance of the marriage experiences of women in determining how they coped after the demise of their husbands. Before his death, Jacob Bristol and Sarah together operated their bakery. With the knowledge and experience thereby acquired, Sarah continued to direct the bakery successfully throughout the 1790s. John Stoy had been a tailor, and not surprisingly his widow Patience earned her living as a seamstress, the line of work they had shared during their marriage. Elizabeth Roberts, however, did not participate with her husband

---

74. Negley K. Teeters, *The Cradle of the Penitentiary: The Walnut Street Jail at Philadelphia* (Philadelphia, 1955), 11. Michael Meranze kindly supplied this reference.

75. The prices of these items are listed in Appendix F.

76. James T. Mitchell and Henry Flanders, comps., *The Statutes at Large of Pennsylvania*, 18 vols. (Philadelphia, 1896–1911), 14:510–511, 15:541–542; "Several Bakers," *Federal Gazette and Philadelphia Daily Advertiser* (Philadelphia), Nov. 7, 1793.

in his job as a tax collector. Failing to develop marketable skills while married, and without an ongoing family business to pursue, Elizabeth relied on her domestic talents to run a boardinghouse.[77]

Continuing toward home, Cook passed the house and shop kept by Mary Allen. Just three years earlier Allen had been one of the increasing number of women in the city to be granted a divorce. She had married Thomas, a cordwainer, in 1786, but he failed to give up his interest in other women. On April Fool's Day in 1794, he moved in with his lover, Margaret Johnson, a widow and shopkeeper living in north Philadelphia. When Mary, left with four children all under ten years old, filed for a divorce on grounds of adultery two years later, her husband did not contest the suit.[78]

Returning home, Cook began preparing the evening meal and continued her washing chores. At some point during the past several years, she had contracted consumption, which was aggravated by her heavy work schedule. When two of her boarders moved out in 1800, her financial situation deteriorated. In July 1801, too sick to care for herself or her children, Cook applied for admittance to the almshouse. The managers initially boarded her with a nurse outside the institution but then readmitted her in August. Several months later Susannah succumbed to her illness.[79]

If he could have accompanied Carle and Cook on their respective walks, William Smith, a shoemaker who had resided in Philadelphia half a century earlier, would have found much about urban life that was familiar.[80] First, the population had expanded enormously, augmented primarily by a large influx of immigrants. Still, the racial and ethnic diversity and the itinerant background of the residents in Smith's time remained characteristic of the inhabitants at the close of the century. Second, the city's overall mortality level had lessened as smallpox, the primary killer before the Revolution, had been gradually brought under control. Yet Smith would not have been surprised by the periodic, devastating epidemics of the 1790s, even though he might not have recognized the new disease, yellow fever. Third, Philadelphia's prosperity had increased significantly during the past five decades, although the city's basic economic structure had not changed fundamentally. The primary business activities still entailed exporting the region's grain products, importing British manufactures, constructing houses and ships, and distributing the handmade goods of urban craftsmen throughout the

77. White, [1785] *Directory*; Biddle, [1791] *Directory*; Hogan, [1795] *Directory*; Stafford, *Philadelphia Directory for 1797*; and Stafford, *Philadelphia Directory for 1800*.

78. Stafford, *Philadelphia Directory for 1797*; Stafford, *Philadelphia Directory for 1800*; *Second Census*; and Divorce Papers.

79. Stafford, *Philadelphia Directory for 1800*; and Admissions and Discharges.

80. Roach, "Taxables in the City of Philadelphia, 1756," 3–41.

Plate 7. "Alms House in Spruce Street," 1799. The brick walls surrounding the almshouse were designed to confine inmates to the grounds. On the eve of the Revolution, Dr. Robert Honyman offered the following description of the structure: "It is built of Brick, & consists of a Main Body & two wings, & in the two corners are two square buildings, higher than the other parts, which are two stories high, besides a ground & Garret story. It has Piazzas round on the Inside" (Philip Padelford, ed., *Colonial Panorama 1775: Dr. Robert Honyman's Journal for March and April* [San Marino, Calif., 1939], 17). From W. Birch and Son, *The City of Philadelphia . . . As It Appeared in 1800.* Courtesy of the Historical Society of Pennsylvania.

area. Even if some signs of the coming industrial order were evident, most artisans continued to work in small shops headed by a master craftsman and only a handful of laborers, mostly women, spent their time in factories.

Smith also would have discovered considerable change. Though the city's affluence had increased, the lines distinguishing the classes actually had become more clearly drawn. Commercial success had been distributed un-equally as the richest citizens had accrued control of more of the wealth. The newly emerging residential segregation by class and ethnicity was but one index of the growing social gulf. A number of mechanics had taken advantage of the available opportunities to enhance their own material circumstances, but Smith might be dismayed that the physical comfort of many among the lower sort had not improved much. Their efforts to acquire the basic necessities were no less painful in 1799 than they had been at midcentury.

As many historians have documented, the political events of the second half of the eighteenth century deepened the commitment of Philadelphians to the notions of freedom, independence, and equality, with critical implications for public political affairs.[81] But those ideas affected the private lives of laboring people in equally significant ways, promoting independence, affection, and equality in most families but also contributing, ironically, to increased domestic turmoil.

William Smith would have found one final aspect of life among late eighteenth-century laboring Philadelphians familiar: they lived in an intensely insecure environment. Disease abruptly ended life, business cycles sent people to the almshouse, material success was often fleeting, working men and women worried daily about how to make ends meet, and family relationships were in transition. The following chapters explore these and other themes in detail, examining the ways in which the lower sort coped with an often difficult, changing, and uncertain world.

81. Gary B. Nash, *The Urban Crucible: Social Change, Political Consciousness, and the Origins of the American Revolution* (Cambridge, Mass., 1979); Richard Ryerson, *The Revolution Is Now Begun: The Radical Committees of Philadelphia, 1765–1776* (Philadelphia, 1978); Steven Rosswurm, *Arms, Country, and Class: The Philadelphia Militia and the "Lower Sort" during the American Revolution, 1775–1783* (New Brunswick, N.J., 1987); Charles S. Olton, *Artisans for Independence: Philadelphia Mechanics and the American Revolution* (Syracuse, N.Y., 1975); Eric Foner, *Tom Paine and Revolutionary America* (New York, 1976); and Sean Wilentz, *Chants Democratic: New York City & the Rise of the American Working Class, 1788–1850* (New York, 1984).

Chapter Two

Deaths and Births
in an Immigrant City

And God blessed them, saying, Be fruitful, and multiply.
—Gen. 1:22

May the God of consolation give me support under this dispensation.
—Nicholas Collin, on the death of his wife in Philadelphia in 1797

THERE IS BUT ONE favorable characteristic of yellow fever: it nearly always kills its victims quickly. Thus it was unusual that Jonathan Grice lingered for a full month with the disease before, like thousands of other Philadelphians in 1793, succumbing to its ravages.[1] A few years later, Susannah Sheed endured an excruciating death from smallpox. After twenty days with a high fever, "her mouth mortified," according to her pastor, then "her teeth came out, most of the fore-teeth, some she pulled out and some dropt. One of her feet was also much affected, inclining to mortify. This pock," he noted dispassionately, "was of the watery bladder-like sort." Children were especially vulnerable to appalling illnesses. The parents of Rebecca Carrick attempted to protect her from smallpox by having her inoculated. The process, which always transmitted at least a mild form of the disease to the patient, caused Rebecca to experience "swellings on her knees, elbows, shoulders, neck and breast, with oozing of acrid matter and dislocation of the bones" before the ailment took her life. Six-month-old Thomas Shillingsford fell victim to worms as, Rector Nicholas Collin observed, "so many others do." But the abundance of parasites that infested the child impressed Collin,

---

1. Burial Records, Old Swedes Church, Gloria Dei, Nov. 1, 1793, GSP, hereafter cited as Burial Records, Old Swedes Church. Selections from these records are available in Billy G. Smith and Susan E. Klepp, "The Records of Gloria Dei Church: Burials, 1800–1804," *PH*, 53 (1986), 56–79.

since Thomas "voided in the course of a week above one hundred, and at once on the 21st of this month, 45. The mother told me that they were all from 1/4 to 1/8 of a yard long, and that in the beginning of the disorder 14 of them were vomited. The kind was the usual white. He had been sick a month."[2]

As numerous and miserable as these sufferings were, Philadelphia still teemed with new life: one birth matched each death in the City of Brotherly Love throughout most of the second half of the eighteenth century. In 1800 Elizabeth Davis helped her friend Margaret Saffern deliver a healthy baby girl.[3] If they followed traditional procedures, a midwife and several female friends assisted and encouraged Margaret throughout her hours of labor. The previous year, Sally Downing chose a new obstetric method, hiring a male doctor who assumed the primary responsibility for the birth and at one point contemplated using forceps, a recently introduced medical instrument, to deliver the baby.[4]

By whatever means Philadelphians entered or exited the world, they faced the eternal human uncertainties about life and death, about how many children they would produce, about what ailments they would suffer, and about how many years they would have on earth. This chapter addresses those questions, analyzing the demographic reality of the city and its laboring people. The vital demographic rates were remarkable by contemporary standards: population grew quickly, mortality levels were high, babies were numerous, and waves of immigrants poured into and through the urban center. The volatile and shifting epidemiological environment combined with heavy migration to shape many of those rates. In addition, migration, morbidity, and mortality varied by class as laboring people, compared to the wealthy, more frequently moved and more often suffered illness and premature deaths.

Scholars have devoted considerable attention to determining Philadelphia's demographic vital rates. Because the first census of the city was not conducted until 1790, historians initially reconstructed the population by multiplying the number of houses and taxpaying citizens by an arithmetic constant. More recent efforts to fit the population changes to theoretical models have provided a very sophisticated analysis of the city's growth (see

2. All three cases are in the Burial Records, Old Swedes Church. Sheed is described in the entry for July 10, 1805, pp. 227–228; Carrick on Jan. 9, 1805, p. 225; and Shillingsford on July 30, 1802, p. 188.

3. Daily Occurrences Docket, Nov. 14, 1800, Guardians of the Poor, PCA, hereafter cited as Daily Occurrences.

4. Catherine M. Scholten, "Changing Customs of Childbirth in America, 1760 to 1825," *WMQ*, 3d Ser., 34 (1977), 426–445; James H. Cassedy, *Medicine and American Growth, 1800–1860* (Madison, Wis., 1986), 181–187.

Appendix B). Between 1750 and 1800 Philadelphia's population multiplied more than fivefold, a growth rate averaging an extremely high 3.4 percent each year (see Figure 1 and Appendix B).[5]

Ironically, the population increased rapidly even as Philadelphians suffered very high levels of mortality. The burials recorded in the city's cemeteries indicate that, on average, between forty and fifty people per thousand inhabitants died each year (see Appendix B), meaning that conditions in the city were far worse than those in most contemporary areas. Various diseases, some of them constantly reintroduced and spread by migrants, pushed the city's mortality rates to astonishing heights. As the principal American immigrant port during the period, Philadelphia experienced the arrival of a trickle of English, approximately twenty-six thousand Irish and Scotch Irish, and nearly forty thousand German newcomers between 1750 and 1775. After pausing during the Revolutionary War, migration resumed as the French and the Irish merged with groups leaving the American countryside to create a new influx of migrants to Philadelphia during the last fifteen years of the eighteenth century.[6]

The long Atlantic voyage, lasting from six weeks to six months, killed many immigrants and left others in a weakened or dying condition on arrival at the city's docks. Afflictions plagued passengers during many of the ocean crossings as dysentery, typhus, and typhoid fever flourished in the overcrowded, unsanitary conditions of the small vessels, and even smallpox and yellow fever sometimes made their appearance. In any combination, these disorders usually resulted in disaster for both passengers and crew. But even

5. See Table B.1 and Appendix B for the data and sources for Figure 1. Records are unreliable for years with missing values.

6. Studies of other contemporary areas include John B. Blake, *Public Health in the Town of Boston, 1630–1822* (Cambridge, Mass., 1959), 112; J. D. Chambers, "Population Change in a Provincial Town: Nottingham 1700–1800," in L. S. Pressnell, ed., *Studies in the Industrial Revolution* (London, 1960), 97–125; and Philip J. Greven, Jr., *Four Generations: Population, Land, and Family in Colonial Andover, Massachusetts* (Ithaca, 1970). Philadelphia's demographic conditions are compared with these other locales in Billy G. Smith, "Death and Life in a Colonial Immigrant City: A Demographic Analysis of Philadelphia," *JEH*, 37 (1977), 863–889. The best analyses of migration to the city are in Marianne Wokeck, "The Flow and the Composition of German Immigration to Philadelphia, 1727–1775," *PMHB*, 105 (1981), 249–278; and Wokeck, "Irish Immigration to the Delaware Valley before the American Revolution" (Paper presented at the Philadelphia Center for Early American Studies, University of Pennsylvania, Oct. 7, 1988). See also Farley Grubb, "British Immigration to Philadelphia: The Reconstruction of Ship Passenger Lists from May 1772 to October 1773," *PH*, 55 (1988), 118–141; and R. J. Dickson, *Ulster Emigration to Colonial America, 1718–1775* (London, 1966), 59. Ralph Beaver Strassburger and William John Hinke estimated that approximately sixty-five thousand Germans arrived in Philadelphia during this period, in *Pennsylvania German Pioneers: A Publication of the Original Lists of Arrivals in the Port of Philadelphia from 1727 to 1808*, Pennsylvania-German Society Publications nos. 42–44 (Norristown, Pa., 1934), 1:xxix, xxxi.

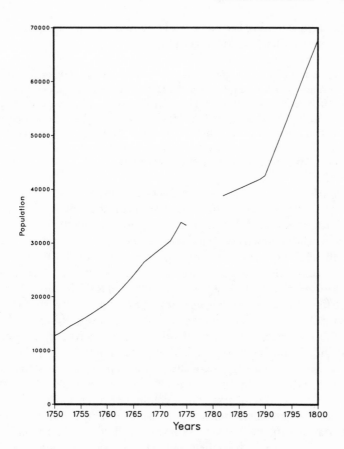

Figure 1. Population of urban Philadelphia, 1750–1800

the immigrants from Ireland may not have suffered as severely as the German redemptioners and indentured servants—the bulk of the migrants—who underwent appalling voyages, some of which, on rare occasions, resembled the horrors of the African "middle passage."[7] Gottlieb Mittelberger, who traveled from Germany to Philadelphia in 1750 as a paying passenger, vividly described some of the difficulties. Captains literally packed transients

7. Wokeck, "Irish Immigration"; John Duffy, "The Passage to the Colonies," *Mississippi Valley Historical Review*, 38 (1951), 21–38; and John Duffy, *Epidemics in Colonial America* (Baton Rouge, La., 1953), 223, 229. Illness and death were omnipresent threats on board ship. Christopher Sauer, editor of a newspaper in a village outside Philadelphia, estimated that 2,000 passengers on fifteen ships, due to arrive in 1758, perished en route. Accounts of individual ship disasters are equally appalling: Johann Keppele reported in his diary that 150 of 312 passengers

onto the ship, assigning each a bedstead measuring a mere two by six feet. "During the Journey," Mittelberger wrote,

> the ship is full of pitiful signs of distress—smells, fumes, horrors, vomiting, various kinds of sea sickness, fever, dysentery, headaches, heat, constipation, boils, scurvy, cancer, mouth-rot, and similar afflictions, all of them caused by the age and the highly salted state of the food, especially of the meat, as well as by the very bad and filthy water, which brings about the miserable destruction and death of many. Add to all that shortage of food, hunger, thirst, frost, heat, dampness, fear, misery, vexation, and lamentation as well as other troubles.[8]

If paying passengers endured such problems, conditions for poorer migrants in steerage berths frequently must have been considerably worse.

On reaching the New World many transients encountered a final disappointment when captains confined passengers who could not pay their full fare to the ship until they were purchased as indentured servants. "In this whole process," Mittelberger commented, "the sick were the worst off, for the healthy are preferred and are most readily paid for. The miserable people who are ill must often still remain at sea and in sight of the city for another two or three weeks—which in many cases means death."[9]

The effects of the harsh North Atlantic passage lingered, creating substantial morbidity and mortality levels among immigrants after the voyage. Some, as Mittelberger suggested, died on a ship docked in Philadelphia's harbor and, although lying in an American grave, never actually set foot on the shore. Others, disembarking in a debilitated condition and facing new climatic and disease environments, succumbed to illness and death. During their initial months in the New World most migrants underwent a "seasoning" period during which they contracted a variety of ailments.[10] Just as

---

died during the voyage, the *Sea Flower* lost 46 of its 106 travelers, and the *Love and Unity* arrived with only 34 of its 150 journeyers. These accounts are from Frank Diffenderffer, *The German Immigration into Pennsylvania through the Port of Philadelphia*, Pennsylvania-German Society Proceedings no. 10 (Lancaster, Pa., 1900), 260; and from Richard Hofstadter, *America at 1750: A Social Portrait* (New York, 1971), 41–42. Basing his analysis on a limited number of voyages, Farley Grubb estimated markedly lower on-board death rates for German migrants than have most other historians, in "Morbidity and Mortality on the North Atlantic Passage: Eighteenth-Century German Immigration," *Journal of Interdisciplinary History*, 17 (1987), 570–571.

8. Gottlieb Mittelberger, *Journey to Pennsylvania*, ed. and trans. Oscar Handlin and John Clive (Cambridge, Mass., 1960), 12–13.

9. Ibid., 16. For similar accounts, see Adolph B. Benson, ed., *The America of 1750: Peter Kalm's Travels in North America*, 2 vols. (New York, 1964), 1:16–17; and William Moraley, *The Infortunate: or, The Voyage and Adventures of William Moraley . . .* (Newcastle, England, 1743).

10. Duffy, *Epidemics*, 218. Farley Grubb estimated the mortality of new arrivals as at least 66 percent higher than Philadelphia's death rates during the eighteenth century. Since his calculations do not include migrants who died after passing through the city, the mortality rate may have been considerably higher; "Morbidity and Mortality," 570–571.

European diseases slaughtered native Americans, new infirmities and unique forms of familiar ones against which their background had provided little immunity took the lives of many who walked down the gangplank at the Pennsylvania docks.[11]

The extent to which the demise of migrants inflated the city's death rate can be estimated in only the crudest fashion. Benjamin Franklin considered the burials in Philadelphia's Strangers' Ground during the 1740s to have consisted primarily of immigrants who died from shipboard diseases.[12] However, while that graveyard undoubtedly served as the principal immigrant cemetery, burials there included many paupers as well.[13] Cost mitigated against the entombment of poor people in a church cemetery; St. Paul's, for example, charged eleven pounds for funerals in 1762, the equivalent of more than two months' wages for a laboring man.[14] Moreover, a great many Philadelphians did not attend any church and thus were eligible only for a plot in a secular cemetery.[15] Perhaps the best estimate, although necessarily imprecise, is that the deaths of immigrants accounted for about one-half of the Strangers' Ground interments, or approximately 14 percent of the city's burials during the second half of the century.

If immigrant deaths added directly to the city's interments, transients carried and disseminated ailments that attacked the health of the residents. Lice and unsanitary water and sewage disposal systems helped to diffuse a variety of common "ship fevers" throughout the city.[16] Smallpox infected

11. For a discussion of increased mortality caused by human migration from one disease environment to another, see Philip D. Curtin, "Epidemiology and the Slave Trade," *Political Science Quarterly*, 83 (1968), 190–216.

12. Leonard W. Labaree et al., eds., *The Papers of Benjamin Franklin*, 24 vols. (New Haven, Conn., 1959–), 3:439.

13. The Philadelphia Common Council, a newspaper editor, and the records of one church all referred to the Strangers' Ground as "Potter's Field." See *Minutes of the Common Council of the City of Philadelphia* (Philadelphia, 1847), 710–711; Zachariah Poulson, *Poulson's Town and Country Almanac . . .* (Philadelphia, 1800), 1; and Birth, Marriage, and Burial Records of Christ Church, vol. 174, GSP, hereafter cited as Birth, Marriage, and Burial Records, Christ Church.

14. Norris Stanley Barratt, *Outline of the History of Old St. Paul's Church, Philadelphia, Pennsylvania, 1760–1898* (Lancaster, Pa., 1918), 43. As a point of reference, the average Philadelphia laborer earned three or four shillings per day in 1762. The Burial Records of Old Swedes Church are filled with examples of poor people requesting the abatement of burial fees.

15. The lack of affiliation with churches by many Philadelphians is discussed by Carl Bridenbaugh and Jessica Bridenbaugh, *Rebels and Gentlemen: Philadelphia in the Age of Franklin*, 2d ed. (New York, 1965), 18. The strict regulations for burial in Gloria Dei's grounds are evident in Burial Records, Old Swedes Church.

16. Duffy, *Epidemics*, 202–237. The arrival of immigrants and their interaction with the city's residents also spread diseases already present in Philadelphia. Francis Packard, *History of Medicine in the United States*, 2 vols. (New York, 1963; orig. 1931), 1:88, blames the severity of the 1756 smallpox epidemic on the spread of the disease caused by the arrival of troops in Philadelphia during that year. According to Packard, the governor of Pennsylvania was alarmed that "the smallpox is increasing among the soldiers to such a degree that the whole town will soon become a hospital." If the arrival of troops in a single year could have such an adverse

practically everyone with whom the newcomer came into contact. And, regardless of elaborate quarantine precautions, sick immigrants fed the mosquitoes thriving in the nearby marshes, thereby enabling yellow fever and, to a lesser extent, malaria to spread among the inhabitants.[17]

These and other immigrant-related diseases created extremely hazardous conditions for Philadelphia's citizens, reflected in their deep concern about health problems. The Assembly and governor of the colony took various steps to regulate overseas immigration. While expressing a large measure of humanitarian sentiment aimed at aiding the newcomers, their proposals included an important component of pragmatic self-protection. Arguments proposing such precautionary measures as constructing a hospital to quarantine new arrivals, fumigating ships with tobacco smoke, inspecting incoming vessels, and restricting the number of passengers transported on each boat nearly always reflected this dual perspective.

Responding to a yellow fever epidemic, the governor in 1741 advocated building a lazaretto to quarantine sick passengers "to prevent the spreading of infectious diseases they may happen to have contracted in their voyage hither." Such action, he felt, was "a suitable Charity and [an] Effectual security for the future" and in "the interest of the Province and the Health of the City."[18] The Assembly endorsed his proposal as "a means to prevent the spreading of infectious Distempers among Us, the effects of which the City of Philadelphia has lately felt."[19] The following year officials designated Province Island in the Schuylkill River as the site of the "pest house" and levied fines on anyone who harbored a patient who had been confined to the hospital.[20] In 1754, spurred by the death of over 250 new arrivals, government authorities appointed a team of doctors to visit arriving ships and the places where ailing immigrants lodged. The physicians reported their findings to the governor, criticizing the Assembly for not having "made the necessary regulations to prevent malignant Diseases being generated by these people, after they came into port, where there is more danger of it than at sea."[21] The Assembly reacted, against the interest of many merchants who

effect, the continuous flow of immigrants must have dramatically inflated the city's overall mortality level.

17. Duffy, *Epidemics*, 17, 205–209; Richard Shryock, "A Century of Medical Progress in Philadelphia: 1750–1850," *PH*, 8 (1941), 7–28. In 1745 Dr. John Mitchell of Philadelphia attributed the outbreak of two yellow fever epidemics to the arrival of infected immigrants, in *The Letters and Papers of Cadwallader Colden*, New York Historical Society Collections no. 3 (New York, 1919), 326.

18. "Minutes of the Provincial Council," *Colonial Records of Pennsylvania* (Harrisburg, Pa., 1851), 4:507, 510; and Duffy, *Epidemics*, 153.

19. Ibid., 508.

20. John F. Watson, *Annals of Philadelphia, and Pennsylvania, in the Olden Time . . .* , 3 vols. (Philadelphia, 1881), 3:333; Diffenderffer, *German Immigration*, 86–87.

21. "A Colonial Health Report of Philadelphia, 1754," *PMHB*, 36 (1912), 479.

trafficked in indentured servants and had close ties to the governor, by imposing much tighter restrictions on vessels, since "infectious Distempers have, notwithstanding previous laws, been introduced and spread in this province."[22] Christopher Sauer, a leading spokesman for the rights of German immigrants, played on the emotions and legitimate fears of Pennsylvania residents, pleading for laws to limit the number of passengers a ship could carry on grounds that they otherwise would "infect the County which receives them," thereby causing an "Increase and Propagation of the Distempers they have brought among us."[23] Judging from the rhetoric and measures adopted, Philadelphians correctly perceived that migrants posed a danger to their own physical well-being.

Despite these precautions, diseases and epidemics formed a routine part of life in the city. Smallpox, recurring every few years, posed the greatest danger during the colonial period, accounting for 18 percent of the decedents in Christ Church's cemetery between 1750 and 1775, a rate twice that of London in the mid-eighteenth century.[24] Residents dreaded the "summer complaints" and the "fall agues" each year, and the peak influx of immigrants during these seasons helped spread fevers and dysentery throughout the city. At least 12 percent of Christ Church's burials during the third quarter of the century resulted from these types of ailments.[25] Typhus, the most common shipboard affliction, also may have been the most prevalent fever in the urban center, although consumption and typhoid fever likewise contributed to the high mortality. At the century's end yellow fever, probably imported on a ship from the West Indies, took the lives of thousands of inhabitants. Venereal disease also ran rampant through the population, killing a great many Philadelphians after years of suffering.[26] To suppress the symptoms of syphilis, most of its victims took mercury pills, but, like so many eighteenth-century remedies, the medicine often created physical problems worse than the illness itself. A variety of other disorders—including diphtheria, scarlet fever, measles, influenza, and pneumonia—took their toll, but physicians could not distinguish among these sicknesses adequately enough to permit evaluation, then or now, of the effects of each.

22. "Minutes of the Provincial Council," *Colonial Records of Pennsylvania*, 6:345. Stricter regulation hurt the merchants' traffic in both people and goods; Diffenderffer, *German Immigration*, 251–255.

23. Diffenderffer, *German Immigration*, 246–247.

24. Smallpox caused about 9 percent of the deaths in London between 1731 and 1765; Duffy, *Epidemics*, 22. The cause of death of Christ Church members is indicated in Birth, Marriage, and Burial Records, Christ Church, vol. 174.

25. As one of the wealthy social groups, the Anglicans enjoyed sufficient food, adequate shelter, and the financial means to escape the area during epidemics. Smallpox and various fevers therefore were undoubtedly more deadly for the city's poorer inhabitants.

26. The epidemic proportions of venereal disease, especially among Philadelphia's destitute citizens, are evident in Daily Occurrences.

Besides causing early death, these maladies burdened the daily lives of Philadelphians. For example, nearly every city resident eventually contracted smallpox and its pustules left many people permanently scarred with "pock marks." Others chronically suffered headaches, upset stomachs, diarrhea, asthma, arthritis, and the like. As one city resident complained, "what a variety of diseases is this poor tabernacle subject to. Man is indeed surrounded with infirmities."[27] And so too are women.

Although the city's crude death rates always were high, they rose and fell during the second half of the century primarily in response to the changing disease environment (see Figure 2).[28] Approximately fifty of every thousand inhabitants died annually during the 1750s, but that figure declined during the next two decades to less than forty per thousand. Even lower death rates characterized the 1780s, but they skyrocketed to as high as ninety-five per thousand during the severe epidemics of the 1790s.

Smallpox was the greatest killer of Philadelphians during the third quarter of the eighteenth century, accounting for most of the annual fluctuations in the death rate before the Revolution as well as for the overall downward trend in mortality after 1760.[29] The bills of mortality indicate that smallpox killed a great many Anglicans in 1751, 1756, 1759, 1762, 1763, 1765, 1769, and 1773, meaning that nearly every peak in the death rate during the century's third quarter resulted from an outbreak of the disease. The decreasing virulence of smallpox tempered the city's death rates at the end of the colonial period. The decline of smallpox-induced deaths is evident among Anglicans during the 1760s and early 1770s: the disease caused 26 percent of their burials during the 1750s, 18 percent between 1761 and 1765, and 11 percent from 1765 to the Revolution. At the same time, epidemics became less severe: the outbreaks of 1756 and 1759 accounted for nearly 60 percent of the deaths among Anglicans, whereas the epidemic years between 1760 and 1775 were marked by a high of only 31 percent.

27. Elizabeth Cope Harrison, ed., *Philadelphia Merchant: The Diary of Thomas P. Cope, 1800–1851* (South Bend, Ind., 1978), 3–39, quote on 7. The variety of ailments that afflicted Philadelphians is evident in Daily Occurrences, and in Elaine F. Crane, "The World of Elizabeth Drinker," *PMHB*, 107 (1983), 25.

28. Data and sources for Figure 2 are in Table B.1 and Appendix B. Records are unreliable for years with missing values.

29. Several other factors influenced the downward trend in death rates during the late colonial period, if in a less dramatic fashion than smallpox. Both declining birth rates (see Figure 3) and continuing population growth depressed death rates during the 1760s and 1770s. Fewer births meant fewer infants in the age groups with the highest mortality levels. And the increase in the number of residents lessened the impact of immigrant burials on the city's overall death rates. For example, because of the city's population expansion, the death of one hundred immigrants inflated the city's death rate by eight per thousand in 1750 but only three per thousand in 1775.

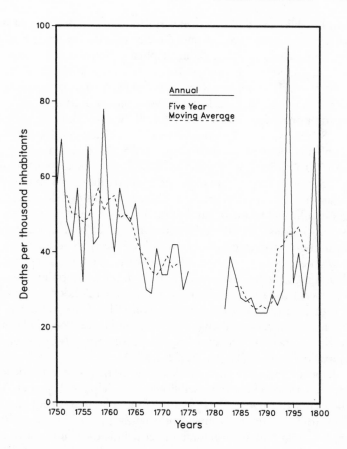

Figure 2. Death rates in Philadelphia, 1750–1800

The declining lethality of smallpox most likely resulted from an increase in variolation (an early form of vaccination). Early in the eighteenth century, physicians learned to inoculate patients with a milder, less dangerous form of the disease to protect them from its worst ravages. And large numbers of wealthy citizens (a few of whom first tested the procedure on their slaves) began to be immunized after 1760. Still, many citizens strongly resisted variolation, fearing correctly that infected patients could spread the disease among the unprotected residents. Thus the process had not gained widespread acceptance even two decades after its introduction into the city in 1736. But in 1759, in the midst of a raging epidemic and with the support of

Benjamin Franklin and the success of variolation in Boston, the first private hospital for inoculation opened and the city quickly became a center for smallpox immunization.[30] Poor Philadelphians, however, often could not afford the new medical technology. Inoculation was expensive, costing the equivalent of nearly a month's wages for a laborer. And patients had to be isolated for two or three weeks to prevent their infecting other people, creating additional expenses for their care and the loss of income during that period.[31] Several physicians recognized these problems, and, alarmed by the great number of poor children who had contracted the disease, they established in 1774 a Society for Inoculation of the Poor, providing service free of charge.[32] Still, the decreasing fatality of smallpox measured among Anglicans, a materially prosperous group, undoubtedly was not shared as widely among less affluent Philadelphians before the Revolution.

These conclusions—based on the figures registered in the bills of mortality—regarding improvements in the health of the city's residents are supported by other evidence. The records of baptisms and burials kept by Christ Church and the Dutch Calvinists shed light on infant mortality, one of the most significant indicators of health conditions. Childhood mortality improved significantly during the years preceding the Revolution. The death rates among infants and children between one and three years old during the final decade of the colonial era averaged approximately 60 percent below their mortality in the 1750s (see Appendix B).

Philadelphians exhibited markedly lower death rates in the decade following the Revolution. The newly established Philadelphia Dispensary inoculated thousands of citizens free of charge, thus helping to bring the disease under control.[33] By the early nineteenth century, James Mease, a city resident, rejoiced that "vaccination is rapidly dispelling the loathsome small pox from the city." In addition, since fewer migrants disembarked at the city's docks during the post-Revolutionary period, they spread less disease among the residents and contributed fewer burials to the cemeteries. As a result,

30. George W. Norris, *The Early History of Medicine in Philadelphia* (Philadelphia, 1886), 107, 113; Donald R. Hopkins, *Princes and Peasants: Smallpox in History* (Chicago, 1983), 255.
31. Carl Bridenbaugh, *Cities in Revolt: Urban Life in America, 1743–1776*, rev. ed. (New York, 1971), 329; John B. Blake, *Public Health in the Town of Boston, 1630–1822* (Cambridge, Mass., 1959), 112; Duffy, *Epidemics*, 40–41, 103; Labaree et al., *Papers of Benjamin Franklin*, 8:284. Inoculation seldom cost less than three pounds, or about a month's wages of a laboring man in 1762; Norris, *Early History of Medicine*, 112. A firsthand report of the arduous process of variolation is available in Cecil K. Drinker, *Not So Long Ago* (New York, 1937), 91–92.
32. Norris, *Early History of Medicine*, 114; Hopkins, *Princes and Peasants*, 256.
33. One out of every five patients at the Philadelphia Dispensary was inoculated for smallpox; see Out Patients Attended and Supplied from the Dispensary of the Pennsylvania Hospital, 1797–1817, Records of the Pennsylvania Hospital, Archives of the Pennsylvania Hospital, Philadelphia, hereafter cited as Out Patients Attended.

Mease claimed, "typhus fevers generally, and the bowel complaint"—two maladies associated with immigrants—"have diminished."[34]

Many citizens attributed the town's healthier conditions to improved sanitation during the 1780s, which may have had some effect, particularly in the affluent neighborhoods.[35] The urban government allocated funds to enhance the center city blocks, paving many streets, hiring scavengers regularly to clean the main thoroughfares, and constructing coverings over Dock Creek, a sewer that meandered through the middle of town. Yet, especially in the impoverished, outlying neighborhoods, pigs, dogs, and rats roamed freely to feed on the garbage in the streets, while residents commonly disposed of their refuse and excrement in the alleys and gutters in front of their homes.[36] Most important, the city's contaminated water supply did not improve until the early nineteenth century. Philadelphians thus took a variety of actions in an effort to safeguard their health, but their ignorance of the actual causes of their afflictions made their protective measures less than effective.[37]

As smallpox subsided, a series of yellow fever epidemics during the 1790s created a new demographic crisis, once again driving up the death rate. Because yellow fever had not appeared in the city for over four decades, Philadelphians possessed virtually no immunity to it. The initial 1793 attack consequently found fertile ground, creating one of the highest mortality levels ever recorded in an American city. Each summer and fall for the succeeding six years the disease struck in successively less disastrous but still very serious proportions. Ships from the West Indies probably first introduced the *Aedes aegypti*—the type of mosquito that carries the disease—as well as the yellow-fever-infected passengers on which the insects fed, and marshes and swamps scattered throughout the urban area subsequently provided a hospitable environment in which the insects bred.[38] Like other

34. Thomas Wilson, *The Picture of Philadelphia, for 1824, containing the "Picture of Philadelphia, for 1811, by James Mease, M.D." with All Its Improvements Since That Period* (Philadelphia, 1823), quotes on pp. 47 and 39, respectively.

35. Ibid., 39. See also William Currie, *An Historical Account of the Climates and Diseases of the United States . . .* (Philadelphia, 1792), 162.

36. Wilson, *Picture of Philadelphia*, 39; John K. Alexander, *Render Them Submissive: Responses to Poverty in Philadelphia, 1760–1800* (Amherst, Mass., 1980), 21–22; J. P. Briscot De Warville, *New Travels in the United States of America, 1788*, ed. and trans. Durand Escheverria and Mara Soceanu (Cambridge, Mass., 1964), 201. Kenneth Roberts and Anna M. Roberts, eds., *Moreau de St. Mery's American Journey* [1793–1798] (Garden City, N.Y., 1947), 260.

37. Their misunderstandings about the causes of diseases sometimes assumed the form of partisan political debates; see Martin S. Pernick, "Politics, Parties, and Pestilence: Epidemic Yellow Fever in Philadelphia and the Rise of the First Party System," *WMQ*, 3d Ser., 29 (1972), 559–586.

38. Henry Rose Carter, *Yellow Fever: An Epidemiological and Historical Study of Its Place of Origin* (Baltimore, Md., 1931), 3, 24–25.

maladies spread by mosquitoes, yellow fever occurred seasonally, beginning in August, peaking in September and October, then ending quickly in November as cold weather froze the harbingers of death.

Philadelphians responded to the epidemic with a variety of measures designed to preserve their lives. They burned bonfires, fired muskets, smoked tobacco, chewed garlic, and carried around pieces of tarred rope, all, of course, to no avail. The only sure protection was to escape the city while the disease raged, and residents departed in record numbers. "Those whose property enabled them to do it," Alexander Graydon wrote, "fled with precipitation." Between a third and a half of the citizens began their hasty exodus in late August. "So great was the general terror," Mathew Carey reported, "that for some weeks, carts, waggons, coaches, and chairs, were almost constantly transporting families and furniture to the country in every direction." Businesses, government affairs, community organizations, and social life all halted for the ensuing months as those who remained behind "shut themselves up in their houses, and were afraid to walk the streets."[39] Conditions in the Quaker City resembled those in European centers during earlier outbreaks of the plague.

Within four months the 1793 epidemic killed at least 5 percent of the original population and one out of every nine residents who did not flee the city. Death carts rumbled through the streets daily, and they picked up more than five hundred bodies in a single five-day period in October.[40] In this, as in most epidemics, poor citizens suffered the highest mortality. As Carey lamented, the disease "had been dreadfully destructive among the poor. It is very probable that at least seven eighths of the number of the dead, was of that class," and the occupations of those who died from the fever confirm his observation.[41] Eating inadequate food, inhabiting overcrowded and under-heated houses, and living in the worst sanitary conditions increased the

39. Alexander Graydon, *Memoirs of His Own Time with Reminiscences of the Men and Events of the Revolution*, ed. John Stockton Littel (Philadelphia, 1846), 365; Mathew Carey, *A Short Account of the Malignant Fever, Lately Prevalent in Philadelphia* (New York, 1970; Philadelphia, 1794), 16–17, 21–22, 77. An account that draws heavily on Carey is John Harvey Powell, *Bring Out Your Dead: The Great Plague of Yellow Fever in Philadelphia in 1793* (Philadelphia, 1949). One of the most dramatic personal accounts of the 1798 epidemic is the Diary of Edward Garrigues, HSP.

40. In Figure 2, the death rate for 1794 (which includes the August through December burials of 1793) is eighty-two per thousand residents. More than four thousand people, or approximately 8 percent of the population, died during the epidemic months. If one-third of the inhabitants fled, then yellow fever killed roughly 12 percent of the citizens who remained. Carey gives the number of daily burials from August through November in *Short Account of the Malignant Fever*, 113–117.

41. Ibid., 27. Carey records the names and occupations of the decedents in ibid., 121–163. Elizabeth Drinker noted that the fever predominated in the poor sections of town, in Elizabeth Evans, ed., *Weathering the Storm: Women of the American Revolution* (New York, 1975), 179.

vulnerability of the lower sort to this and other diseases. More important was the inability of the poor to escape the afflicted area. As one newspaper essayist recognized, leaving the city was impossible for "the poor who have neither places to remove to or funds for their support, as they depend on their daily labour, for daily supplies."[42]

Their greater geographic mobility and the hazards peculiar to their work meant that laboring Philadelphians generally suffered more illnesses and earlier deaths than did their more affluent neighbors. Poor citizens migrated more often than wealthier ones,[43] thereby exposing the urban lower sort to different epidemiological environments that contained new diseases to which old immunities afforded scant protection. And the city was ripe with maladies that continually afflicted the lower classes. Approximately one out of every four poor patients treated at the Philadelphia Dispensary during the late 1790s, for example, suffered from a contagious disease.[44] These ailments, as contemporaries recognized, took a high toll both in lives and in the physical damage inflicted on their victims.[45]

Laboring people suffered a variety of work-related accidents and illnesses.[46] The records of the almshouse, the Pennsylvania Hospital, and the Philadelphia Dispensary are replete with cases of men in such distress. Daniel McCalley was hurt while working in a mast yard, John Shay was disabled when his wheelbarrow fell on him, and Dennis Haines broke his collarbone when a wagon overturned. All three were thereby "rendered incapable of labouring for a livelyhood" by these injuries.[47] Seamen risked particular danger, and they often entered the almshouse or hospital with hurt or broken hands, feet, legs, thighs, and fingers. Thomas Pain "received his lameness by severity & hardships he suffered on board the Ship *Drake*."[48] John Richards broke his thigh when he slipped and fell from the ship's mast. Thomas Boyd "had his feet mashed on board." By "beating and other Hard Treatment,"

42. "A Useful Hint," *Mercury Daily Advertiser* (Philadelphia), Aug. 19, 1797.

43. Tracing people among the six tax lists during the second half of the century revealed that the rate of migration varied inversely with income and property ownership. See chapter 5 for a complete discussion of this issue.

44. Out Patients Attended.

45. Currie, *Historical Account*, 94–95, 117; Carey, *Short Account of the Malignant Fever*, 27, 121–163; Evans, *Weathering the Storm*, 179. Newspapers commented on the high mortality from smallpox among laboring people in the Feb. 2, 1774 issues of both the *Pennsylvania Gazette* (Philadelphia) and the *Pennsylvania Journal* (Philadelphia). That poor neighborhoods suffered considerably more than wealthier ones in the epidemic of 1793 is evident in the number of deaths recorded in various parts of the city in Edmund Hogan, *The Prospect of Philadelphia and Check on the Next Directory* (Philadelphia, 1795).

46. These are discussed in the *Pennsylvania Journal and Weekly Advertisers* (Philadelphia), Sept. 27, 1786.

47. Daily Occurrences, Apr. 13, 1790; Jan. 1, 1795; and Sept. 8, 1801.

48. Ibid., Mar. 15, 1790.

Captain Morison inflicted a "Scorbatic Habit and Sinuous Ulcer in the thigh" of mariner William Walker. Of course, privateering and warfare likewise took a high toll.[49]

Mechanics were liable to a variety of other ailments associated with their employment. John Cheeson served on the frigate *Constellation* for sixteen months, during which time, in the words of the almshouse clerk, "he got miserably frost bitten in both his feet and one of his hands whereby he is rendered unable to support himself."[50] Laborer Daniel Seaman likewise entered the almshouse because "both his feet are badly Frost-bitten."[51] Others suffered from asthma and rheumatism. Some, such as Hugh Porter, undoubtedly aggravated their condition since they "worked at hard Labour" their entire lives. Tailor Anthony Dawson and cordwainer Thomas Kelby grew so badly afflicted by rheumatism that they could not earn their living by their trade.[52] Many tailors suffered from eyesight problems. One nineteenth-century tailor described their quandary, unaltered until the invention of the light bulb: "It is not the black clothes that are trying to the sight—black is the steadiest of all colours to work at . . . scarlet, such as is used for regimentals, is the most blinding, it seems to burn the eyeballs, and makes them ache dreadful . . . everything seems all of a twitter, and to keep changing its tint. There's more military tailors blind than any others."[53]

Venereal disease was another scourge of poor Philadelphians, although it hardly afflicted only members of their class. Still, mariners seem to have been unusually distressed by the "pox." James Steward, Thomas Johnson, "Negro" Harry, John Rigg, and Peter Goubel are only a few of the scores of "venereal sailors" who passed through the city's welfare institutions each year.[54]

The bodies of many mariners reflected their travails. Smallpox had marked the faces of approximately one of every three sailors (a figure twice that in eighteenth-century London), suggesting the perils of coming into contact with so many varieties of the disease. Thus Samuel Ward was "considerably pockmarked" and Robert Sinclair "very much Pitted." George Lyman bore various "Trophies of War," and the six scars on John Williams's shoulder, the four on his leg, and yet another on his chin indicated that he had seen some

49. Thomas G. Morton, *The History of the Pennsylvania Hospital, 1751–1895* (Philadelphia, 1897), 226.

50. Daily Occurrences, Jan. 26, 1801.

51. Ibid., Sept. 10, 1800.

52. Ibid., June 2, June 6, and Apr. 7, 1800.

53. Henry Mayhew, *London Labour and the London Poor*, 3 vols. (London, 1862), 1:342–343.

54. Daily Occurrences, Steward entry on Dec. 24, 1789; Johnson entry on Aug. 11, 1796; and the final three men are noted in the Admission Forms, 1797–1817, Records of the Pennsylvania Hospital, Archives of the Pennsylvania Hospital.

hard times, perhaps while enslaved. John Way was lame, John Curtis had a broken thigh, John Campbell had a broken finger, and Stephen Kinney had lost a toe, although apparently none of the sailors wore a peg leg.[55]

The perils associated with their work could kill the lower sort quickly or by degrees. The wills left by mariners attest their familiarity with the dangers: "Intending a Voyage to Sea in a Marine Capacity," William Edgar took note of the "uncertainty of this Transitory life particularly to persons in such Employment." Captain James Russel likewise wrote his last testament "calling to mind the dangers of the sea."[56] Few seamen continued in their occupation into their old age; only 3 percent of a sample of 304 mariners in 1803 were older than forty-five.[57] While the loneliness and difficulty of their work undoubtedly discouraged many from serving too long, accidents, illnesses, and diseases shortened their lives and brought them to watery graves.

The continuous heavy physical activity of dock and construction workers also had its detrimental effects. One newspaper contributor may have exaggerated little when he complained that "most who are used to hard labour without doors begin to fail soon after thirty, especially if they have been obliged to live on a poor diet that afforded but little nourishment or was unwholesome."[58] James Breahere is but one example of a laborer who because of "hard work, and frequent colds . . . [was] rendered unable to support himself by any kind of work."[59] Unending toil, exhaustion, malnutrition, and inferior clothing and shelter did not kill as swiftly or as dramatically as epidemics, but these conditions slowly wore people down over the course of their lives.

Morbidity and mortality rates thus were higher among poor Philadelphians than among wealthier ones. By the reckoning of one historian, at the end of the century laboring people were four times more likely than the upper classes to die of yellow fever, three times more likely to die in childbirth, and two times more likely to die from tuberculosis.[60] The ailments that

55. These descriptions are based on information contained in the Seamen's Protective Certificate Applications, 1797, 1798, and 1799, Records of the Bureau of Customs, Record Group 36, NA; and in the Ship's Crew Lists, Records of the Bureau of Customs, 1803, Record Group 36, NA, hereafter cited as Ship's Crew Lists. On the pockmarks among Londoners, see Keith Thomas, *Religion and the Decline of Magic* (New York, 1971), 7.

56. Will Book S, p. 24, and Will Book K, p. 203, Wills, Philadelphia County Probate Records, 1683–1901, RW.

57. Ship's Crew Lists.

58. "Phileleutheros," *Pennsylvania Gazette* (Philadelphia), Feb. 2, 1780.

59. Daily Occurrences, Mar. 26, 1801.

60. Susan E. Klepp, "Philadelphia in Transition: A Demographic History of the City and Its Occupational Groups" (Ph.D. diss., University of Pennsylvania, 1980), 190, 292. A contemporary physician agreed with these estimates, in Currie, *Historical Account*, 94–95, 117. On the higher death rates among blacks—the city's most impoverished citizens—than among whites,

attacked poor immigrants during their seasoning period continued to plague them throughout their stay in the city. Some of the diseases, such as yellow fever and smallpox, often killed their victims outright, but other maladies, such as typhus, dysentery, and venereal disease, slowly ravaged the body, sometimes inflicting physical damage that lingered for a lifetime.

Although suffering from remarkably high mortality, Philadelphians produced children in great abundance. Birth rates generally ranged between forty and sixty per thousand inhabitants (see Figure 3 and Appendix B), making them considerably higher than many contemporary areas in either North America or England.[61] Data on the age and gender structure of the city suggest that females during their fertile years bore, on average, a child every 24 to 36 months. Women who married in their early twenties and lived to their midforties thus might expect to deliver between seven and nine babies.

The youthful age structure, the large influx of migrants, and the loosening of constraints on marriage among the new arrivals all encouraged the city's elevated birth rates, although the evidence is too scattered to evaluate accurately the differential impact of these factors. Like most contemporary urban centers, Philadelphia's population consisted disproportionately of people in their twenties and thirties.[62] Since young adults composed the majority of

see Klepp, "Black Mortality in Early Philadelphia, 1722–1859" (Paper presented at the Meeting of the Social Science History Association, Chicago, November 1988).

61. See Table B.4 and Appendix B for data and sources of Figure 3. Records are unreliable for years with missing values. Historians have estimated a birth rate of approximately fifty per thousand for late eighteenth- and early nineteenth-century America. See A. J. Lotka, "The Size of American Families in the Eighteenth Century," *Journal of the American Statistical Association*, 22 (1927), 165; J. Potter, "The Growth of Population in America, 1700–1860," in D. V. Glass and D.E.C. Eversley, eds., *Population in History* (London, 1965), 646, 672; Warren S. Thompson and P. K. Whelpton, *Population Trends in the United States* (New York, 1933), 263; and Yasukichi Yasuba, *Birth Rates of the White Population in the United States, 1800–1860: An Economic Study* (Baltimore, 1962), 99. A review of colonial fertility studies is available in John J. McCusker and Russell R. Menard, *The Economy of British America, 1607–1789* (Chapel Hill, N.C., 1985), 211–235. Scholars who have found evidence of high fertility among married women in Philadelphia include Klepp, "Philadelphia in Transition," 142–230; Roslyn Stone Wolman, "Some Aspects of Community Health in Colonial Philadelphia" (Ph.D. diss., University of Pennsylvania, 1974), 334–354; Louise Kantrow, "Philadelphia Gentry: Fertility and Family Planning among an American Aristocracy," *Population Studies*, 34 (1980), 21–30; and Robert V. Wells, "Family Size and Fertility Control in Eighteenth-Century America: A Study of Quaker Families," *Population Studies*, 25 (1971), 73–83.

62. In 1800, the first date for which reliable age figures are available, more than a third of free whites were younger than sixteen, and half were between sixteen and forty-four years old. The age structure undoubtedly was even more skewed when itinerants disembarked at the docks in large numbers during the closing decades of the colonial era. These figures are recorded in the U.S. Census Office, *Return of the Whole Number of Persons within the Several Districts of the United States: Second Census* (Washington, D.C., 1800).

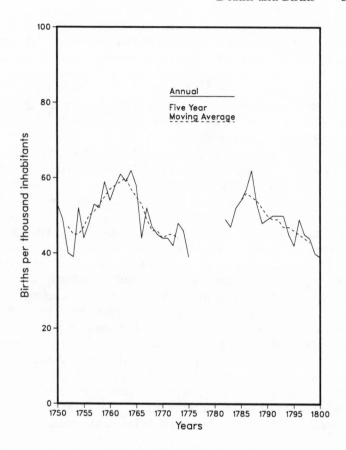

Figure 3. Birth rates in Philadelphia, 1750–1800

immigrants, they skewed the city's age structure and contributed heavily to the great number of births.[63] Some migrants baptized the infants born during or shortly after their voyage in one of the city's churches, while, according to one observer, "people living at a distance from Philadelphia bring in their children to be baptized, on occasions of market or other business." Both activities obviously inflated the urban birth rate.[64]

63. Because migrants generally are youthful, immigrant centers tend as a rule to be character-ized by younger age structures and higher birth rates than nonimmigrant centers; see George Barclay, *Techniques of Population Analysis* (New York, 1958), 231.

64. Johann David Schoepf, *Travels in the Confederation* [1783–1784], ed. and trans. Alfred J. Morrison (New York, 1968; orig. 1911), 68. Births to transient immigrants affected the birth rates in Boston in a similar fashion as rates among the Irish climbed to sixty-seven per thousand

In addition, new settlers may have married at a relatively young age, thereby adding to the overall fertility level. Our knowledge of the marriage ages of Philadelphians is limited, but in one church that served the working people, men generally wed in their early twenties and women a few years younger. Migrants to the Quaker City found that traditional restrictions no longer bound them to postpone marriage. Many were freed of the necessity to obtain the consent of their parents, who were left hundreds or even thousands of miles behind, while others did not have to wait to inherit a farm before establishing a household. As a result, migrants sometimes quickly exercised their new-found control over their own marriage plans.[65] Still, acute morbidity and mortality prevented the birth rates from reaching even greater heights than actually achieved, as marriages were broken and pregnancies ended by illness and deaths.

While maintaining an elevated plateau, the city's birth rates fluctuated during the second half of the century. Rates increased significantly during the late 1750s, peaked in the early 1760s, then declined until the Revolution. The evidence is more fragmentary during and immediately following the war, but the rates fell steadily in the century's final fifteen years.

Economic and demographic factors best explain these ebbs and surges. The trends in the birth rates during the late colonial period conformed roughly (albeit with a lag of a few years) to vacillations in the economy, in large part because more people could afford to wed during periods of prosperity. The relatively low rates of the early 1750s corresponded to a period of economic depression; rising rates during the years of the French and Indian War matched a period of general prosperity; and falling birth rates during the decade preceding the Revolution responded to a downturn in the economy.[66]

Alterations in Philadelphia's age structure also played a role in the changing birth rates. Migration usually influences the age composition of a community, with in-migration creating a younger age configuration than out-migration. Minimal overseas immigration and warfare on Pennsylvania's frontier characterized the late 1750s.[67] From the middle of the decade until

---

in 1845; see Oscar Handlin, *Boston's Immigrants: A Study in Acculturation* (New York, 1969), 117.

65. The young marriage ages of laboring Philadelphians are considered here in chapter 7 and in Klepp, "Philadelphia in Transition," 65, 75. The impact of immigration and the age structure in nineteenth-century Philadelphia are explored by Michael R. Haines, "Fertility and Marriage in a Nineteenth-Century Industrial City: Philadelphia, 1850–1880," *JEH*, 40 (1980), 156.

66. Increasing real wages during the late 1750s and early 1760s, for example, drove the marriage rate up precipitously. The number of marriages is from Smith, "Death and Life," 883–884; the real wages are computed in chapter 4.

67. Gary B. Nash, "Slaves and Slaveowners in Colonial Philadelphia," *WMQ*, 3d Ser., 30 (1973), 232–233; and Wokeck, "Irish Immigration."

the defeat of Pontiac in 1764, conflict raged in western Pennsylvania and native Americans frequently enjoyed a superior position, at one time reaching to within thirty miles of the Pennsylvania capital.[68] This threat drove some frontier inhabitants to the city for safety while restricting emigration from it, further skewing the urban age structure. Birth rates consequently may have increased as the war curtailed the normal emigration of potential migrants, primarily individuals in their child-producing years. Low levels of migration to the city during the post-Revolutionary period affected the age composition, and thus the birth rates, in the opposite fashion.[69] The demographic crises of the 1790s offset the decade's high level of prosperity to drive birth rates down. Theoretically, more Philadelphians should have married and produced children after 1793 than before, as their incomes increased. Instead, the severe yellow fever epidemics dampened fertility by disrupting families and ending pregnancies prematurely.

Philadelphia's population grew very rapidly during the second half of the century. Like most contemporary urban centers, the city expanded primarily because of immigration, although it grew by natural means as well (see Table 1). Deaths exceeded births during the 1750s, but natural increase accounted for one percent of the annual growth rate between 1760 and 1775. Rising birth rates created this initial spurt in natural increase before the Revolution, whereas declining death rates were responsible for the excess of births over deaths during the 1780s and early 1790s.[70] Beginning in 1793, the yellow fever epidemics held population increase by natural means in check.

Immigration defined the city's growth rate as well as its ethnic and racial composition. Both the magnitude and the character of migration to Phila-

68. Thomas A. Gordon, *The History of Pennsylvania* (Philadelphia, 1829), 348, 385–397; Agnes Repplier, *Philadelphia: The Place and the People* (New York, 1904), 141–157.

69. The 1762 and 1775 Constables' Returns for Walnut Ward (located in the PCA) provide the only direct measurement of the ages of Philadelphians during the colonial era. These records indicate that the city's residents were older on average during the postwar years than during the prewar period. Among households with children, the oldest child was younger than five years of age in 32 percent of the families in 1762 and in only 17 percent of the families in 1775. In 57 percent and 50 percent of the families in 1762 and 1775, respectively, the oldest child was younger than ten years of age. Although other extraordinary events may account for these differences, it appears that relatively more women were in the child-bearing age categories in 1762 than in 1775. Based on their analysis of the 1775 Constables' Returns, Sharon V. Salinger and Charles Wetherell conclude that the city had a somewhat older age structure than I have calculated, in "A Note on the Population of Pre-Revolutionary Philadelphia," *PMHB*, 109 (1985), 380–382. But their calculations (discussed more fully in Appendix B) do not show agreement with the age structure in 1800, as indicated above in n. 62.

70. A similar pattern of growth is evident when only the six Philadelphia churches in which baptisms and burials were recorded are considered. The transitional period among these churches also occurred during the late 1750s and early 1760s, when the number of baptisms expanded faster than the number of burials.

delphia ebbed and flowed during the second half of the century. Before the French and Indian War, Germans were the largest immigrant group, with the Irish and the Scotch Irish not far behind. For example, more than five thousand Palatinates arrived annually between 1750 and 1755, making this a period of high net migration into the city (see Table 1). The war curtailed the arrival of passenger ships for the next seven years, accounting for the decline in the net migration rate; undoubtedly it would have fallen more precipitously except that hostilities with native Americans discouraged many temporary residents from moving to the frontier. The number of African-Americans in Philadelphia increased dramatically during these years as inhabitants bought slaves to substitute for the scarcity of European indentured servants. After the Seven Years' War, the Irish, the Scotch Irish, and, to a lesser extent, the Germans resumed disembarking at the city's docks in large numbers.[71]

After being disrupted by the Revolution, overseas immigration began again during the late 1780s and 1790s, although it did not achieve its earlier magnitude. But Americans from the countryside, especially newly freed and escaped slaves, flooded into the city. Combined with European migration, this movement of people was sufficient to account for the rapid population expansion of the 1790s even as the city experienced little surplus in the number of births over deaths.[72]

Three important characteristics distinguish the nature of migration during the 1790s from that of the previous four decades. First, the Irish and Scotch Irish dominated among overseas immigrants during the last dozen years of

71. As rack-renting and a setback in the linen trade forced many people off the land and out of jobs in Ulster, the Scotch Irish landed in Philadelphia in great numbers during the interim between the French and Indian War and the Revolution. See Wokeck, "Flow and Composition of German Immigration," 249–278; Wokeck, "Irish Immigration"; Dickson, *Ulster Emigration*; Audrey Lockhart, *Some Aspects of Emigration from Ireland to the North American Colonies between 1660 and 1775* (New York, 1976); and Nash, "Slaves and Slaveowners," 233. The changing ethnic patterns among residents are evident in the distribution of burials in the city's cemeteries, as recorded in the Bills of Mortality. During the quarter century before the Revolution, burials among predominantly German and Scotch-Irish religious groups—Lutherans, Calvinists, and Presbyterians—increased, while interments among the more established Anglicans and Quakers proportionally declined.

72. Both contemporaries and historians estimate that between four and six thousand people entered the country each year during the 1790s and probably even fewer during the Confederation Era. An average 2,934 people disembarked in the city annually between 1789 and 1793 according to the Health Officer's Register of Passenger's Names, Record Group 41, PHMC, hereafter cited as Health Officer's Register. See also Adam Seybert, *Statistical Annals* . . . (New York, 1969; orig. 1818), 29; George M. Stephenson, *A History of American Immigration, 1820–1924* (Boston, 1926), 99; Douglass C. North, *The Economic Growth of the United States* (New York, 1966), 32; and Maldwyn Allen Jones, *American Immigration* (Chicago, 1960), 64–65. On the forced migration of blacks to Philadelphia, see Billy G. Smith, "Black Family Life in Philadelphia from Slavery to Freedom, 1750–1800," in Catherine Hutchins, ed., *Shaping a National Culture: The Philadelphia Experience, 1750–1800*, forthcoming.

Table 1. Estimated population growth, natural increase, and migration rates, 1750–1800

Period	Annual percentage of population growth	Annual percentage of natural increase	Annual net migration per hundred residents
1750–1755	4.2	−0.9	5.1
1755–1760	3.7	−0.2	3.9
1760–1765	5.0	+1.0	4.0
1765–1770	3.7	+1.1	2.6
1770–1775	2.9	+.9	2.0
1782–1787	1.1	+2.0	−0.9
1788–1795	4.2	+1.2	3.0
1796–1800	4.2	+.3	3.9

Source: Population growth was calculated from population figures in Table B.1 of Appendix B, using the geometric method to measure growth, as explained in George Barclay, *Techniques of Population Analysis* (New York: 1958), 206–207. Natural increase represents the differences between the annual number of births and deaths during each time frame, and the rates were computed according to the same geometric method. Net migration represents the differences between the percentage of population growth and the percentage of natural increase.

Note: Data for the years 1776–1781 are not included because records are unreliable.

the century. Like earlier immigrants, they came primarily from the poor and middling ranks of society. Second, a large group of French settled in Philadelphia during the early 1790s, refugees from revolutions in their own country and in the West Indies. They differed from most earlier migrants to the Quaker City in that many belonged to the wealthier classes, including merchants, doctors, lawyers, planters (many of whom brought their West-Indian slaves with them). Even such important political figures as Louis Philippe and Talleyrand lived briefly in Philadelphia.[73] Third, a substantial proportion of the migrants during the last decade of the century arrived from the nearby countryside. In particular, hundreds of slaves who had acquired their freedom during the Revolution flocked to the city in search of economic opportunities and a community of other blacks with whom to live.[74]

Because of their proximity to Philadelphia, American migrants were more likely than their European counterparts to be aware of and responsive to the "pull" factors of economic conditions in the city. Those who undertook the

73. The influx of the French and the Irish is evident in the growth of their interments in the city's Catholic cemeteries, as recorded in the Bills of Mortality. Of the immigrants arriving in Philadelphia's harbor between 1789 and 1793, 53 percent were from Ireland and 27 percent from France or the French West Indies, as cataloged in Health Officer's Register. The economic characteristics of the French refugees are discussed in Powell, *Bring Out Your Dead*, 6–7; and Marcus Lee Hansen, *The Atlantic Migration, 1607–1860* (New York, 1940), 58.

74. Gary B. Nash, "Forging Freedom: The Emancipation Experience in the Northern Seaport Cities, 1775–1820," in Ira Berlin and Ronald Hoffman, eds., *Slavery and Freedom in the Age of the American Revolution* (Charlottesville, Va., 1983), 4–11; and Smith, "Black Family Life in Philadelphia."

long ocean voyage often were misinformed about life in Philadelphia. Thus, European migrants of the late colonial era most likely arrived in the city in a more random, less economically rational fashion than migrants from America during the 1790s.

Philadelphia was an extremely hazardous place to live, considerably more unhealthy than contemporary American rural areas and many European cities. Sickness and death formed an integral part of the day-to-day lives of the residents of the city. Smallpox, the greatest menace in the early years, was gradually brought under control, at least for those both willing and financially able to undergo immunization. But residents still worried about contagious diseases, particularly since yellow fever devastated the inhabitants at the century's close. Constantly introducing and spreading infections, new arrivals to the area both caused and suffered much of this misery. Philadelphia posed special danger for them because, even if they survived the ocean voyage, they still encountered a new disease environment in which they likely would contract a serious illness within a short time after they disembarked.

Elevated birth rates coexisted with and added to the city's high mortality. Infants filled the city, their numbers often fluctuating with economic conditions, and they were most vulnerable to the dangerous surroundings. The remarkable birth rates offset the high death rates to create a small natural increase of the population throughout much of the period. This growth, combined with the large influx of migrants, skewed the city's age structure: children and young adults greatly outnumbered those in the older age groups.

Laboring Philadelphians thus lived in a city characterized by high mortality, high fertility, a skewed age distribution, and large-scale immigration. Several factors make it likely that the lower classes suffered a mortality rate greater than most other residents. Not only were many of the lower sort migrants, but their poor diets, hazardous jobs, crowded housing, and inability to afford inoculation or to flee epidemics increased their susceptibility to disease. Their lives were foreshortened accordingly.

Chapter Three

Laboring People and
the Urban Economy

For unto every one that hath shall be given, and he shall have abundance:
but from him that hath not shall be taken away even that which he hath.
—Matt. 25:29

PHILADELPHIA WAS the wealthiest American urban center during the
second half of the eighteenth century. "The rapid growth of this beautiful
city, in size, wealth, and splendor, and its increase of trade" impressed one
visitor at the turn of the century as having "seldom been equaled in commercial history."[1] While scholars usually have concurred with this assessment,
they have differed about the extent to which the increased riches benefited all
Philadelphians.[2] The numerous boom and bust cycles that buffeted most
inhabitants make generalizations difficult, but the wealthiest classes appear
to have been financially much better off at the end of the period than at its
beginning. Yet, laboring people did not enjoy a corresponding overall improvement in their welfare as measured either in relative or in absolute
terms.[3] This chapter attempts to explain that paradox. Specifically, it explores
the structure and operation of the city's economy; the participation of the
lower classes and their employment opportunities in three major economic
sectors; and the changes wrought in the distribution of wealth during the last
five decades of the eighteenth century.

1. Charles William Janson, *The Stranger in America, 1793–1806*, ed. Carl S. Driver (New
York, 1971), 181.
2. Two excellent studies that differ about the nature and impact of the city's economic
development during this period are Thomas M. Doerflinger, *A Vigorous Spirit of Enterprise:
Merchants and Economic Development in Revolutionary Philadelphia* (Chapel Hill, N.C., 1986);
and Gary B. Nash, *The Urban Crucible: Social Change, Political Consciousness, and the Origins of
the American Revolution* (Cambridge, Mass., 1979).
3. The material standards of laboring people are evaluated in chapter 4.

Occupational Structure

The city's economy rested squarely on the foundation of commerce. "Everybody in Philadelphia deals more or less in trade," Lord Adam Gordon observed, and Dr. Alexander Hamilton agreed: "Their chief employ, indeed, is traffick and mercantile business."[4] Both statements oversimplify but still capture the essence of the city's economic life. Most workers, directly or indirectly, depended on commerce with people scattered throughout the Atlantic world, from small farmers and storekeepers in the neighboring countryside to large manufacturers and merchants operating from the West Indies to Lisbon and London. Numerous vessels docked at the wharves, unloading foreign manufactures to be sold throughout the Delaware Valley and stowing the abundant grain and livestock products that made the region the breadbasket of the Atlantic basin. The construction of ships and houses likewise formed important components of the city's economy, although both enterprises depended heavily on the course of overseas trade.[5]

The majority of males worked in jobs related in some manner to commerce.[6] Engaged directly in maritime trade, mariners accounted for as many as one of every five workers, making them the largest occupational group in the city (see Figure 4 and Appendix C). Together with merchants and their clerk assistants, the men employed in the commercial sector constituted close to one-third of the free work force.[7] A great many other people relied on trade as well: laborers, carters, porters, draymen, shallopmen, and flatmen transported goods to and from the city and stowed and unloaded ship's cargoes; coopers fashioned barrels to hold items bound for the sea; shopkeepers and grocers sold foreign merchandise; distillers and sugar boilers used West Indian molasses and sugar; innkeepers and tavernkeepers catered to the men who moved merchandise across the roads and the sea; and smiths,

---

4. "Journal of Lord Adam Gordon," in Howard H. Peckham, ed., *Narratives of Colonial America, 1704–1765* (Chicago, 1971), 262; Carl Bridenbaugh, ed., *Gentleman's Progress: The Itinerarium of Dr. Alexander Hamilton, 1744* (Westport, Conn., 1973), 23.

5. On the importance of overseas trade as a driving force in the economy of British America, see John J. McCusker and Russell R. Menard, *The Economy of British America, 1607–1789* (Chapel Hill, N.C., 1985), esp. chap. 4. Sean Wilentz has formulated an important model of "metropolitan industrialization" for New York City from 1788 to 1850, but its applicability to Philadelphia is limited until the end of the 18th century; *Chants Democratic: New York City & the Rise of the American Working Class, 1788–1850* (New York, 1984), 107–144.

6. The analysis in the following paragraphs draws on the tax lists discussed in Appendix C. The occupational structure among working women was, of course, vastly different, but it cannot be systematically reconstructed from the records. Chapter 4 discusses the range of women's employment for wages.

7. See Table C.1 for data and Appendix C (n. 1) for sources for Figure 4. Tax assessors overlooked a great many mariners, as explained in Appendix C.

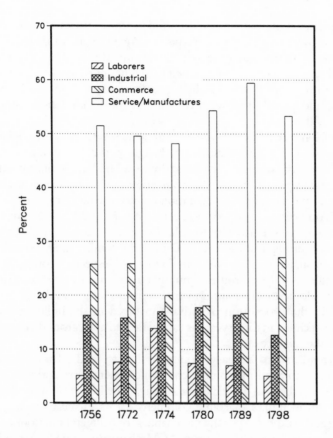

Figure 4. Occupational structure of Philadelphia, 1756–1798

farriers, wheelwrights, riggers, sailmakers, and chandlers cared for the horses, carts, and ships.

Slightly fewer than half of the taxpayers produced goods and performed services for the local retail market, which itself often was heated by the fuel of overseas trade.[8] The carpenters, bricklayers, and joiners who constructed houses accounted for one out of every ten workers who paid taxes, while one in five taxpayers made and sold clothes, shoes, hats, bread, and the like to their fellow citizens. "Industrial" workers who built ships and furniture,

8. Even though the service and domestic manufacturing sector is the largest employment category among taxpayers in Figure 4, the majority of males actually worked in jobs directly or indirectly related to commerce since so many mariners and others dependent on trade often were out of town when the tax assessors made their rounds.

fashioned metal and leather products, and processed various foodstuffs numbered roughly one in every six taxpayers. Again, many of them, especially those involved in shipbuilding and metal crafts, were closely linked to commerce since they built and maintained vessels designed to carry commodities to and from other ports. Finally, constables, cryers, jail and workhouse keepers, and postal employees constituted the handful of governmental officials in the city.

Philadelphia remained fundamentally a mercantile city throughout the second half of the century, although changes in the nature of its commerce affected the city's occupational structure in subtle but significant ways. An astonishing increase in the number of laborers and a decline in the commercial sector on the eve of the Revolution marked the most important shifts in the city's occupational composition between 1756 and 1774. The disruption of trade during and after the Revolution kept the commercial sector relatively small throughout the 1780s. During the conflict itself, the number of service, manufacturing, and industrial workers—especially cordwainers, tailors, saddlers, and gunsmiths—multiplied to produce war materials and goods for domestic consumption that were no longer available from England. But the proportion of artisans involved in shipbuilding and construction declined in those years as capital flowed away from their enterprise and into the military effort.

This trend toward a smaller commercial sector and a larger service and domestic manufacturing component, which characterized the 1780s, reversed during the final decade of the century. The European wars after 1793 spurred Philadelphia's maritime commerce to its greatest heights, as the carrying and reexporting of the merchandise of belligerent nations added to the overseas shipment of local produce. Mechanics profited from this expansion of the overseas trade, although not as greatly as merchants, brokers, and their clerk assistants. The tax lists indicate that the proportion of flatmen, shallopmen, watermen, wheelwrights, and smiths (the men responsible for transporting goods to and from the countryside) actually shrank. And because reexports generally were not unloaded from the arriving ships, the relative number of laborers, carters, draymen, and porters who moved the cargo diminished, and the demand for coopers to fashion barrels declined.

Although Philadelphia's industrialization began early in the nineteenth century, the occupational profile of the tax-inscribed population during the 1790s affords little hint of future mechanized developments.[9] The vast majority of "industrial" workers fashioned items by hand rather than machine, and even their relative number decreased during the century's final

9. Diane Lindstrom, *Economic Development in the Philadelphia Region, 1810–1850* (New York, 1978), esp. chap. 2.

years. Following the Revolution, a steady decrease of workers in textiles, shipbuilding, and food and drink processing offset the previous growth of craftsmen who manufactured goods during the Revolutionary War years. However, the tax lists obscure a few tentative steps toward mechanization. Several small "manufactories," staffed by women and children who were not included on the tax rolls, operated in the city after 1785.[10] Still, industrialization remained unimportant throughout this period, and the city housed few factory operatives until well into the nineteenth century.

The service and domestic manufacturing sector expanded and changed in character during the final quarter of the eighteenth century. The exigencies of the Revolutionary War stimulated its initial growth, encouraging the proliferation of shopkeepers and grocers, for example, to meet the high demand for articles in the city and environs; their numbers continued to grow throughout the 1780s. As discussed above, the service sector contracted in the 1790s in response to the changing nature of Philadelphia's commerce and the concomitant decrease in demand for many service jobs. The available services changed in number and type during the post-Revolutionary decades. Luxury services expanded greatly as coachmakers, coachmen, hairdressers, dancing masters, jewelers, booksellers, bookbinders, printers, and toy makers appeared on the tax lists with increasing frequency or for the first time. Simultaneously, more doctors, druggists, and attorneys provided additional professional help (or harm). To some degree this process belonged to a general pattern of increasing specialization in American urban centers which was required to meet the needs of their rapidly growing hinterlands. But many of these men attended wealthy French émigrés and other newly opulent residents.

Maritime Commerce

In evaluating the city's economic conditions, historians have focused primarily on the value of imported and exported goods.[11] However, employ-

---

10. Cynthia J. Shelton, *The Mills of Manayunk: Industrialization and Social Conflict in the Philadelphia Region, 1787–1837* (Baltimore, Md., 1986); George W. Geib, "A History of Philadelphia, 1776–1789" (Ph.D. diss., Univ. of Wisconsin, 1969), 238–239; and Curtis P. Nettels, *The Emergence of a National Economy, 1775–1815* (New York, 1962), 70–71.

11. Scholars have used incomplete data on the value of trade to produce excellent studies of Philadelphia's economy, many of which differ in their interpretations. See, for example, Doerflinger, *Vigorous Spirit of Enterprise*; Doerflinger, "Philadelphia Merchants and the Logic of Moderation, 1760–1775," *WMQ*, 3d Ser., 40 (1983), 197–226; Nash, *Urban Crucible*; Nash, "Poverty and Poor Relief," *WMQ*, 3d Ser., 33 (1976), 3–30; Nash, "Urban Wealth and Poverty in Pre-Revolutionary America," *Journal of Interdisciplinary History*, 6 (1976), 545–584; Marc Egnal, "The Pennsylvania Economy, 1748–1762: An Analysis of Short-Run Fluctuations

ment opportunities for mariners, laborers, stevedores, carters, draymen and the like depended as much if not more on the *volume* as on the *worth* of merchandise that passed through the city's port. The growth in the tonnage of exported grain, for example, had a more immediate impact on the number of available jobs for men who loaded it into ships than did the increase in the price of wheat.

To obtain the best possible index of job opportunities in the commercial sector, I compare the magnitude of trade to the number of inhabitants in the city. Three records catalog the volume of trade, each depicting similar overall patterns (see Figures 5–7 and Appendix D). The most accurate continuous account of commerce is the annual number and registered tonnage of ships entering the port.[12] The "official" values of Pennsylvania's commerce with England, which reflect fluctuations in the amount rather than the worth of the traffic, and desultory statistics on the export of bread and flour likewise chart the course of maritime activity.[13] Measured statistically on a per capita basis, the number and tonnage of ship arrivals decreased, the volume of imports from and exports to Great Britain fell, and the shipment of bread and flour subsided during the third quarter of the century.[14] Maritime commerce

---

in the Context of Long-Run Changes in the Atlantic Trading Community" (Ph.D. diss., University of Wisconsin, 1974); Arthur L. Jensen, *The Maritime Commerce of Colonial Philadelphia* (Madison, Wis., 1963); Harry D. Berg, "Economic Consequences of the French and Indian War for the Philadelphia Merchants," *PH*, 13 (1946), 185–193; Linda Kerrigan Salvucci, "Development and Decline: The Port of Philadelphia and the Spanish Imperial Markets, 1783–1823" (Ph.D. diss., Princeton University, 1985); and Helen Louise Klopfer, "Statistics of Foreign Trade of Philadelphia, 1700–1860," MS, 1936, Eleutherian Mills-Hagley Library, Wilmington, Del. Trade between Philadelphia and its hinterlands was naturally very important, although difficult to measure accurately. But see David E. Dauer, "Colonial Philadelphia's Intraregional Transportation System: An Overview," in Glenn Porter and William H. Mulligan, Jr., eds., *Working Papers from the Regional History Research Center*, vol. 2 (Greenville, Del., 1979), 1–16; and John Flexer Walzer, "Transportation in the Philadelphia Trading Area, 1740–1775" (Ph.D. diss., University of Wisconsin, 1968).

12. Because the size of vessels varied widely, the tonnage of ships docking at the wharves is more reliable than their number in estimating the quantity of merchandise arriving by sea. For example, the ships, brigantines, and snows that regularly sailed across the ocean dwarfed the sloops and schooners that plied coastal waters. Furthermore, the size of transatlantic vessels grew markedly during this period as owners sought to take advantage of the economies of scale. See John J. McCusker, "Sources of Investment Capital in the Colonial Philadelphia Shipping Industry," *JEH*, 32 (1972), 150–151. See Table D.1 and Appendix D for data and sources for Figure 5. Records are not available for years with missing values.

13. See John J. McCusker, "The Current Value of English Exports, 1697 to 1800," *WMQ*, 3d Ser., 28 (1971), 607–628. Data and sources for Figure 6 are available in Table D.2 and the U.S. Bureau of the Census, *Historical Statistics of the United States: Colonial Times to 1970*, 2 vols. (Washington, D.C., 1975), 2:1176, hereafter cited as *Historical Statistics*. Data and sources for Figure 7 are in Table D.3. Records are not available for years with missing data in both figures. The dotted lines in Figure 7 connect points of known data separated by more than one year.

14. The most unbiased measurement of the trend is the slope of the least-squares lines. Those slopes of the lines on a per capita basis for the 1750 to 1775 period are as follows: − .0002 for

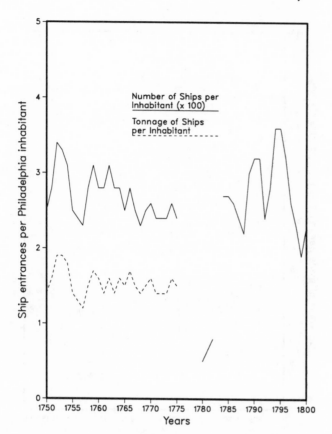

Figure 5. Ship entrances per Philadelphia inhabitant, 1750–1800

the number of ships; −.0057 for the tonnage of ships; −.0515 for the official value of imports; −.0326 for the official value of exports; and −.0047 for the tons of bread and flour exported. (The official values of imports and exports in 1775 were not included in these calculations because of their extreme abnormality.) Peculiarities in the records minimize the extent of the actual decline in shipping. Because the data on arriving vessels are most complete for the closing years of the colonial period, the recorded entrances for the 1750s are too low. Thus, the volume of trade per capita, as measured by the number and tonnage of ship entrances, decreased more precipitously during the twenty-five-year period of 1750–1775 than what appears either in Figure 5 or in the slopes of the trend lines. Measurement of the trend using the method of least squares is explained in Hubert M. Blalock, Jr., *Social Statistics* (New York, 1972), chap. 17. These data confirm James Shepherd's conclusion that Pennsylvania's volume of shipping stagnated during the decades preceding the Revolution, in "British America and the Atlantic Economy," in Ronald Hoffman et al., eds., *The Economy of Early America: The Revolutionary Period, 1763–1790* (Charlottesville, Va., 1988), 12, 42.

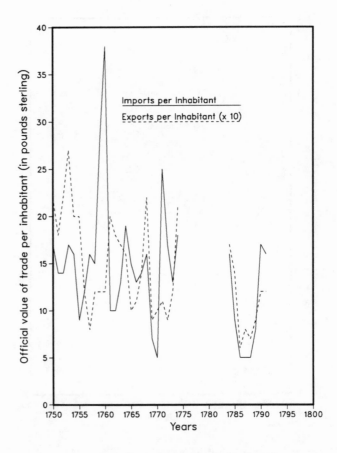

Figure 6. Volume of Pennsylvania's trade with England per Philadelphia inhabitant, 1750–1791

plummeted during the Revolutionary War, recovered briefly as hostilities ended, declined once again in the mid-1780s, then flourished during the century's final decade.

These long-term trends are vital to evaluating changes over decades, but they camouflage the shorter cycles in the city's ocean trade, which more immediately influenced the lives of Philadelphians of all ranks. These variations can be traced in the above data on the quantity of goods shipped, data on the port of embarkation of arriving vessels (see Figure 8), and previous

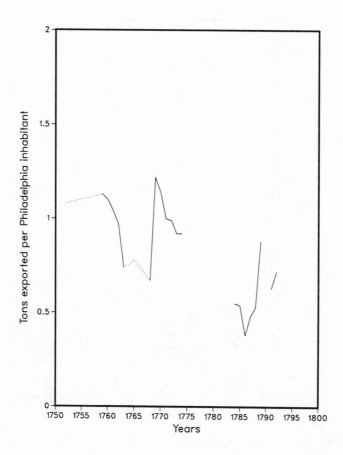

Figure 7. Bread and flour exports per Philadelphia inhabitant, 1752–1792

historical accounts. The volume of commerce expanded rapidly during the early 1750s as ships, greater in number and larger in size than prior arrivals, docked at the wharves. Foreign manufactures and cloth accounted for much of this gain, apparent both in the relatively high proportion of vessels arriving from Great Britain and in the near tripling of the official value of British imports. As Philadelphia's businessmen broke their dependence on New England merchants and more aggressively developed a direct trade relationship with overseas partners, imports from the British Isles increased.

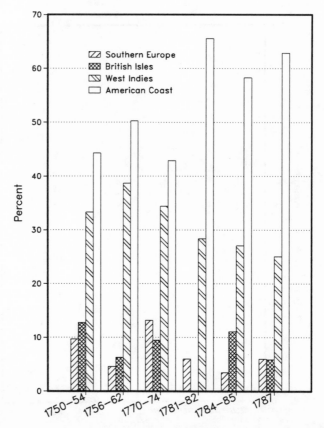

Figure 8. Ships entering Philadelphia from select geographic areas, 1750–1787

Meanwhile, the affluence of Pennsylvania's farmers combined with the area's rapidly expanding population to boost demand for foreign manufactures. Prosperity in Britain further encouraged English merchants to ship a record number of provisions to the mid-Atlantic market.[15]

Trade slumped in the mid-1750s as hostilities between European nations early in the Seven Years' War and embargoes on the export of products from the Delaware Valley discouraged transatlantic shipping. Reports of fighting

15. Egnal, "Pennsylvania Economy," 69–70, 97, 108–109, 111–112; Jensen, *Maritime Commerce*, 116–118; Jacob M. Price, "Economic Function and Growth of American Port Towns," *Perspectives in American History*, 8 (1974), 152–53; Nash, *Urban Crucible*, 233–263, 312–338; McCusker and Menard, *Economy of British America*, 193–195; and Gary M. Walton and James F. Shepherd, *The Economic Rise of Early America* (Cambridge, England, 1979), 100. Table D.4 contains data and sources for Figure 8.

and the disruption of prosperity in the Pennsylvania countryside created uncertainties and led to a decline in the demand for imported goods. The impressive increase in ship entrances in 1758 and 1759 signaled the boom that often accompanies wars. Military spending underlay much of the economic surge as Philadelphians helped provision the Royal Navy in Nova Scotia, the Caribbean forces, and troops in the backcountry. Exports of bread and flour and ship arrivals from the West Indies rose as the city's merchants expanded the trade with both the British and the French islands. Favorable economic conditions in Britain and rising consumer demand in the middle colonies (owing to their renewed prosperity) promoted large imports in 1759 and 1760.[16]

The prosperity of the late 1750s ended in a commercial slump during the final years of the war. Arriving vessels decreased in number and volume as British imports plummeted against the background of an economic crisis in England. Proportionally fewer ships from Europe or Britain docked in Philadelphia, and, for the first time, more than half of the entering vessels came from other American ports. The 1762 war with Spain gave commerce a much needed boost, and shipping activity remained on a relatively high plateau for the next several years. But the precipitous decline in Pennsylvania's exports of flour and bread in 1763, as well as the numerous business failures of the early years of the decade, attest that for many of the city's inhabitants this was a period of financial hardship.[17]

Philadelphia emerged from its difficulties as shipping activity quickened in 1766, moderated during the next two years, then again picked up its pace in 1769 and 1770. Even though the colonial nonimportation agreements severely curtailed the import of English goods, the proportion of ships entering from Great Britain during 1769 and 1770 remained relatively high, a consequence in part of the large number of immigrant vessels arriving from Ireland. A decade of rack-renting and a faltering linen trade pushed many people off the land and out of jobs in that country, providing cargoes of indentured servants as substitutes for the proscribed British manufactures.[18]

16. Egnal, "Pennsylvania Economy," 149–150, 158–161, 178–179; Jensen, *Maritime Commerce*, 74, 91–92, 117–119; and Gary B. Nash, "Up from the Bottom in Franklin's Philadelphia," *Past & Present*, no. 77 (1977), 70–71. For a different interpretation of the business cycles before the Revolution, see Doerflinger, *Vigorous Spirit of Enterprise*, 168–180.

17. Berg, "Economic Consequences of the French and Indian War," 185–193; Jensen, *Maritime Commerce*, 118–122; Egnal, "Pennsylvania Economy," 82, 217, 225; and Nash, *Urban Crucible*, 233–263.

18. R. J. Dickson, *Ulster Emigration to Colonial America, 1718–1775* (London, 1966), 64–78; and Marianne Wokeck, "Irish Immigration to the Delaware Valley before the American Revolution" (Paper presented at the Philadelphia Center for Early American Studies, University of Pennsylvania, Oct. 7, 1988).

Poor harvests in southern Europe further stimulated overall shipping activity in 1769 and 1770. Many of the city's merchants reaped sizable profits selling foodstuffs to Spain and France, while others took advantage of American nonimportation restrictions to clear their stock of English manufactures.[19]

The volume of trade continued to rise and fall during the five years preceding the Revolution. From a peak in 1770, shipping activity decreased the following year, swung gently upward in 1772, reached a new high in 1774, then fell once the fighting began. British imports followed a similar pattern. Their official value skyrocketed in 1771 as merchants scrambled to resupply depleted stocks, but the excessive imports of that year flooded the city's markets and, together with the British credit crisis of 1772, discouraged new imports for the next several years. In anticipation of yet another ban on trade, American merchants bought more merchandise from Britain in 1774. Bread and flour exports meanwhile slowed during the years immediately preceding the war.[20]

The Revolutionary War played havoc with the city's ocean trade, although the concomitant disruption of record keeping makes it impossible to piece together fully the puzzle of the economy. In general, the conflict curtailed the Delaware Valley's production of foodstuffs for overseas shipment, closed vital markets in the British Empire, and drove up the price of imported goods by restraining maritime commerce. Americans compensated by trading illegally with Europe and the West Indies and by fabricating articles to substitute for imports, but these measures were only partially successful. Thomas M. Doerflinger has traced four phases in the city's wartime economy. During the eighteen months beginning in the spring of 1776, an embargo and the blockade by the Royal Navy created a scarcity of foreign manufactures. The British occupation of the city from September 1777 until mid-1778 caused many residents to scatter and did little to improve the financial climate. The economic nadir was reached during the following two years as the price of food and other essential items rose sharply, thereby contributing to the considerable unrest among the city's laboring people. As the fighting moved south in 1781, conditions improved. Still, ship arrivals in 1781 and 1782 remained far below their pre-Revolutionary levels.[21]

19. Jensen, *Maritime Commerce*, 67, 122, 292–293; and Klopfer, "Statistics of Foreign Trade," 118–119.

20. Jensen, *Maritime Commerce*, 122–125; and Nash, "Up from the Bottom," 71.

21. Doerflinger, *Vigorous Spirit of Enterprise*, 207–221; Shepherd, "British America," 19–23; Anne Bezanson, "Inflation and Controls, Pennsylvania, 1774–1779," *JEH*, 8 (1948), supplement, 1–20; and Anne Bezanson et al., *Prices and Inflation during the American Revolution: Pennsylvania, 1770–1790* (Philadelphia, 1951). On the response to the rising prices, see the excellent studies by Steven Rosswurm, *Arms, Country, and Class: The Philadelphia Militia and 'Lower Sort' during the American Revolution, 1775–1783* (New Brunswick, N.J., 1987); Eric Foner, *Tom Paine and Revolutionary America* (London, 1976), chap. 5; and John K. Alexander,

The city's commerce boomed at the war's end as Great Britain flooded American markets with manufactured goods. The number of arriving vessels, the proportion of those ships embarking from the British Isles, and the quantity of English imports during 1783 and 1784 nearly matched their prewar levels. However, shipping activity collapsed during the next several years as the city's economy suffered a deep depression. When stores in the Delaware Valley bulged with unsold foreign goods, imports dried up. Trade restrictions imposed by the major European nations (particularly the closing of the British West Indies to American shipping) likewise cut deeply into Philadelphia's exports. Boats arriving from the Caribbean consequently fell from their previous high of 40 percent to about 25 percent of the total entrances. Commerce with other states of the Confederation dominated the city's trade while Pennsylvania merchants desperately attempted to open new markets and to recapture old ones.[22] Baltimore's concurrent emergence as the premiere port of Chesapeake Bay carved inroads into Philadelphia's trade with its hinterlands.[23]

Shipping activity recovered during the early years of the new nation, suffered a brief setback in 1792, and then expanded in the mid-1790s to unprecedented heights, as indicated by both the number of ship entrances and the arrivals per inhabitant.[24] The real value of Pennsylvania's total exports and the customs duties on imports corroborate this pattern of shipping activity during the 1790s.[25] Even though Philadelphia's merchants were not as proficient as their counterparts in New York and Baltimore in

"The Fort Wilson Incident of 1779: A Case Study of the Revolutionary Crowd," *WMQ*, 3d Ser., 31 (1974), 589–612.

22. While scholars disagree about the severity of the depression and the timing of the recovery throughout the country, most concur that Philadelphia experienced difficult times during the mid-1780s. See Klopfer, "Statistics of Foreign Trade," 215–218; Anna C. Clauder, *American Commerce as Affected by the Wars of the French Revolution and Napoleon, 1793–1812* (Clifton, N.J., 1972), 15–23; Geib, "History of Philadelphia," 216–217; Geoffrey Gilbert, "The Role of Breadstuffs in American Trade, 1770–1790," *Explorations in Economic History*, 14 (1977), 378–387; Gordon C. Bjork, "The Weaning of the American Economy: Independence, Market Changes, and Economic Development," *JEH*, 24 (1964), 541–560; Bjork, *Stagnation and Growth in the American Economy, 1784–1792* (New York, 1985), 54–57, 61–62, 73–79, 160–164; James F. Shepherd and Gary M. Walton, "Economic Change after the American Revolution: Pre- and Post-War Comparisons of Maritime Shipping and Trade," *Explorations in Economic History*, 13 (1976), 397–422; and Doerflinger, *Vigorous Spirit of Enterprise*, 246.

23. James Weston Livingood, *The Philadelphia-Baltimore Trade Rivalry, 1780–1860* (Harrisburg, Pa., 1947), 1–27; Shepherd, "British America," 31; James T. Lemon, *The Best Poor Man's Country: A Geographical Study of Early Southeastern Pennsylvania* (Baltimore, Md., 1972), 129; and Ronald Hoffman, *A Spirit of Dissension: Economics, Politics, and the Revolution in Maryland* (Baltimore, Md., 1973), 74–80.

24. Because much of this growth was based on transatlantic shipping, the actual increase in the aggregate tonnage of entering ships (if those figures were available) probably was even more impressive than indicated for the middle years of the decade, while the declining shipping activity of the last several years of the century would be somewhat moderated.

25. Klopfer, "Statistics of Foreign Trade," 221–223.

capturing the important trade with the Spanish Empire, the rising demand for Delaware Valley foodstuffs throughout the Atlantic community stimulated the city's commerce.[26]

The explosion of maritime activity in the mid-1790s responded primarily to developments in the reexport trade during the European wars. At the outbreak of hostilities in 1793, Americans, as neutrals, carried cargoes between the belligerent European nations and their colonies. American captains needed only to call at an American port and pay a small duty on the cargo to fulfill British restrictions on shipping goods to and from most areas. Despite occasional harassment of ships by the Royal Navy, this carrying trade dominated Philadelphia's maritime commerce during the final decade of the century. According to the earliest registers, reexports constituted two-thirds of the total value of Pennsylvania's exports between 1803 and 1810, and they likely formed an equally large proportion of the city's exports during the previous decade. An increase in British seizures of American vessels transporting foodstuffs to France and its West Indian colonies accounted for some of the dwindling overseas trade during the century's concluding years. One important corollary to the changes in commerce in the 1790s was the rapid expansion of the United States fleet, vessels that provided additional opportunities for Philadelphia's merchant marines.[27]

Just as maritime trade moved in cycles, it also varied with the seasons, which affected the working lives of many laboring people. In a rhythm matching that of most economic activities in a preindustrial society, ships docked at the city's wharves in fewest number during winter, rose to a peak in early spring and summer, then tapered off during late autumn (Figure 9).[28] Weather conditions partly dictated these fluctuations since ice in the Delaware River slowed or halted vessels. The natural rhythm of agriculture further encouraged this periodicity of shipping activity because the greatest number of vessels were required during the harvest season to carry off the grain.[29] As maritime commerce vacillated, so did employment opportunities

26. Salvucci, "Development and Decline."

27. Klopfer, "Statistics of Foreign Trade," 221–243; Clauder, *American Commerce*, 25, 67–72; Douglass North, *The Economic Growth of the United States, 1790–1860* (New York, 1966), 24–25.

28. The ship arrivals in Figure 9 are my tabulations from weekly reports in the *Pennsylvania Gazette* (Philadelphia) for 1756 through 1762, and the data for 1785 through 1788 are from Geib, "History of Philadelphia," 218. The percentages of ships arriving in January to December in all of these years combined are, respectively, 3, 2, 5, 10, 12, 9, 10, 11, 10, 10, 10, and 7.

29. Contemporary comments about weather-related disruptions of shipping traffic are in Janson, *Stranger in America*, 182, 187–188; Adolph B. Benson, ed., *The America of 1750: Peter Kalm's Travels in North America*, 2 vols. (New York, 1964), 1:15, 27; and James Mease, *The Picture of Philadelphia* . . . (New York, 1970; Philadelphia, 1811), 41. See also Jensen, *Maritime*

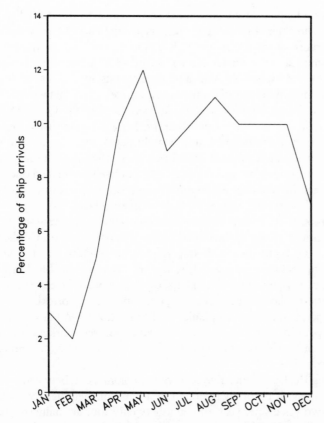

Figure 9. Seasonality of ship arrivals in Philadelphia, by month, 1756–1762 and 1785–1788

for mariners, dock workers, carters, and day laborers. The resulting competition for jobs during colder months forced many citizens with few extra resources to draw their purse strings tighter.

Shipbuilding

Shipbuilding, a second essential component of the city's economy, provided employment to a host of artisans and lesser-skilled workers. Pennsyl-

---

Commerce, 102. Immigrant vessels likewise followed a seasonal pattern, as discussed by Wokeck, "Irish Immigration."

vanians had invested an enormous sum—close to 835,000 Pennsylvania pounds—in their shipbuilding industry by the end of the colonial period, and workers in the Delaware Valley constructed more tonnage than any other American area outside New England.[30] At midcentury, Philadelphia's shipwrights drew on the oak and pine forests in the region for timber, planking, and masts to build small, inexpensive vessels that would ply coastal waters or sail to the West Indies. As merchants in the Quaker City established trade directly with English and other European firms, they ordered large carriers from neighboring boat builders, and, by the early 1770s, transatlantic craft accounted for 94 percent of the tonnage produced in the city's shipyards.[31] The construction of large vessels intensified once again for a few years immediately following the Revolution and during the 1790s to meet the demand for ships that could cross the ocean.

The manufacture of sailing vessels, especially those designed to traverse the Atlantic, was one of the largest economic enterprises undertaken in early America. To build each such ship required a year's work of at least thirty craftsmen, including shipwrights, joiners, ropemakers, blockmakers, sailmakers, carpenters, riggers, caulkers, carvers, cabinetmakers, smiths, founders, braziers, glaziers, painters, coopers, tanners, and bricklayers. Laborers cut timber, sawed it in to planks, and hoisted it from place to place. The entire operation could occupy more than a hundred workers, and, on average, one or two lesser-skilled men assisted every skilled craftsman employed in a shipyard.[32]

During the last twenty-five years of the colonial era, between a dozen and fifteen shipyards regularly operated in urban Philadelphia. Each turned out one or two vessels per year, or roughly twenty-four annually (see Figure 10 and Appendix D).[33] While the number of craft that floated off the docks decreased slightly from the high at midcentury, the size of the vessels grew considerably. From a mean volume of sixty-nine tons apiece during the 1750s, newly constructed ships averaged ninety-six tons between 1765 and 1775. Their bulk expanded considerably more in the decades after the Revolution.

30. Philadelphia's shipyards produced approximately 8 percent of the total colonial output on the eve of the Revolution and as much as 3 percent of all of the British Empire. McCusker, "Sources of Investment Capital," 154; *Historical Statistics*, 2:1195.

31. John J. McCusker, "The Pennsylvania Shipping Industry in the Eighteenth Century," MS, 1973, HSP, 108, 115, 117–119.

32. Carl Bridenbaugh, *The Colonial Craftsman* (Chicago, 1961), 92–94; and McCusker, "Sources of Investment Capital," 154.

33. McCusker, "Pennsylvania Shipping Industry," 144–147. See Table D.5 and Appendix D for data and sources for Figure 10. Records are not available for years with missing data. The dashed line in Figure 10 connects points of known data separated by more than one year.

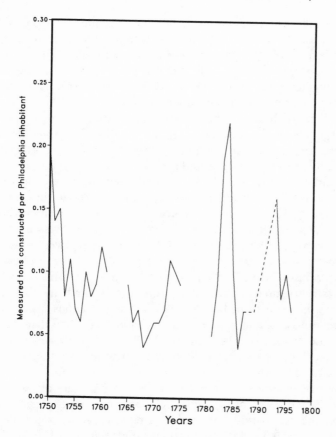

Figure 10. Shipbuilding in Philadelphia, select years, 1750–1796

The change in the tonnage of ships produced per capita provides one of the best barometers of the employment opportunities available to laboring men in the shipbuilding industry. Not surprisingly, the demand for ships broadly corresponded to the volume of maritime commerce. From a high point in 1750, when workers assembled one ton of a vessel for every five inhabitants, ship construction declined to one ton for every seventeen citizens by the middle of the decade. The commercial prosperity of the late 1750s inspired local investors to commission more vessels to carry their merchandise, pushing the tonnage of new boats registered in the port upward during the early 1760s. Slumping trade at the war's end limited the capital available to finance more vessels, but since ships were ordered well in advance, the downward cycle of construction lagged several years behind that of commerce. The full impact of the economic downturn thus did not affect the shipyards until well into the 1760s. Shipwrights increasingly picked up their tools during the early 1770s to satisfy orders for large vessels designed to carry goods to and from Europe.

The War for Independence disrupted the construction of new vessels. Even though the Continental Congress commissioned three dozen ships from the nation's shipyards and Pennsylvania's government ordered a number of row galleys, riverboats, and fire rafts directly from Philadelphia ship-makers, these contracts could not offset the nearly nonexistent demand by local and British merchants for sloops, schooners, snows, brigantines, and other craft.[34] When commerce improved during the years immediately following the peace settlement, the number and tonnage of vessels constructed in the Pennsylvania capital escalated. New carriers replaced those that had been lost during the war and satisfied the needs of American businessmen who previously had worked in partnership with British firms but now found it necessary to purchase their own means of transport.[35] In 1784 and 1785 the city's shipyards turned out vessels averaging 201 tons apiece, reflecting the intention of local merchants to open commercial routes that spanned not merely the Atlantic but the entire world. But as these dreams faded during the mid-1780s, the number and tonnage of new vessels plummeted, adding to the city's economic woes.

Although quantitative evidence for the closing years of the century is spotty, a few signs point to a high level of ship production during the initial years of the new nation, followed by a rapid expansion once the wars in Europe began. After 1793 the carrying trade stimulated demand and its profits enabled merchants to finance more ocean-crossing vessels than previously possible. During the middle of the decade, when ship construction peaked, Americans fabricated more than 100,000 tons annually. The records of Philadelphia's shipbuilding end in 1796, but activity in the city's shipyards may well have declined for the next two years and then revived at the turn of the century.[36]

While the fortunes of the shipbuilding industry waxed and waned, its relative importance as a source of employment for urban residents declined slightly over the course of the entire fifty-year period.[37] The value of each

34. William M. Fowler, Jr., *Rebels under Sail: The American Navy during the Revolution* (New York, 1976), 254; John W. Jackson, *The Pennsylvania Navy, 1775–1781* (New Brunswick, N.J., 1974), 11–25; and Doerflinger, *Vigorous Spirit of Enterprise*, 229.

35. John G. B. Hutchins, *The American Maritime Industries and Public Policy, 1789–1914* (Cambridge, Mass., 1941), 184–187.

36. Ibid.

37. The slopes of the least-square lines of tonnage built per inhabitant are as follows: −.0024 for 1750 to 1775, −.0046 for 1781 to 1787, and −.0250 for 1793 to 1796.

new ton of vessel rose, but the number of jobs in the shipyards depended more on the physical volume than on the worth of the vessels produced.[38] The data disguise the trend in employment somewhat since the figures on shipbuilding include the production of ships in the entire region around the city. But since shipyards in other areas of the Delaware Valley accounted for ever larger proportions of the total ship tonnage manufactured, relatively fewer of the city's residents worked in ship construction at the close of the century than in 1750. The declining percentage of shipbuilding artisans among the city's taxpayers (2.3 percent in 1756 and 1.6 percent in 1798) corroborates the somewhat reduced role of shipbuilding in the working lives of laboring people.

Housing Construction

Philadelphia's rapidly expanding population, augmented continually by heavy overseas immigration, fired a vigorous housing construction industry. Occasionally, as in modern-day California, real estate values burned red hot. Investments in land and housing provided one of the most reliable and lucrative sources of income for many citizens. Part of the affluence of such merchant families as the Shippens and Whartons, for example, rested on their real estate portfolios in the southern suburbs, while speculators such as Michael Hillegas reaped huge profits from rough-hewn dwellings in the Northern Liberties.[39]

Building contractors hired a large, disparate group of workers to construct brick homes on the major avenues, frame shacks in the alleyways, wooden tenements on the outskirts of town, warehouses near the docks, and public structures throughout the city. Nearly one of every ten taxpayers toiled as a carpenter, glazier, mason, bricklayer, painter, plasterer, plumber, stone cutter, or joiner. Laborers assisted these specialists by draining swamps and clearing ground for new structures, digging foundations and cellars, sawing wood, hauling dirt, bricks, and stones, and paving sidewalks and streets. All of these mechanics benefited from periodic housing spurts, and a few (especially those who operated as contractors) enjoyed substantial success; bricklayer Samuel Powel, for example, owned nearly a hundred rental units at his death. On the other end of the scale, most construction workers lacked the resources to invest successfully in real estate and were subjected to the whims of the market, obtaining jobs during booms but losing them during busts.

38. The cost per ton of vessels constructed generally increased during the half century before the Revolution; McCusker, "Sources of Investment Capital," 150.

39. These examples are from the 1772 Provincial Tax List, PCA, hereafter cited as Provincial Tax List. On real estate speculation by merchants, see Doerflinger, *Vigorous Spirit of Enterprise*, 178.

The housing industry responded to a variety of forces, including business cycles, wars, and the shifting streams of migration. While construction could not sustain prosperity in large cities (as it did in smaller towns such as Annapolis), it nevertheless provided employment for a substantial number of laboring people.[40]

Periodic house counts enable us to track the cycles in the construction industry and the employment opportunities in that sector for the lower classes. One effective method of analysis is to compare the number of homes and taxpayers in the city (see Figure 11). From a relatively slow period around midcentury, construction picked up after 1753, and the number of structures expanded by 29 percent during the next seven years. Dwellings rose at an astonishing rate (51 percent) during the subsequent decade as, according to Carl Bridenbaugh, "the unprecedented demand for housing forced real-estate values to dizzy heights, enriching those fortunate enough to own lots and encouraging speculative enterprises." Several factors created this housing explosion. Commercial prosperity, military contracts, and privateering profits during the Seven Years' War financed new warehouses, shops, soldiers' barracks, and mansions for the newly rich. And as thousands of German and Scotch-Irish immigrants swelled the city's population, craftsmen and laborers hastily erected new dwellings.[41]

Building activity initially sagged during the 1770s, then another brief round of construction began to shelter the new influx of the Scotch Irish. Mechanics forged fewer domiciles in the final years of the colonial era than earlier, but some displaced workers located jobs in such large-scale projects as the New College at the University of Pennsylvania, Carpenters Hall, churches for the Lutherans, Anglicans, and Presbyterians, the Bettering House, the Walnut Street Prison, and a second wing of the Pennsylvania Hospital.[42]

Housing construction moved sluggishly during the Revolution, increasing by only 10 percent, and most of that gain may have been realized in the war's closing years. Both the general difficulties plaguing the city's economy and the slow growth of the population combined to dampen activity during the remainder of the 1780s. The relatively slow expansion in dwellings (a rate of 13 percent) outstripped the even slower increase in the number of

40. Carl Bridenbaugh, *Cities in Revolt: Urban Life in America, 1743–1776* (New York, 1955), 15, 231; and Doerflinger, *Vigorous Spirit of Enterprise*, 131–133. On the importance of the construction of magnificent townhouses to the economy of pre-Revolutionary Annapolis, see Edward C. Pappenfuse, *In Pursuit of Profit: The Annapolis Merchants in the Era of the American Revolution, 1763–1805* (Baltimore, Md., 1975), 5–34.

41. Bridenbaugh, *Cities in Revolt*, 225, 231. Data and sources for Figure 11 are included in Table B.2.

42. Nash, *Urban Crucible*, 314.

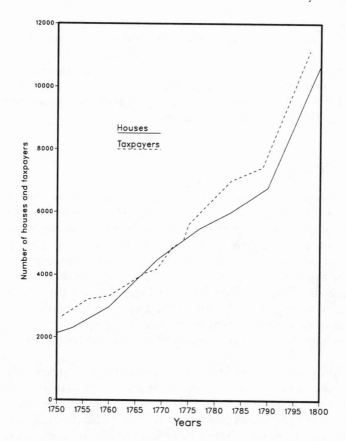

Figure 11. Housing construction in Philadelphia, 1750–1800

inhabitants during the 1780s, leaving many homes unoccupied and minimizing the demand for new structures. Though given to hyperbole, Benjamin Rush may have exaggerated little when he claimed that at the end of the 1780s "bricklayers and house carpenters and all the mechanics and labourers who are dependent upon housing construction were unemployed."[43]

Growing commercial prosperity and renewed migration to the city revived the housing industry during the final decade of the century. In 1795 officials prohibited new wooden structures within the heart of the city, reserving the

43. George W. Corner, ed., *The Autobiography of Benjamin Rush* (Princeton, N.J., 1948), 160; and Doerflinger, *Vigorous Spirit of Enterprise*, 222.

downtown district for brick buildings and the suburbs for cheaper frame shelters, thereby endorsing a pattern that had already begun to take shape. Fearing that these restrictions would curtail their business, contractors and construction artisans protested the ordinance, ultimately to no avail. Still, the 60 percent increase in the number of houses during the 1790s—the highest rate of growth for the entire half century—attests the robust health of the building industry in spite of regulation.

Wealth Structure

The evidence presented above about the dimensions of maritime commerce, shipbuilding, and housing construction indicates that the overall trend in employment opportunities for laboring men was stagnation at best during the final five decades of the century. However, as most historians agree, the actual wealth produced in these economic sectors almost certainly increased over the same period. For example, both the value of exports from England and Wales to Philadelphia (see Figure 12) and the worth of Pennsylvania's exports grew on an absolute and a per capita basis during the third quarter of the eighteenth century.[44] Although complete data are not available, the capital invested in the production of ships and houses probably rose as well.

Yet the profits realized from these ventures spread very unevenly among the residents. The pounds and dollars that filled the pockets of successful merchants, speculators, officials, shopkeepers, and other businessmen far exceeded the shillings and pennies that fell into the hands of laboring people. "Riches do not consist in having more Gold and Silver," John Locke wrote, "but in having more in proportion . . . than our Neighbours."[45] By that definition, one group of Philadelphians became rich as their neighbors grew poor during much of the second half of the century. The remainder of this chapter measures the slices that various groups cut out of the city's economic pie and explains the factors responsible for their varying sizes.

Table 2 confirms that a small segment of the inhabitants acquired owner-

44. Data for Figure 12 are from McCusker, "Current Value of English Exports," 624–625. The slope of the least-squares line of current values per inhabitant is .16 for 1750 through 1774. While the volume of bread and flour exports did not increase on a per capita basis, their price rose considerably; see Anne Bezanson, Robert D. Gray, and Miriam Hussey, *Prices in Colonial Pennsylvania* (Philadelphia, 1935), 12–15. Also see Jacob M. Price, "New Time Series for Scotland's and Britain's Trade with the Thirteen Colonies and States, 1740 to 1791," *WMQ*, 3d Ser., 32 (1975), 325.

45. John Locke, *An Essay Concerning Human Understanding*, ed. Peter H. Nidditch, 2 vols. (Oxford, England, 1975), 417.

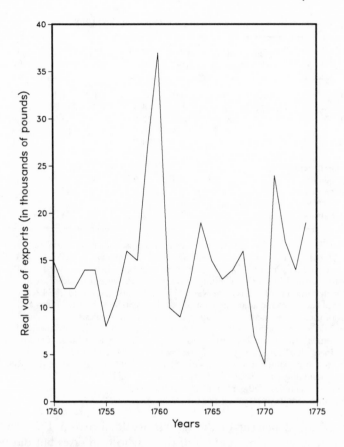

Figure 12. Real value of exports from England and Wales to Philadelphia, 1750–1774

ship of a large portion of the community's taxable resources during the closing decades of the colonial period.[46] The increase of the Schutz coefficient of inequality from .45 in 1756 to .61 in 1767 denotes the widening gap between rich and poor, particularly during and just after the Seven Years' War. Members of the richest decile benefited most as their share stretched

46. Nash found this to be true for inventoried wealth as well, in "Urban Wealth and Poverty," 548–554. The probate data, however, primarily reflect changes among the affluent taxpayers. When the names of decedents with inventoried estates between 1773 and 1775 are matched against the 1772 Provincial Tax List, only 3 percent of decedents are found among the

Table 2. Distribution of taxable wealth in Philadelphia, 1756–1798

Tax bracket (%)	1756[a] (%)	1767 (%)	1769 (%)	1772 (%)	1774 (%)	1780[b] (%)	1789[c] (%)	1798[b] (%)
0–30	1.6	1.8	0.0	1.7	1.1	1.1	0.7	2.7
31–60	14.0	5.5	1.2	4.4	4.0	6.3	3.4	9.2
61–90	37.8	27.0	26.8	22.6	22.6	32.9	31.6	27.6
91–95	12.6	16.2	18.3	16.5	16.8	17.6	19.3	15.9
96–100	34.0	49.5	53.7	54.7	55.5	42.0	45.1	44.6
Schutz coefficient of inequality	.45	.61	.68	.65	.66	.58	.64	.55
Percentage of tax-payers without taxable property	27.4	41.2	49.0	42.2	52.2	34.3	45.0	35.7

Source: The 1756 tax list was published by Hannah Benner Roach, comp., "Taxables in the City of Philadelphia, 1756," *Pennsylvania Genealogical Magazine,* 22 (1961), 3–41. Transcripts of the Tax Assessors' reports for 1767 are at the Van Pelt Library, University of Pennsylvania, Philadelphia. The 1769, 1772, 1780, 1789, and 1798 Provincial Tax Lists are in the PCA. The wealth distribution for 1774 is from Nash, "Urban Wealth and Poverty," 549. See Appendix E for an explanation of the adjustments made to the 1756 wealth distribution and an extended analysis of the measurement and meaning of these wealth profiles.

Note: The Schutz coefficient of inequality measures relative mean deviation, where 0 equals perfect equality and 1 equals perfect inequality; see Robert R. Schutz, "On Measurement of Income Inequality," *American Economic Review,* 41 (1951), 107–122.

[a]Adjusted as explained in Gary B. Nash, "Urban Wealth and Poverty in Pre-Revolutionary America," *Journal of Interdisciplinary History,* 6 (1976), 551–552.

[b]Based on a sample of 60 percent of the tax list.

[c]Based on a sample of 80 percent of the tax list.

from 47 to 72 percent of the taxable wealth between 1756 and 1774. Simultaneously, the proportion of those who paid taxes but did not own taxable property nearly doubled, swelling from about one-quarter to slightly more than half of all taxpayers.

Changes in tax assessment methods complicate the analysis of the wealth structure during the century's final twenty-five years (as explained in Appendix E). Although the data in Table 2 overstate the shifts that occurred, they still accurately portray the trends in the distribution of wealth. Taxable property became slightly more equitably distributed between 1774 and 1780. Among the most prosperous half of the taxpayers, the 60-to-90 percent bracket enhanced their relative affluence, primarily at the expense of

poorest 40 percent of the tax-inscribed population, while 89 percent of decedents who left inventories belonged to the richest 40 percent of taxpayers. A similar pattern appears when inventories between 1757 and 1760 are linked with the 1756 Provincial Tax List. Alterations in Philadelphia's inventoried wealth structure thus indicate changes among the affluent taxpayers. I thank Gary B. Nash for computer printouts of the probate data.

people in the richest decile. Taxpayers in the top 5 percent suffered the biggest setback, in part because a number of very wealthy Loyalists fled the city, leaving their property vulnerable to seizure and sale.[47] Meanwhile, the proportion of taxpayers without any assets declined, and the bottom half of taxpayers generally fared somewhat better.

Like a magnet changing its poles, inequality reversed its course twice in the next two decades, intensifying during the 1780s and then declining in the 1790s. The top decile of taxpayers held their own throughout most of the two decades, but poorer citizens rode an economic rollercoaster. Measured by the proportion of propertyless taxpayers and the share of wealth owned by members of the bottom tax brackets, the poorest 60 percent of taxpayers lost their assets during the 1780s and then recouped them in the following decade.

The nature of economic change accounts for the increasing concentration of wealth in Philadelphia before the Revolution.[48] Shifts in the city's economy during the third quarter of the eighteenth century benefited some classes of citizens much more than others. By skill, luck, dedicated effort, and occasional exploitation of other humans, some people were able to amass fortunes substantial enough to alter the aggregate distribution of wealth. At the same time (as discussed in subsequent chapters), members of the laboring classes experienced a mixed fate—some up, some down, some immobile. But since their possessions initially were so few, gains or losses among poor citizens had little impact on the overall stratification of wealth.

Modifications in the structure of the mercantile community and in the disparate allotment of profits earned from maritime commerce account for some of the growing inequality. The scale of activity among Philadelphia's merchants changed significantly after midcentury. Previously they had imported many European manufactured goods by way of Boston and other northern ports in exchange for Pennsylvania foodstuffs. Small merchants who engaged in trade with the Caribbean and along the coast had predominated in the city. Matters began to change during the 1750s as the city's businessmen assumed more control over the European import traffic to their region and aggressively pursued commerce throughout the Atlantic world. The city on the Delaware thus increasingly took on the functions of an entrepôt in the dispersement of imported merchandise. Trade in English manufactures and cloth created hefty profits for local wholesalers and re-

---

47. Doerflinger, *Vigorous Spirit of Enterprise*, 218–223.
48. Some scholars have argued that demographic rather than economic factors may have accounted for the nature of and the changes in the distribution of wealth in Philadelphia and other urban centers. For a review of the literature on this subject and a rebuttal of that thesis, see Billy G. Smith, "Inequality in Late Colonial Philadelphia: A Note on Its Nature and Growth," *WMQ*, 3d Ser., 41 (1984), 629–645.

tailers, providing the credit and capital necessary for their continued expansion. Large firms such as Willing and Morris filled the demands of the international market, establishing connections with London merchant houses, raising funds to finance bigger transatlantic ships, and handling the wider domestic distribution of goods.[49]

The Seven Years' War and the increasing demand for cereals in southern Europe further encouraged the trend toward larger and wealthier merchant partnerships. Lucrative contracts to provision various military forces afforded windfall profits to some firms. Meanwhile, poor harvests in Europe pushed up the price of grain and stimulated the growth of merchant houses to organize the export of wheat products to Lisbon and Barcelona.[50] As large businesses came to dominate much of the maritime commerce, opportunities for small merchants declined. Between 1756 and 1774 the proportion of merchants among the city's taxpayers decreased by 40 percent, and the earnings from this international commerce fell into the hands of fewer and fewer businessmen.[51]

Many merchants experienced considerable adversity during and after the Revolutionary War, although some, such as Robert Morris, were able to take advantage of unique opportunities offered by the conflict to make fortunes quickly. As one historian has reminded us, not all merchants were wealthy; some were grocers who lived no better than prosperous master craftsmen. But the pillars of the mercantile community sometimes earned fabulous returns on their wartime investments, and a small number of firms controlled the majority of maritime imports during the 1780s. The commercial boom after 1793 proved a bonanza for many businessmen, enabling them to amass estates far beyond the dreams of an earlier generation.[52]

As some men profited from trade, others built riches from privateering, shipbuilding, and real estate. John McPherson, for example, captured eighteen French vessels on one voyage in 1758, making him one of the wealthiest men in the city. The lure of quick riches seduced lower-class landlubbers to risk their lives in such ventures even though shipowners reaped the major portion of the harvest of prizes. While individual owners might realize £1,500 or £2,000 for each ship snared, seamen earned £10 or £15 apiece.[53]

49. Price, "Economic Function," 152–155; Egnal, "Pennsylvania Economy," 79; Jensen, *Maritime Commerce*; and Berg, "Economic Consequences of the French and Indian War," 185–193. For a different interpretation, but one that still contends that some merchants were growing much wealthier during the late, compared to the early, colonial period, see Doerflinger, *Vigorous Spirit of Enterprise*, 17–45, 167–180; and Doerflinger, "Philadelphia Merchants."

50. Price, "Economic Function," 152–155; Nash, *Urban Crucible*, 235–237.

51. Merchants accounted for 12.5 percent of taxables with identified occupations in 1756 and 7.5 percent in 1774, according to the Provincial Tax Lists for those years. Also see Doerflinger, *Vigorous Spirit of Enterprise*, 17.

52. Doerflinger, *Vigorous Spirit of Enterprise*, chaps. 1, 5, and 6.

53. I culled figures for the division of the booty from the Admiralty Court Papers, HSP; and Nash, *Urban Crucible*, 236–240.

Other Philadelphians found their way to wealth through judicious investments in vessels, houses, and land.[54]

In general, men with available capital earned the greatest rewards. In a city whose economy rested on commerce, merchants not surprisingly were the majority of the economic elite. Not only were some merchants very rich, but their fortunes increased dramatically in both absolute and relative terms during the final three decades of the colonial era. For example, the total value of the ten largest estates left by merchants in the decade before the Revolutionary War exceeded by 161 percent those left by their ten counterparts during the period from 1746 to 1755. The value of the estates of all decedents in the city grew by only 25 percent during the same time frames. In addition, whereas hardly any merchant possessed more than £20,000 during the 1750s, such fortunes became commonplace by the 1790s. A very few men grew enormously rich: William Bingham may have been worth £668,000 in the mid-1790s.[55]

Philadelphia's elite often spent their newly acquired wealth in ways that afforded limited economic benefits for poorer inhabitants. Many envisioned themselves as merchant princes who, according to one historian, "were obsessed with wealth and the social status it bought." They emulated the lesser British gentry by constructing opulent town houses and large country estates, furnishing them with tables, divans, beds, and chandeliers from abroad, and acquiring servants and slaves as cooks, waitingmen, and maids. The grandeur of their homes required matching refinement in their carriages, and elegant coaches rolled through the streets in ever increasing numbers. They also invested in foreign objets d'art, laid out formal gardens, and founded clubs for horse racing and fox hunting. Their taste naturally extended to clothing (including the latest English fashions, down to silk undergarments) and to expensive wines, rums, Madeiras, Asian spices, and tropical fruits, as well as to the proper glassware from England and plates from China. One obvious sign of their growing prosperity and pretentiousness was that the proportion of taxpayers designated as "gentleman" or "esquire" tripled between 1756 and 1772 and then multiplied another five times during the following quarter century.[56]

54. Doerflinger, "Philadelphia Merchants," 208.

55. Nash provided me with the evidence on inventories of estates from RW. Doerflinger's claim that Philadelphia did not possess a "merchant aristocracy" is surely exaggerated. By his own reckoning, more than half of the richest 15 percent of citizens were active or retired merchants. Moreover, an additional 41 percent of the top tax bracket were designated as either "gentlemen" or "unknown," some of whom undoubtedly came from the ranks of merchants. On this and other topics presently discussed, see Doerflinger, *Vigorous Spirit of Enterprise*, 16, 20–36, 65, 123–134, 236–242.

56. For a wonderful portrait of the lifestyle of the city's rich and famous, see Doerflinger, *Vigorous Spirit of Enterprise*, 20–36, quote on 30. Among the many studies of the increasing opulence of the elite during the late colonial period are Carl Bridenbaugh and Jessica Bridenbaugh, *Rebels and Gentlemen: Philadelphia in the Age of Franklin*, 2d ed. (New York, 1965),

This gentrified life-style with its emphasis on ostentatious consumption, particularly of foreign baubles, meant that the spending habits of the rich had rather limited multiplier effects within the local economy, apart from increasing the demand for specific luxury services. Constructing country estates and furnishing them with elegant finery benefited some of the city's skilled master carpenters, cabinetmakers, carvers, silversmiths, goldsmiths, and clock makers. And a gracious social life provided employment for a few master tailors, limners, dancing masters, and china makers and effected a tenfold growth in coachmakers during the twenty years before the Revolution. However, the demand for luxuries did not create a great many new jobs for unskilled workers and lesser artisans. When the city's elite invested as much as a third of their fortunes in articles of personal consumption, relatively little was left to seep down to laboring people.[57]

The middling classes, comprised primarily of tradesmen and artisans, enjoyed mixed success during this period of commercial advance. As the city became more of an entrepôt, the position of merchandise retailers improved. The proportion of shopkeepers among the top half of taxpayers, for example, increased from 70 to 90 percent between 1756 and 1772. At the same time, their number among the richest decile of decedents tripled to 15 percent. Likewise, artisans engaged in the construction of houses and ships often capitalized on the growth of these economic sectors. But advances on the part of some craftsmen were balanced by the decline of others. Overall, the taxable status of average artisans improved slightly, while the very wealthiest among them lost ground. A variety of factors caused the material standards of laborers, mariners, and lesser artisans to fluctuate throughout the second half of the century, a subject that is considered later.

Even though shipbuilding, housing construction, and other enterprises played important roles, maritime commerce to a great extent shaped Phila-

chap. 6; Jensen, *Maritime Commerce*, 61; Theodore Thayer, "Town into City, 1746–1765," in Russell F. Weigley, ed., *Philadelphia: A 300-Year History* (New York, 1982), 93–96; and Harry M. Tinkcom, "The Revolutionary City, 1765–1783," ibid., 120–122. This phenomenon impressed contemporaries as well; see Johann David Schoepf, *Travels in the Confederation* [1783–1784], ed. and trans. Alfred J. Morrison (New York, 1968; orig. 1911), 100; Kenneth Roberts and Anna M. Roberts, *Moreau de St. Mery's American Journey* [1793–1798] (Garden City, N.Y., 1947), 334; Elizabeth Evans, ed., *Weathering the Storm: Women of the American Revolution* (New York, 1975), 289; Janson, *Stranger in America*, 188. The elegance of dress of the city's elite is evident in the Ledger of Joseph Graisbury, Tailor, 1759–1773, Forde and Reed Papers, HSP. Also see advertisements for fashionable attire in the *Pennsylvania Ledger* (Philadelphia), Jan. 7, 1783; and the *Aurora General Advertiser* (Philadelphia), Nov. 14, 1799. The proportions of gentlemen and esquires are calculated from the 1767 Tax Assessors' Reports, Van Pelt Library, University of Pennsylvania, Philadelphia, and the 1772 and 1798 Provincial Tax Lists.

57. Doerflinger estimates the average amount that merchants invested in personal consumption, in *Vigorous Spirit of Enterprise*, 25, 67.

delphia's economy. The city's trade, in turn, depended on other regions throughout the Atlantic world. Philadelphia's traffic in goods constituted but one strand in an intricate weave of commercial fibers that interconnected the Atlantic basin. Twists in any of the threads could affect the coporeal tapestry of the lives of the city's residents. Poor harvests in southern Europe, declining wheat production in England, tropical storms in the Caribbean, wars among European nations, social and economic dislocation in the Palatinate or in Ireland, slave revolts in St. Domingue, political conflict between Great Britain and its colonies, and hostilities among whites and Indians on the frontier all reverberated in the pocketbooks of Philadelphians.

Local as well as international forces that lay beyond the control of the city's laboring people affected their welfare. Cycles in Philadelphia's economy helped define employment opportunities. In general, the early and late 1750s and the mid-1790s were particularly good times, whereas the early 1760s through much of the 1780s were difficult ones. Laboring people likewise experienced the seasonal rise and fall of economic activity, enjoying greater job options in the warmer months and fewer ones during the colder season.

Equally important were the long-term trends during the second half of the century. Although marked by frequent oscillations, Philadelphia's economy was bustling and prosperous during much of this period. But the way in which the economy grew advantaged some residents greatly and others hardly at all. To return to the paradox identified earlier, the laboring classes generally did not improve their position either in relative or in absolute terms, while the wealthy enjoyed much greater affluence in the 1790s than in the 1750s.

The rich, to paraphrase Ernest Hemingway's famous retort to F. Scott Fitzgerald, have always lived differently than the common people. And the gap between the life-styles of the upper and lower classes widened considerably in Philadelphia between 1750 and 1800. Of course, this is not to say that all of the rich got richer, for they, too, were tossed about by a variety of forces. Still, those near the top possessed resources that often allowed them to cushion fiscal shocks and even to take advantage of opportunities during periods of economic crisis. As wealthy citizens grew increasingly opulent and self-consciously spent their fortunes in ways designed to identify their social status, the distance between the upper and lower classes sharpened.

If the lower classes did not enjoy relative gains, neither did they benefit greatly from the city's economic growth in concrete terms. Employment in the three major economic sectors—commerce, shipbuilding, and housing construction—barely kept pace with population growth. One consequence, as we see in the succeeding chapters, is that the income, living standards, and economic and occupational mobility of the lower classes did not improve during the century's last fifty years.

Material Conditions

I am a true labourer: I earn that I eat, get that I wear.
—William Shakespeare, Corin, *As You Like It*

JOHN SHENTON, a Philadelphia mariner, sailed four times to Antigua on the snow *Mary* between October 1750 and November 1752. He earned between £13 and £15 per voyage, plus 3.5*s.* for each day he worked unloading or stowing cargo, for an annual income of approximately £32 during those years. Shenton's personal expenses must have been minimal, for room and board were provided on ship, and the only financial difficulties he may have encountered would have resulted from supporting a wife and children, if he had such. The material conditions he and his hypothetical family experienced, however, are not clear to us.

Fifteen years later, Joseph Graisbury earned approximately £180 annually by outfitting some of Philadelphia's wealthiest citizens in the latest fashions, from Holland cloth britches to silk vests. He bought a house worth £120 in Lower Delaware ward, in which he resided with his wife, at least seven children, all under eight years of age, and a slave. But the standard of living provided by his tailoring and the ways it varied during the decade before the Revolution are unknown.

Late in the 1780s, John and Elizabeth Baldwin performed occasional jobs for the Pennsylvania Hospital for the Sick Poor. John whitewashed fences and walls for 5*s.* 5*d.* per day and spread dung on the hospital's garden for 1.5*s.* each day. Elizabeth washed clothes, cleaned rooms, made candles, cooked, and nursed, usually for 2.5*s.* per day. The couple and their two children lived in a "brick tenement" rented from the hospital for £12 annually and may at times have paid 9*d.* for a meal at the hospital. Again, the material circumstances of their lives and the nature of their struggle to make ends meet cannot be clearly understood from these fragmentary data.[1]

---

1. These vignettes are drawn from information contained in the U.S. Bureau of the Census, *Heads of Families of the First Census of the United States taken in the Year 1790: Pennsylvania*

These vignettes provide glimpses into the material world of urban laboring people in America during the second half of the eighteenth century. They are a summons to research the day-to-day lives of ordinary Americans rather than a basis for easy generalizations about their physical existence. Despite limited evidence, historians at times have described the living standards of the urban lower classes as comfortable, perpetuating the hoary myth that labor scarcity in early America inevitably meant high wages for anyone who cared to work. Thus Sam Bass Warner, Jr., finds Revolutionary Philadelphia a city of "abundance for the common man." "An unskilled laborer without connections," Warner claims, "could find work with board and wages to begin accumulating a little money for tools," and the "earnings of the ordinary artisan . . . could support a wife and children without their having to take outside employment."[2] Carl Bridenbaugh states that the lower sort received "very high wages" and that "a hard-working man could support his wife and family and even lay by a little money for the future."[3] Philadelphians, in particular, Carl and Jessica Bridenbaugh believe, "enjoyed continuing prosperity and a steady rise in the standard of living."[4] In the Quaker City, as in the colonies generally, according to John J. McCusker, "not only were the rich getting richer but the poor were also."[5] Jackson Turner Main concurs that "the general standard of living was high." Indeed, conditions in the Pennsylvania capital were so favorable that even the "poor laborer," Main avers, "could normally expect to become a small property owner."[6]

Similarly, paucity of evidence has not restrained historians from using the

---

(Washington, D.C., 1908), 245, and in the following manuscript records: Business Papers of Samuel Coates and John Reynell, 1755–1767, Coates and Reynell Papers, HSP, hereafter cited as Coates and Reynell Papers; Ledger of Joseph Graisbury, Tailor, 1759–1773, Forde and Reed Papers, HSP, hereafter cited as Ledger of Graisbury; transcripts of the 1767 Tax Assessors' Reports, Van Pelt Library, University of Pennsylvania, Philadelphia, hereafter cited as Tax Assessors' Reports; Philadelphia City Constables' Returns for 1775, PCA, hereafter cited as Constables' Returns; and Matron and Steward's Cash Books, Pennsylvania Hospital Records, APS, hereafter cited as Matron and Steward's Cash Books.

2. Sam Bass Warner, Jr., *The Private City: Philadelphia in Three Periods of Its Growth* (Philadelphia, 1968), 7. See also David Hawke, *In the Midst of a Revolution* (Philadelphia, 1961), 38; and Stephen E. Lucas, *Portents of Rebellion: Rhetoric and Revolution in Philadelphia, 1765–1776* (Philadelphia, 1976), 20.

3. Carl Bridenbaugh, *Cities in Revolt: Urban Life in America, 1743–1776* (New York, 1955), 148, 284.

4. Carl Bridenbaugh and Jessica Bridenbaugh, *Rebels and Gentlemen: Philadelphia in the Age of Franklin* (New York, 1942), 10–11, 13.

5. John J. McCusker, "Sources of Investment Capital in the Colonial Philadelphia Shipping Industry," *JEH*, 32 (1972), 146–157. See also James F. Shepherd and Gary M. Walton, "Trade, Distribution, and Economic Growth in Colonial America," ibid., 128–145; and Alice Hanson Jones, "Wealth Estimates for the American Middle Colonies, 1774," *Economic Development and Cultural Change*, 18 (1970), 127–140.

6. Jackson Turner Main, *The Social Structure of Revolutionary America* (Princeton, N.J., 1965), 194, 279.

supposedly favorable economic circumstances of laboring people to interpret their political motivations and behavior. Charles S. Olton argues that "the mechanic class" in Revolutionary Philadelphia was "preponderantly composed of independent entrepreneurs" whose "common interests" help explain their political activity.[7] Other historians, generalizing on the meaning of the Revolution, assert that it did not result from "belly factors" or "rising misery" but "took place in a basically prosperous . . . economy." Americans in general, it is said, did not confront and were not roused to rebellion by the "predicament of poverty."[8]

Gary B. Nash, John K. Alexander, and Steven Rosswurm paint a less rosy portrait of the lives of laboring people.[9] Nash discovers growing problems of poverty and unemployment during the late colonial period, which he regards as symptomatic of structural weaknesses in the urban economy, and he undertakes to show how changes in the "material conditions of life . . . for city dwellers" generated a "revolutionary commitment within the middle and lower ranks of colonial society."[10] Still, relatively little has been done to test the welfare of the urban "lesser sort" by measuring their living standards. Main's analysis of the social structure of Revolutionary America took a very important step in this direction, but, as Philip S. Foner concludes in his review of the literature, "we can but guess at the actual wages of eighteenth-century workers," a fundamental issue, because "we have no reliable statistics on pay scales."[11]

We still lack a systematic investigation sensitive to changes in the material welfare of the urban laboring classes during the late eighteenth century. Historians seldom have studied the relation between wages and living costs, the regularity of employment opportunity, or the cyclical factors that affected income, prices, and work availability. Basic questions consequently remain unanswered. How did the supposedly high wages translate into

7. Charles S. Olton, *Artisans for Independence: Philadelphia Mechanics and the American Revolution* (Syracuse, N.Y., 1975), 8–9.

8. Bernard Bailyn, "The Central Themes of the American Revolution: An Interpretation," in Stephen G. Kurtz and James H. Hutson, eds., *Essays on the American Revolution* (Chapel Hill, N.C., 1973), 12. See also Hannah Arendt, *On Revolution* (New York, 1963), esp. chap. 1.

9. Gary B. Nash, "Poverty and Poor Relief in Pre-Revolutionary Philadelphia," *WMQ*, 3d Ser., 33 (1976), 3–30; Nash, "Urban Wealth and Poverty in Pre-Revolutionary America," *Journal of Interdisciplinary History*, 6 (1976), 545–584; Nash, "Up from the Bottom in Franklin's Philadelphia," *Past and Present*, no. 77 (1977), 57–83; John K. Alexander, *Render Them Submissive: Responses to Poverty in Philadelphia, 1760–1800* (Amherst, Mass., 1980); and Steven Rosswurm, *Arms, Country, and Class: The Philadelphia Militia and 'Lower Sort' during the American Revolution, 1775–1783* (New Brunswick, N.J., 1987).

10. Gary B. Nash, "Social Change and the Growth of Prerevolutionary Urban Radicalism," in Alfred F. Young, ed., *The American Revolution: Explorations in the History of American Radicalism* (De Kalb, Ill., 1976), 7; Nash, *The Urban Crucible: Social Change, Political Consciousness, and the Origins of the American Revolution* (Cambridge, Mass., 1979).

11. Main, *Social Structure*, 192–195; Philip S. Foner, *Labor and the American Revolution* (Westport, Conn., 1976), 12.

purchasing power? How did the seasonality of work affect income? How close to the margin did working people live, and how seriously did fluctuations in the economy affect them? How often did they experience periods of hardship or prosperity? Were the material conditions of their lives generally improving or deteriorating? The evidence available to answer such questions is more limited than that for the study of the wealthy or even of the institutionalized poor for whom government records exist. But it is possible, nonetheless, to find out a good deal about the material lives of laborers, mariners, and artisans.

My purpose in this chapter is to measure as precisely as the sources permit the household budgets, wages, and material conditions among the lower sort. Specifically, the primary focus of this and the succeeding chapter is on two categories of lesser artisans—cordwainers (shoemakers) and tailors—and two less-skilled groups—laborers and mariners. The following pages give an account of the costs of four basic necessities—food, rent, fuel, and clothing—in order to construct a typical household budget. A consideration of actual and real wages (the latter adjusted by the cost of living), of income, and of the material conditions of the four occupational groups then follows.[12]

Food was the most important item in every household budget. The eighteenth-century Philadelphia price series of foodstuffs painstakingly gathered by Anne Bezanson and her associates have been widely employed by economic historians. Unfortunately, these data are not very useful in estimating the actual expense of nourishment to laboring people. Bezanson's data represent the *wholesale* cost of staples as they were exported from the port rather than their *retail* value at the city's local markets, and we do not know the relationship between the two prices. Bezanson assembled figures for the price of goods sold in large bulk, and it is not evident how to translate the wholesale price paid by a merchant for several barrels of beef into the cost of a quarter pound of meat bought by a consumer at the local market.[13] Fortunately, a better record of the retail prices for food is available. Accounts

12. A word of caution concerning the data in this chapter is needed. No historical statistics are completely accurate, and figures from the eighteenth century are generally less dependable than those from later eras of American history. The best one can hope for is reliable estimates. In this study the relative values—the indices of change of prices, budgets, and wages—are more reliable than the estimates of absolute budgets and wages.

13. The authors acknowledged the shortcomings of their studies that constructed only wholesale price series, which could not then be translated accurately into retail prices, in Anne Bezanson, Robert D. Gray, and Miriam Hussey, *Prices in Colonial Pennsylvania* (Philadelphia, 1935), 8. See also Anne Bezanson et al., *Prices and Inflation during the American Revolution: Pennsylvania, 1770–1790* (Philadelphia, 1951); and Anne Bezanson et al., *Wholesale Prices in Philadelphia, 1784–1861*, 2 vols. (Philadelphia, 1936–1937). It is also likely that foodstuffs produced for the local market differed in quality (and price) from exported staples, especially when the latter were designated for consumption by slaves in the West Indies.

of daily purchases, specifying the quantity and price of each commodity by the Pennsylvania Hospital from the mid-1750s until well into the nineteenth century, provide a wealth of information about both the cost of goods and the consumption standards of the lower sort.[14]

The hospital's purchases reveal that Philadelphians could select from an impressive variety of food. Flour, bran, oats, barley, and rice products constituted a large part of their diet; they also dined on fresh and salted pork, mutton, veal, and beef (including calf's head); chicken, goose, turkey, pigeon, and rabbit; and such seafoods as shad, herring, oysters, and clams. Vegetables included white and sweet potatoes, turnips, parsnips, corn, beans, peas, asparagus, and cucumbers, and Philadelphians ate apples, oranges, peaches, lemons, raisins, currants, and cranberries in season. Butter, cheese, and eggs seem to have been plentiful, while salt, pepper, mustard, horseradish, sugar, molasses, syrup, and vinegar were used to flavor food. The Quaker City residents washed all this down with milk, coffee, several types of tea, chocolate, and unfermented cider, and they lifted their spirits with hard cider, rum (both the local and the more expensive West Indian variety), wine, and "small" and "strong" beer.

The cost of items purchased by the hospital provides an annual average retail price of each foodstuff during the second half of the century.[15] To construct an accurate food budget index that measures the cost of sustenance for an individual or family, a weighting system based on the quantity of each of the foodstuffs consumed is necessary. For the purposes of the present investigation, reliable food consumption patterns of Philadelphia's lower sort can be derived from the records of the Pennsylvania Hospital. Because the hospital was a publicly funded institution established for the poor, and because it experienced continuous financial problems, we may reasonably assume that the types and proportions of foods eaten by laboring people resembled the diet of the patients.[16]

To establish a reliable laborer's diet, I have computed the proportion of each of the nineteen most common foodstuffs purchased by the hospital in

14. Matron and Steward's Cash Books.

15. To account for seasonal variation in the cost of food, prices from February, May, August, and November of each year have been collected and the mean prices during each of the four months have been weighted equally to compute the average annual cost of each commodity. The price relative of each item and the evenly weighted index of all the foods are available in Appendix F and in Billy G. Smith, "'The Best Poor Man's Country': Living Standards of the 'Lower Sort' in Late Eighteenth-Century Philadelphia," in Glenn Porter and William H. Mulligan, Jr., ed., *Working Papers from the Regional Economic History Research Center*, vol. 2 (Greenville, Del., 1979), 50, 64–68.

16. William H. Williams, "The 'Industrious Poor' and the Founding of the Pennsylvania Hospital," *PMHB*, 97 (1973), 431–443; Nash, "Poverty and Poor Relief," 7–8. Eighteenth-century medical practice discouraged wealthy citizens from entering hospitals, and the diet standards provided there undoubtedly reflected that fact.

1772.[17] The caloric requirements of laboring Philadelphians have been used to determine the amount of each food they consumed. The Nutritionists calculate that a twentieth-century man of average physical activity needs between 3,000 and 3,200 calories each day; males engaged in heavy labor require approximately 4,550.[18] Men of the colonial period perhaps needed somewhat fewer calories because of their slightly smaller stature compared to the twentieth-century standard, though this may well have been offset by the additional energy expended in the absence of modern labor-saving machinery.[19] It seems unlikely that an eighteenth-century laborer could long have been adequately sustained on much less than 3,000 to 3,200 calories daily. Accordingly, I have constructed a diet with that caloric intake, in which nineteen of the most common foodstuffs are consumed in the same proportion as they were purchased by the Pennsylvania Hospital (see Table 3).[20]

Although the method of establishing this diet is not completely satisfactory, comparisons with other real and estimated patterns of food consumption indicate that the Philadelphia worker's diet was minimal in both quality and cost. Grains constituted the mainstay of the American table generally. Daily rations of the Continental army in 1775 included one pound of bread and a small amount of cornmeal, whereas prisoners in early nineteenth-century Philadelphia ate 1.25 pounds of bread, supplemented by cornmeal.[21] James T. Lemon finds that the wills of Pennsylvania farmers specified that their widows receive five hundred pounds annually, or 1.37 pounds per day of grain products.[22] David Klingaman calculates .6 pounds of wheat

17. The amount the Pennsylvania Hospital spent on various foods between May 3, 1772 and May 3, 1773, is in its report to the assembly. See Charles F. Hoban, ed., *Votes of the Assembly*, vol. 7 of *Pennsylvania Archives*, 8th ser., ed. Samuel Hazard et al. (Philadelphia and Harrisburg, Pa., 1852–1949), 7069.

18. Mary Davis Rose, *Laboratory Handbook for Dietetics*, ed. Clara Mae Taylor and Grace Macleod, 5th ed., rev. (New York, 1949), 15–36.

19. Eighteenth-century Americans apparently were not as short as it is sometimes believed. Sixty-seven inches was the mean height of 130 mariners who applied for certificates of citizenship in Philadelphia between 1795 and the end of the century, in Seamen's Protective Certificate Applications to the Collector of Customs for the Port of Philadelphia, Records of the Bureau of Customs, Record Group 36, NA. In addition, the 1,324 runaway slaves advertised in the *Pennsylvania Gazette* (Philadelphia) between 1728 and 1790 averaged sixty-eight inches in height. See Billy G. Smith and Richard Wojtowicz, *Blacks Who Stole Themselves: Advertisements for Runaways in the Pennsylvania Gazette, 1728–1790* (Philadelphia, 1989).

20. Caloric estimates are from Rose, *Laboratory Handbook*. Neither fish nor peas are included in the diet because the records do not permit calculation of their unit price.

21. Data for soldiers are from the U.S. Bureau of the Census, *Historical Statistics of the United States: Colonial Times to 1970*, 2 vols. (Washington, D.C., 1975), 2:1175; hereafter cited as *Historical Statistics*. James Mease recorded the diet of prisoners, in *The Picture of Philadelphia . . .* (New York, 1970; Philadelphia, 1811), 167.

22. James T. Lemon, "Household Consumption in Eighteenth-Century America and Its Relationship to Production and Trade: The Situation among Farmers in Southeastern Pennsylvania," *Agricultural History*, 41 (1967), 63–64, 68.

Table 3. Estimated Philadelphia worker's diet

Foodstuff	Annual quantity consumed (in pounds)	Daily caloric intake	1762 cost per week in pence
Wheat flour[a]	365.0	1,600	12.73
Cornmeal	45.0	199	.71
Rice	15.7	68	.68
Bran	52.6	110	.69
Meat		528	11.65
Beef	100.2		
Mutton	18.2		
Pork	9.1		
Veal	47.0		
Potatoes	6.6	7	.19
Turnips	27.6	12	.50
Butter	12.8	117	5.09
Milk	38.1[b]	281	7.81
Salt	21.9	c	.37
Pepper	.1	c	.06
Sugar	16.8	83	2.16
Molasses	4.9[b]	174	3.16
Beverages			.92
Coffee	.7	c	
Tea	.2	c	
Chocolate	.2	c	
Total		3,179	46.72

Source: See text.
[a]Includes both "middling" and "common" flour.
[b]In gallons.
[c]Not included in caloric calculations.

flour as the daily adult per capita consumption before the Revolution.[23] The proposed diet of laboring Philadelphians, which allows 1.31 pounds of grains each day, closely resembles that of soldiers, prisoners, and widows and exceeds the adult per capita consumption of grains.

Meat furnished a significant portion of the caloric intake of Americans. The Continental army allotted 1 pound of beef a day to soldiers; Philadelphia prisoners ate .5 pounds; .41 pounds has been estimated as the daily fare of both Pennsylvania widows and American adults generally.[24] The worker's diet, as constructed, includes .48 pounds of meat daily, similar to that of prisoners and widows, and to the overall American consumption, but not quite half the ration of soldiers. Contemporary comments indicating that "most labourers and mechanics eat a portion of [meat] at breakfast and

23. David Klingaman, "Food Surpluses and Deficits in the American Colonies, 1768–1772," *JEH*, 31 (1971), 559–560.
24. These figures are computed from *Historical Statistics*, 2:1175; Mease, *Picture of Philadelphia*, 167; Lemon, "Household Consumption," 63; and Klingaman, "Food Surpluses," 559–560.

supper" suggest that, if anything, the diet estimate cuts the meat allotment to the bone.[25]

Milk, sugar, and molasses served as less important energy sources. Most colonists drank milk or, when it turned to curd on warm days, ate it as "bonny clabber." Both Bostonians of the "middling figure" in the early eighteenth century and Continental soldiers consumed a quart a day, while Philadelphia laborers are estimated to have drunk .4 quarts each day.[26] Sugar and molasses were important food flavorings, and the latter also served to make the small beer popular among Philadelphians.

If the laborer's diet included more grains and less meat than other real and estimated patterns of consumption, it was also cheaper to purchase. Retail prices gathered from the hospital records indicate that in 1762 (the base year for all the indices constructed in this chapter) Philadelphians would have paid 3.88s. per week, or £10.12 per year, for the diet served up in Table 3.[27] Estimates by Main and Klingaman exceed this amount. Main puts the cost of food for a single man at £10–13 annually during this period, and Klingaman calculates the per capita food budget in Philadelphia at £11.88 per year between 1768 and 1772. The Continental army rations, because they included more meat than the diet specified in Table 3, cost even more: £14.38 per year at 1762 Philadelphia prices.[28] Other miscellaneous records of expenditures for food corroborate the conservative nature of this budget.[29]

25. Mease, *Picture of Philadelphia*, 121. The diet in Table 3 also resembles that consumed by the occupants of Philadelphia's almshouse during the late eighteenth century. In 1792 and 1793 the almshouse supplied its inhabitants with .32 pounds of meat for every pound of cereals, and the diet in Table 3 allots .36 pounds of meat for every pound of cereals. Calculated from the Daily Occurrences Docket, Feb. 5, 1793, Guardians of the Poor, PCA, hereafter cited as Daily Occurrences.

26. *Historical Statistics*, 2:1175; Carl Bridenbaugh, "The High Cost of Living in Boston, 1728," *The New England Quarterly*, 5 (1932), 800–811; and Charles William Janson, *The Stranger in America, 1793–1806*, ed. Carl S. Driver (New York, 1971), 187.

27. All values in this chapter are in Pennsylvania currency unless otherwise indicated. Conversion rates to sterling before the Revolution are available in *Historical Statistics*, 2:1198. For the 1790s values are converted from dollars to Pennsylvania pounds at the rate of 7.5s. per dollar. The superior data on prices and wages available for the year 1762 determined its selection as the base year for all the indices in this chapter. The war years 1777 through 1782 were excluded from all indices because prices and wages fluctuated so violently during these years that their levels could not be accurately determined from the number of observations. For accuracy and convenience, money values are often given in decimal notation: £10.12 is equivalent to £10 and 2s..

28. The currency of Main's estimate is unclear. If it is pounds sterling, the equivalent in Pennsylvania currency is between £16.67 and £21.67; *Social Structure*, 115. Klingaman's estimate in pounds sterling is converted into Pennsylvania currency at the rate of .6 pounds sterling per each Pennsylvania pound and then adjusted to the 1762 food prices found in this chapter; "Food Surpluses," 567. Data on the Continental army rations are in *Historical Statistics*, 2:1175.

29. During the third quarter of the eighteenth century, sea captains and their "boys" both customarily received one shilling per day "diet money." See the Journal of John and Peter Chevalier, Nov. 29, 1770, July 19, 1773, HSP; Clifford Papers, vol. 3, 1760–1762, HSP; Coates and Reynell Papers, 1751–1754 and 1755–1767. In the 1770s, John Fitch's journey-

Although the diet in Table 3 is imprecise, for the purposes of this book it need be only a reliable estimate, and it does appear reasonable, if minimal, sustenance for Philadelphia's lower sort both in pattern of consumption and in price. In any case, minor alterations of the diet will not significantly affect the overall conclusions here.

Using this diet and the food price series developed above, I have constructed a food budget index that measures the cost of the diet in each year relative to its cost in 1762 (see Table 4).[30] For example, in 1762 the diet cost £10.12; in 1770 its cost was 90 percent of that, or £9.11. Food prices climbed more than 20 percent from the war years of the 1750s to 1763 (see Figure 13),[31] fell to their prewar level by the late 1760s, and then rose gradually until the outbreak of the Revolutionary War. The diet's cost was 50 percent higher during the early 1780s but decreased steadily until 1788, when it again began to rise steeply, increasing more than 100 percent by the mid-1790s.

The food budget index functions as a barometer of a family's expenditures for sustenance. Nutritionists consider that, on average, an adult female and a child require 83 percent and 60 percent, respectively, of the calories needed by an adult male.[32] The median size of families in the four occupational

---

men silversmiths paid 8s. 2d. weekly for board, in Ledger of John Fitch, Case 33, HSP, hereafter Ledger of John Fitch. At the same time, master tailors thought that it cost 1.5s. per day to feed a journeyman, as calculated from information in the Minutes of the Taylors' Company, HSP, hereafter cited as Minutes of the Taylors' Company. Board in the Pennsylvania Hospital and in the workhouse cost 10s. per week before the Revolution. After the Revolution, the hospital both paid and charged workmen 9d. per meal, while the lowest price for patients' board fluctuated between 7.5s. and 12.5s. per week; Matron and Steward's Cash Books.

30. The formula used to construct this index is

$$I = \frac{\Sigma \, P_o Q(P_i/P_o)}{\Sigma \, P_o Q},$$

where I = food budget index, P_o = prices of each foodstuff in base year 1762; P_i = prices of each commodity in a given year; and Q = quantities of each food consumed by families in 1772. This is the most widely used measurement in cost-of-living studies. A slight upward bias is built into this measurement as it is assumed that the pattern of consumption remains constant. Consumption patterns change, however, as consumers tend to purchase more of those items whose prices rise least or fall most over time. Arithmetic rather than geometric indices are used in this chapter because the former make more economic sense even though the latter possess superior mathematical qualities. For an explanation of the construction of an index and a discussion of the benefits and liabilities of arithmetic and geometric indices, see R.G.D. Allen, *Index Numbers in Theory and Practice* (Chicago, 1975), 1–48 ; and Irving Fisher, *The Making of Index Numbers: A Study of Their Varieties, Tests, and Reliability*, 3d ed., rev. (New York, 1927).

31. Table 4 contains the data for and an explanation of years with missing values in Figure 13. Rising food prices during the early 1760s may have been even more dramatic than the food budget index indicates. In 1761 the assembly passed a law regulating the assize of bread; in changing the measurement of loaves from troy to avoirdupois weight, the law reduced the size of the cheapest loaf by approximately 25 percent. James T. Mitchell and Henry Flanders, comps., *The Statutes at Large of Pennsylvania from 1682 to 1801*, 18 vols. (Philadelphia and Harrisburg, Pa., 1896–1911), 2:61–63, 6:69–71.

32. Rose, *Laboratory Handbook*, 15–36.

Table 4. Household budget indices (base year = 1762), 1754–1800

Year	Food budget index	Rent index	Firewood price index	Clothing price index	Household budget index
1754	94		59[b]	92	89
1755	89		60	83	84
1756	99		52		92
1757	98[a]		78[b]		95
1758	80[a]		56[b]		76
1759	89		95[b]		90
1760	95		91		94
1761	86		88		86
1762	100	100	100	100	100
1763	115		91	100	107
1764	101		116[b]	94	102
1765	91		96[b]	82	94
1766	90		58[b]	73	90
1767	94	112	81[b]	88	96
1768	86		71	81	90
1769	81		71	83	88
1770	90		73	88	94
1771	96		71	79	95
1772	99		91	85	99
1773	90		76[c]	76	92
1774	100		61	79	96
1775	89	111	76	80	92
1776	97		82	251	121
1783	154	252	118	188	180
1784	147		160	99	164
1785	123		116	92	143
1786	124		111	110	142
1787	119		105	99	134
1788	99		74	139	123
1789	107	165	76	82	115
1790	134		79	92	131
1791	130		97	92	131
1792	131		106	110	136
1793	143		111	119	144
1794	161		130	137	158
1795	207		197	114	186
1796	227		215	132	201
1797	192		212	150	185
1798	183	184	182	129	176
1799	188		174	105	174
1800	201		177	125	185

Source: See text.

Note: The food budget index is based on nineteen items weighted by the diet in Table 3. The firewood includes only oak and pine and the prices used are for April through June of each year unless otherwise noted. Except for the years before 1762, the household budget index is based on the cost of food, rent, firewood, and clothing. In 1754 and 1755 it is calculated from the cost of food, firewood, and clothing, whereas in 1756 through 1761 it is computed from the price of food, rent, and firewood. The years 1777–1782 are not included because the extreme volatility of prices makes the records for those years unreliable.

[a]Interpolated from the wholesale cost of nine food items in Anne Bezanson, Robert D. Gray, and Miriam Hussey, *Prices in Colonial Philadelphia* (Philadelphia, 1935), 422–423.

[b]Index based on mean price for entire year.

[c]Interpolated from index in 1772 and 1774.

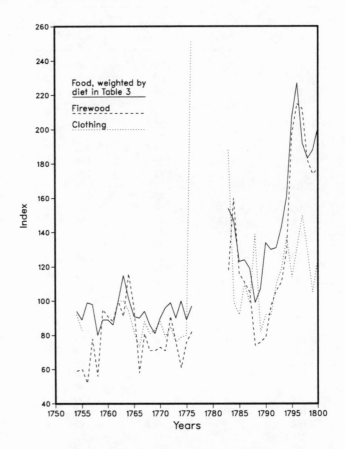

Figure 13. Indices of food, firewood, and clothing, 1754–1800

groups in Philadelphia during the mid-1770s was four, two adults and two children, and that composition forms the basis of all computations of household budgets in this chapter.[33] Consumption at these rates, when applied to the £10.12 cost of the diet in Table 3 for 1762, produces an estimated family food budget of £30.66 in the base year of the food budget index.

Even though Philadelphia was located in a grain- and animal-producing

33. Household size (discussed further in chapter 7) was calculated by matching people in the four occupational groups on the 1772 Provincial Tax List, PCA (hereafter cited as Provincial Tax List) with the Constables' Returns of 1775, which give the name of the household head and composition of the household.

region, its people could not buy food as cheaply as might be expected. Because foodstuffs composed the primary export of the area, overseas demand drove up local prices and caused rapid and wide fluctuations in food costs. The assize of bread, for example, was legally bound to the value of wheat or flour, and as the export prices of those products increased, so did the expense of loaves in the city's bakeries.[34] Several foreign visitors took note of the high fare for food. Comparing costs in Philadelphia with those in London, Joseph Poultney found "meat nearly the same price, butter much dearer, and bread as dear," and Dr. Robert Honyman agreed that "provisions are much dearer than I expected."[35]

During difficult times, laboring families adopted several strategies to trim food costs. They could produce their own food, although the crowded alleys where most lived made gardening impractical and owning a cow even less feasible.[36] Many undoubtedly kept hogs, notching the animals' ears for identification and allowing them to roam freely through their neighborhoods to feed on garbage. Poor residents most often reduced their food costs by eating large quantities of flour, cornmeal, and rice, foods with the highest caloric yield for the money. Carried to its extreme—the consumption of grains only—a family food budget could be cut by as much as 45 percent, though this resulted in a bland, nonnutritious diet. Such a strategy would have been debilitating, increasing susceptibility to the diseases that plagued the city.

The cost of shelter constituted the second major component of the household budget. Constables' returns and tax assessors' reports for various years provide sufficient data to construct an index of rents (see Table 4).[37] Real

34. *Statutes at Large*, 2:61–63, 6:69–71, 8:130–138, 308–309, 429–435, 14:510–511. Philadelphians continually complained that forestalling and engrossing drove up the cost of food. Because of these "different manoevers," one drayman grumbled, "a number of worthy families were sorely distressed, and the common day laborers almost starved"; in "A Drayman," *Independent Gazetteer* (Philadelphia), Apr. 9, 1791.

35. Letter of Joseph Poultney, Dec. 15, 1783, *PMHB*, 52 (1928), 95, hereafter cited as Letter of Joseph Poultney; and Philip Padelford, ed., *Colonial Panorama 1775: Dr. Robert Honyman's Journal for March and April* (San Marino, Calif., 1939), 17.

36. Only 3 percent of the members of the four occupational groups were taxed for a cow in 1772.

37. Constables' Returns for Walnut Ward in 1762, and for all ten city wards in 1775, give the name, occupation, and amount of annual rent paid by each householder who was not an inmate in another household. The 1767 Tax Assessors' Reports record the annual rent of each taxpayer, except inmates, in the ten city wards and suburbs of Southwark and the Northern Liberties. House valuations in five wards—Dock, Chestnut, High Street, Upper Delaware, and Walnut—are specified on the 1783, 1789, and 1798 Provincial Tax Lists, and since houses were assessed at six times the annual rent of the house, rents in these years can be easily computed. The rent index for 1775 was calculated from the mean rent in the ten city wards in 1775 and 1767. Indices for 1783, 1789, and 1798 were computed from the mean rents of the five wards in those years and in 1767. A comparison of all rents in Walnut ward in 1762 and 1767 indicated an

estate prices were high, reflecting the pressure of the quickly growing population on the available resources. According to one English visitor, rents were unusually elevated in Philadelphia, perhaps even "dearer than in London." Laboring families lived predominantly as tenants and boarders; fewer than one in ten owned their homes.[38] In 1767, laborers, mariners, cordwainers, and tailors paid average annual rents of £10.08, £11.86, £21.98, and £22.81, respectively.[39] During the decade before Independence, housing costs remained stable, as cheap dwellings multiplied on the outskirts of the city. Rents of poor Philadelphians doubled during the Revolutionary War (reflecting the general inflation), declined during the Confederation era, and then climbed slightly during the following decade.[40]

Philadelphians cooked their meals and heated their homes with firewood, an essential ingredient in their household budgets. Private business documents and records of the Pennsylvania Hospital permit the construction of an index of firewood prices (see Table 4).[41] Only the costs of oak and pine are tabulated, for these were the cheapest available fuels and the ones most likely used by the lower sort. The cost of wood spiraled upward from the war years of the 1750s to a peak in 1764 (see Figure 13), plummeted for the next two years, then fluctuated until Independence. Like food expenses and house

---

increase in rents of 12 percent during those years, and the rent indices with base year 1767 were accordingly adjusted to base year 1762. These rents represent the minimal expense for shelter since they do not include the ground rent and taxes that many tenants complained they had to pay. See "A Poor Tradesman," *Pennsylvania Packet, and Daily Advertiser* (Philadelphia), July 16, 1784; "A Tenant," *Pennsylvania Evening Herald, and American Monitor* (Philadelphia), July 16, 1785.

38. Letter of Joseph Poultney, 95. Only 4 percent of laborers and mariners and 14 percent of cordwainers and tailors owned their own homes, according to the Provincial Tax Lists of 1767, 1783, 1789, and 1798 and the Constables' Returns of 1775. This differs from Jackson Turner Main's conclusion that the "great majority of artisans . . . were homeowners." Main believes that more than half of cordwainers owned their own homes and that "three-fourths of all artisans were homeowners"; *Social Structure*, 80, 132.

39. The calculation of the average rent included the rent paid by inmates. The 1775 Constables' Returns indicate that 12 percent of laborers, 28 percent of mariners, 6 percent of cordwainers, and 7 percent of tailors were inmates, and nearly all of them were unmarried. While no direct record of their rent is available, it seems reasonable that they paid roughly half of the cost of leasing the cheapest house, or about £5 in 1767. The number of inmates is sufficiently small that an error in this estimate would alter the overall mean rent only slightly.

40. On rising rents during the 1790s, see "Several Bakers," *Federal Gazette and Philadelphia Daily Advertiser*, Nov. 7, 1793; and Mathew Carey, *A Short Account of the Malignant Fever, Lately Prevalent in Philadelphia* (New York, 1970; Philadelphia, 1794), 13.

41. Matron and Steward's Cash Books. The following are at the HSP: Samuel Morris's Day Book, 1755–1767, hereafter cited as Morris's Day Book; Bills, Receipts, and Accounts of the Shippen Family, vols. 28–30, 1754–1822, hereafter cited as Shippen Family Papers; Journal of John and Peter Chevalier; Incoming Correspondence: Bills and Receipts of John Cadwalader, Cadwalader Collection, Boxes 1–6, 12–14, hereafter cited as Cadwalader Collection; Business Papers of Levy Hollingsworth, Hollingsworth Collection, sec. 7: Bills, 1751–1789, and sec. 3: Invoices, 1764–1789, hereafter cited as Hollingsworth Collection; and Thomas A. Biddle Shipbook. Charges for cording and carting the firewood are included.

rents, fuel prices climbed during the Revolutionary War, declined during the 1780s, and rose again in the subsequent decade.

In 1762 Philadelphians spent an average of 22s. 11d. for the cheapest cord during the spring months. Poor citizens, usually buying quantities smaller than a full cord and most often during the winter months when prices were at their peak, must have paid two or three times that amount.[42] The quantity of firewood used by the average household is difficult to determine because of the paucity of evidence and the seasonal variations in the use of fuel. One historian has estimated that it took between 30 and 40 cords of wood annually to heat the homes of New Englanders, whereas a contemporary believed that wealthy Philadelphians used 25 cords each year. Four journeymen silversmiths in the Quaker City each burned an average of 4.88 cords per year from 1772 to 1775.[43] This appears to be a very conservative estimate of use by poor Philadelphians; much less would hardly have sufficed for their cooking and heating requirements, particularly in their draughty wooden homes. Thus a poor family spent a substantial sum, an estimated £5.60 in 1762, for fuel.[44]

The great demand for wood by both private and commercial users undoubtedly drove up its cost. Households alone burned at least 20,000 cords in 1772. Bakers, brickmakers, blacksmiths, and iron manufactures likewise needed fuel, while coopers, house carpenters, shipwrights, and lumber exporters must have added to the city's wood requirements. So vital was firewood that local regulations proscribed its purchase for resale in the city between September and March.[45] As the forests surrounding the city were depleted, small boats brought wood from throughout the Delaware Valley; as the carrying distance increased, so too did the price of fuel. Traveling through the area at midcentury, Peter Kalm observed that "the woods with

42. The price of firewood varied seasonally, often costing twice as much in winter as in spring. Constructing a working-class budget in Philadelphia during the nineteenth century, Mathew Carey estimated that a cord was nearly twice as high when bought in small parcels; *An Appeal to the Wealthy of the Land* . . . (Philadelphia, 1833), 10. In 1748, Peter Kalm wrote that "the price of wood went up rapidly" once winter began, and that when wood was first brought into the city in "early autumn, it is bought up at once by the wealthy and thoughtful, who then get their supply at a lower price"; in Adolph B. Benson, ed., *The America of 1750: Peter Kalm's Travels in North America*, 2 vols. (New York, 1964), 2:656.

43. The estimate for New England is in William Cronon, *Changes in the Land: Indians, Colonists, and the Ecology of New England* (New York, 1983), 120. Joseph Nourse commented about the amount of fuel burned by a "genteel" Philadelphia family during the 1790s, in Ellis Paxon Oberholtzer, *Philadelphia: A History of the City and Its People*, 4 vols. (Philadelphia, 1912), 1:400. The calculation for journeymen silversmiths is from the Ledger of John Fitch, 1773–1775.

44. The £5.60 figure is the product of the 1762 average price per cord, 22.92s., and the estimated 4.88 cords burned per year. One artisan in Charleston, South Carolina thought firewood cost him £3 sterling each year, or £5 Pennsylvania currency, and winters are much milder in Charleston than in Philadelphia; see Main, *Social Structure*, 118.

45. Mease, *Picture of Philadelphia*, 125–126; Bridenbaugh, *Cities in Revolt*, 27, 235.

which Philadelphia is surrounded would lead one to conclude that fuel must be cheap there. But is is far from being so." Kalm predicted that "in future times Philadelphia will be obliged to pay a high price for wood." The problem evoked numerous charity drives to supply wood to the city's poor, as well as recurrent demands to regulate the amount charged by carters and boatmen for carrying firewood.[46]

Reasonable estimates of clothing costs can be made. The city's workhouse spent at least £3 annually to outfit John Peter Operting, a "Labouring lunatic," during the 1760s. Main has calculated £4.17 as an average annual clothing allowance for adult males during this period.[47] In 1770, the most essential and least expensive attire could be purchased in Philadelphia for about £3.74. For that sum a man could buy one pair of coarse laborer's shoes (9s.), a pair of stockings (2s. 6d.), one pair of cloth britches (15s. 7d.), a cloth coat (29s. 5d.), two shirts (6s. 2d. each), and one felt hat (6s.).[48] This wardrobe would have been minimal, not quite equaling the standards of dress annually issued the inmates of the city's almshouse during the early nineteenth century.[49] If materials were purchased, and the coat, breeches and shirts made at home, clothing costs could be cut to £2.50.[50] This figure, 40 percent below Main's estimate, can be used to compute the clothing costs for a laboring family. The price of women's clothes probably matched that of men's, while cordwainers' and tailors' records indicate that children's shoes, breeches, and coats cost about 70 percent of those for men.[51] Thus in 1770 a laboring family of four would have spent roughly £8.5 for attire.

Prices for basic articles of clothing other than shoes are unavailable for the entire period, but an index constructed from the cost of materials (thread, flax, tow, flannel, and linen) for certain items of apparel (stockings, breeches, shirts, and coats) can serve as a proxy for the changes in the cost of clothing.[52] This index, combined with the price index of shoes, each weighted

46. Benson, *America of 1750*, 150–151. See Bridenbaugh, *Cities in Revolt*, 27, 235; and Bridenbaugh and Bridenbaugh, *Rebels and Gentlemen*, 235. On similar conditions on Manhattan Island, see Graham Russell Hodges, *New York City Cartmen, 1667–1850* (New York, 1986), 35.

47. Gertrude MacKinney, ed., *Votes and Proceedings of the House of Representatives of the Province of Pennsylvania*, vol. 6 of Samuel Hazard et al., *Pennsylvania Archives*, 5451, 6345; *Pennsylvania Gazette* (Philadelphia), July 14, 1763; and Main, *Social Structure*, 116.

48. Ledger of Graisbury; Matron and Steward's Cash Books.

49. Clothing Issues Ledger, 1805–1831, Guardians of the Poor, PCA.

50. Spinning the yarn and weaving the cloth domestically might save a bit more money, but this would have been difficult for many poor households because of the considerable time and skill required, as well as the substantial investment. A spinning wheel cost £1, or about four days' wages for a laborer, in 1788; Matron and Steward's Cash Books.

51. Ledger of Graisbury. Main estimates that the cost to clothe a child ran about 80 percent of the expense of outfitting an adult, or about £3.33 (Pennsylvania currency) annually during this period; *Social Structure*, 116.

52. Prices of these articles are from the Matron and Steward's Cash Books. Unfortunately, these records are incomplete and do not contain any data on clothing costs from 1756 through 1761.

according to its proportion of the 1770 clothing budget estimated above, provides a clothing price index (see Table 4 and Figure 13).

The family budget for laborers, mariners, cordwainers, and tailors constructed from calculations of the price of food, rent, fuel, and clothing averaged £60.82 in 1762.[53] The costs of the items in this budget are below other observed costs and estimates made by other scholars. Not only is the budget thus minimized, but many necessities for a "decent competency" have been excluded. Rum, apparently a vital element of the lives of eighteenth-century Americans,[54] may have cost laboring Philadelphians £3 annually but has not been included in the household budget. Taxes likewise are excluded; they amounted to £1–2 per year for those in the lowest brackets.[55] Although the Pennsylvania Hospital provided low-cost services, medical treatment was expensive. Smallpox variolation cost £3, not including wages lost during the required quarantine period of one or two weeks, and the inoculation had to be renewed every four or five years.[56] Death imposed a financial burden; in the early 1760s interment in private cemeteries could cost as much as £11.[57] Childbearing also was dear: midwives charged about 15s. before the Revolutionary War.[58] All of these necessities, along with soap, starch, candles, chamber pots, brooms, cutlery, and furniture, have been excluded from the estimated budget.

The index of the average household budget of the four occupational groups, which measures the relative cost of purchasing the 1762 budget in nearly every year from 1754 to 1800, is presented in Table 4 and is graphed in Figure 14.[59] The cost of this budget increased sharply toward the end of

53. In 1762, food, fuel, and clothing cost £30.66, £5.60, and £9.66, respectively. Laborers, mariners, cordwainers, and tailors paid rent of £9.00, £10.58, £19.63, and £20.37, respectively, or an average £14.90 for the four groups. These expenses are further confirmed and clarified through a comparison with other eighteenth- and nineteenth-century budgets in Smith, "'The Best Poor Man's Country,'" 14, 53.

54. W. J. Rorabaugh, *The Alcoholic Republic: An American Tradition* (New York, 1979), 7–11.

55. Nash, "Up From the Bottom," 76; and Nash, *Urban Crucible*, 403.

56. George W. Norris, *The Early History of Medicine in Philadelphia* (Philadelphia, 1886), 112.

57. Norris Stanley Barratt, *Outline of the History of Old St. Paul's Church, Philadelphia, Pennsylvania, 1760–1898* (Lancaster, Pa., 1918), 43.

58. Matron and Steward's Cash Books.

59. Except for the years 1754 through 1761, the annual costs of food, rent, fuel, and clothing are summed for each year and divided by the estimated 1762 budget to compute the index of household budgets. Because of limitations in the data, the household budget index for 1754 and 1755 is calculated by dividing the total expenditure for food, fuel, and clothing in those years by the total cost of these items in 1762. Similarly, the index for 1756 through 1761 is constructed by dividing the outlay for food, fuel, and rent in those years by the total price of these items in 1762. Rent and clothing accounted for 25 percent and 14 percent, respectively, of the total 1762 household budget. Unless the cost of those two items fluctuated very significantly during the few years for which data are not extant—and there is no reason to believe that they did—the household budget index for 1754–1761 should accurately reflect variations in the cost of the budget. Table 4 explains years with missing values in Figure 14.

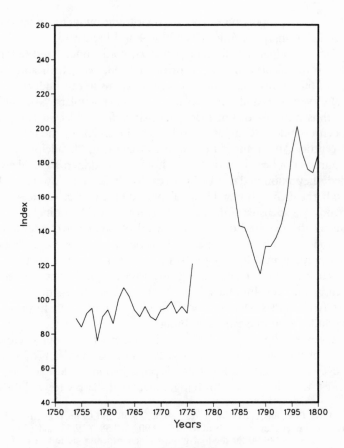

Figure 14. Index of household budget, 1754–1800

the French and Indian War, fell precipitously in 1765 to its prewar level, and rose gradually during the following decade. The significant jump in 1776 marked the beginning of the exorbitant inflation during the Revolutionary War. The index plummeted from 1783 to 1789 and then climbed rapidly back to a peak more than twice as high as the maximum of the 1770s.

Laborers, mariners, cordwainers, tailors, and their families frequently found it difficult to earn enough money to meet their basic expenses. Relatively low wages (compared to the cost of living) and irregular employment made life unpredictable for laboring people and undercut their attempts to achieve more than a minimal degree of physical well-being or economic security. The following section compares the wages and incomes of the four groups with the cost of their household budgets and considers a few of the factors responsible for their struggle to maintain their subsistence.

Laborers formed the second largest occupational group in the city, their numbers exceeded only by mariners.[60] More than any other group of freemen, they congregated at the bottom of the economic hierarchy: in 1772, assessors appraised nine of every ten laborers at the minimum rate. Using data on laborers' earnings contained in the ledgers of the Pennsylvania Hospital, government records, and a host of private business accounts, I have constructed an index of laborers' actual wages, and I have used the household budget index as an inflationary scale to produce an index of laborers' real wages (see Table 5). Real wages peaked during the French and Indian War (see Figure 15), plunged during the last two years of that conflict, rose during the mid-1760s, and then declined steadily during the last decade before the Revolutionary War. Although they fluctuated, real wages in the 1780s approximated those of the 1770s and began to rise during the final decade of the century.[61]

If employed for six days each week throughout the year, a laborer would have earned £59.3 in 1762, the base year of the wage indices. Because this hypothetical annual income assumes full employment, however, it must be considered a maximum figure, rarely attained. A variety of factors limited the supply of jobs: the cycles of nature slowed work during the winter, epidemics halted the city's economy, personal illnesses prevented laboring people from earning wages, and downturns in the business cycle curtailed employment opportunities.[62]

A comparison of incomes and household budgets discloses the nature of the struggle to make ends meet. In 1762, a laborer would have spent about £55 for food, rent, fuel, and clothing for himself and his family. If fully employed, his total annual wages of nearly £60 met these basic expenses. If

60. See Appendix C.

61. Only workers performing unskilled tasks and receiving wages "not found" (not supplied board) were considered. Hardly any short-term laborers received board. I calculated the indices of all real wages by solving the following equation for each year:

$$I_R = I_W/I_H,$$

where I_R = index of real wages, I_W = index of actual wages, and I_H = index of household budget. See Table 5 and Table 6 for data, sources, and an explanation of years with missing values in Figure 15.

62. These issues are discussed more fully elsewhere: chapter 2 considers epidemics and the health problems of workers; chapter 3 analyzes business cycles and the adverse impact of cold weather on the economy; and chapter 5 treats the difficulties faced by laboring people each winter.

Table 5. Indices of laborers' wages (base year = 1762), 1751–1800

Year	Laborers' actual wages	Laborers' real wages	Number of observations	Sources
1751	92		6	a
1752	90		11	a
1753	89		15	a
1754	86	97	18	a,i
1755	85	101	28	a,b,c
1756	92	100	11	a
1757	92	97	1	c
1758	90	118	13	b,c
1759	92	102	7	b,d
1760	118	126	34	b,e,m,p,t
1761	116	135	3	r,v
1762	100	100	17	b,c,k,p,w
1763	90	84	18	b,h,p,y
1764	86	84	12	b,c,f,m,x
1765	92	98	3	b,c,k
1766	105	117	6	b,f,k
1767	105	109	10	b,f,k
1768	101	112	11	f,k,m,s
1769	84	95	14	b,c,j,m
1770	89	95	35	b,m,n,q
1771	87	92	12	b,n
1772	82	83	5	b,z
1773	68	74	12	b,n,o,z
1774	79	82	13	b,m
1775	74	80	13	b
1776	93	77	8	b,m
1783	125	69	9	b,x
1784	110	67	22	b,u,x,zl
1785	126	88	57	b,l,n,u,x,zl
1786	120	84	16	b,u,x
1787	104	78	29	b,u,x,zl
1788	117	95	15	b,u
1789	88	77	17	b,m,x,zl
1790	86	66	14	b,l,zl
1791	97	74	25	b,g,zl
1792	119	88	15	b,zl
1793	117	81	11	b,n,zl
1794	143	90	28	b,zl
1795	174	94	12	b,l,zl
1796	170	85	12	b,zl
1797	178	96	2	b,zl
1798	197	112	9	b,zl
1799	197	113	11	b,zl
1800	162	88	10	b,l,zl

Sources: See Appendix F.
Note: The years 1777–1782 are not included because the extreme volatility of wages makes the records unreliable for those years.

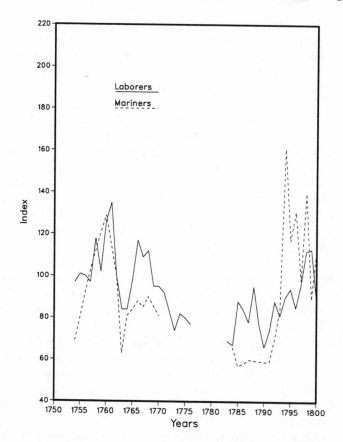

Figure 15. Indices of real wages of laborers and mariners, 1754–1800

he were partially employed (a more reasonable assumption) for five out of every six work days, or ten of every twelve months, his income fell £6 shy of these necessities. Other members of his family therefore had to work to secure its subsistence. Women toiled as nurses, clothes washers, chimney sweeps, potato diggers, cooks, maids, servants, whitewashers, soap makers, bakers, and in a variety of other capacities. The range of money-making activities for children were more limited. They gathered twigs to sell for fuel, tended cattle, cleaned chimneys, and carried dairy produce from the countryside.

Data on the wages received by several hundred women in the city suggest that they earned roughly one-half the wages of less-skilled men, and children considerably less than that.[63] A working woman in 1762 thus might have contributed an additional £25 to the household. Her income would have covered the deficit for the four necessities and the extra expenses of taxes, medical bills, candles, soap, and other essential items, while perhaps even providing a few luxuries such as tobacco or "sweet meats." This degree of comfort was most likely to have been achieved when the index of real wages was one hundred or greater, as during the French and Indian War, the mid-1760s, and the late 1790s.

Much more prevalent was a situation in which the income of the family barely matched the cost of basic necessities. This condition characterized the postwar depression of 1762–1765 and most of the 1770s, 1780s, and early 1790s, when real wages fluctuated 20–25 percent below their 1762 level and posed severe economic problems for laborers and their families. At the partial level of employment assumed above, a laborer's earnings would have averaged £14 below the cost of essentials. The combined income of husband and wife would barely have covered food, fuel, rent, and clothing, and the few remaining pounds could not have met additional expenses, much less permitted savings or minor luxuries.[64]

Unskilled workers and their families in Philadelphia generally lived on the edge of, or occasionally slightly above, the subsistence level, and both spouses had to work simply to maintain that position. Life was hard during the best of times and disastrous during the worst. Consequently, institutional aid to the poor rose to unprecedented heights during the second half of the century.[65]

Most sailors were concentrated at the bottom of the economic ladder of freemen; tax collectors assessed 70 percent of them the minimum tax in 1772. From mariners' wage rates recorded by merchants engaged in the

63. The types of jobs and wages earned by women are reported in the Matron and Steward's Cash Books; Minutes, Overseers of the Poor, 1768–1774, PCA; Samuel Coates's Memorandum of Wages Paid, 1784–1806, Coates and Reynell Papers, HSP; and by Elizabeth Drinker, as recorded in Elaine F. Crane, "The World of Elizabeth Drinker," *PMHB*, 108 (1983), 28. This ratio is apparently a common wage proportion between the sexes in the nineteenth century. See Edith Abbot, *Women in Industry: A Study in American Economic History* (New York, 1910), 262–316.

64. In 1774, the cost of the four basic necessities was £52.72, while a laborer, employed at 83 percent of full capacity, and his wife might earn £58.30. The resulting per capita estimated income of £8.74 sterling for a laborer's family of four agrees with the calculations of other historians. David Klingaman computes the per capita income in Philadelphia in about 1770 at between £6.5 and £9 sterling; "Food Surpluses and Deficits," 569. Alice Hanson Jones figures a range of £8.4 to £14 sterling per capita income in the American colonies in 1774; "Wealth Estimates," 128, Table 51.

65. Nash, "Poverty and Poor Relief"; George W. Geib, "A History of Philadelphia, 1776–1789" (Ph.D. diss., University of Wisconsin, 1969), 203–205.

overseas trade, I have constructed indices of the actual wages of seamen, mates, and captains, and, deflating by the household budget, an index of seamen's real wages (see Table 6).[66] In 1762, common seamen earned an average of £4.1 per month, and mates £5.4.[67] The maximum annual income of seamen, £49, fell short of the cost of the four basic necessities and also of the maximum earnings of day laborers. Longer periods of continuous employment and the food and lodging supplied sailors on board ship somewhat offset this occupational difference. As with laborers, however, periodic unemployment prevented seamen from earning the maximum income. Job opportunities varied seasonally, the slowest time being the winter months.[68] More important was the turnaround time of ships in port, on the order of thirty-six days in Philadelphia at midcentury.[69] In foreign ports sailors filled part of that slack period unloading and stowing cargo. In Philadelphia, however, in the words of an Admiralty Court judge, "merchants find it more for their interest . . . to hire other than the mariners to lade and unlade vessels" because it was cheaper to employ stevedores by the day than to pay the crew monthly wages and supply them with provisions.[70]

Living on the edge of subsistence, merchant seamen with families faced many of the same economic problems as those faced by laborers. When John Machman was unable to get a berth on a ship during winter, when John Quail suffered from rheumatism and venereal disease, when James Union

66. Based on the following HSP documents: Coates and Reynell Papers, 1751–1754 and 1755–1767, hereafter cited as Coates and Reynell Papers; Clifford Papers, Correspondence, vol. 3, 1760–1762, hereafter cited as Clifford Papers; Account Book, Folder: Brigantine *Elizabeth* Accounts, Richard Waln Collection; Ships and Shipping Folder, Etting Papers; Customs House Papers; Dutilh and Wachsmuth Papers, Miscellaneous Boxes 1726–1856 and 1704–1800; Thomas Mason's Journal, 1775, Miscellaneous Letters of Thomas and John Mason, Henry Pleasant's Papers; Journal of John and Peter Chevalier, 1770–1781; Philip Benezet's Account with Sloop *Sally*, Dreer Collection; Claude W. Unger Collection; Boats and Cargoes, Society Miscellaneous Collection; Thomas A. Biddle Shipbook, 1784–1792. See also Business Records of Stephen Girard, APS; Donald R. Adams, Jr., "Wage Rates in Philadelphia, 1790–1830" (Ph.D. diss., University of Pennsylvania, 1967), 213.

67. These figures do not include the privilege of carrying their own freight aboard ship to sell in their home port, but this more often was reserved for captains than extended to the entire crew.

68. An act of Parliament in 1696 required sailors on vessels owned by a citizen of the British Empire to pay a tax of 6*d.* for each month's wages to support the Greenwich Hospital for disabled seamen. Philadelphia's mariners paid only 12 percent of their taxes during the winter months, reflecting the sluggishness of jobs during that season. The collections from the city's mariners during several years before the Revolution are recorded in the Customs House Papers, vol. 11, HSP.

69. James F. Shepherd and Gary M. Walton, *Shipping, Maritime Trade, and the Economic Development of Colonial North America* (Cambridge, England, 1972), 198.

70. Richard Peters, *Admiralty Decision in the District Court of the United States, for the Pennsylvania District, by the Hon. Richard Peters* . . . (Philadelphia, 1807), 1:255, 2:413. The practice of hiring men other than mariners to stow and unload the cargo seems to have been common in pre-Revolutionary Philadelphia as well. See, for example, Coates and Reynell Papers, 1755–1767.

Table 6. Indices of mariners' wages (base year = 1762), 1750–1800

Year	Seamen's actual wages	Seamen's real wages	Mates' actual wages	Captains' actual wages
1750	73		79	80
1751	72		79	80
1752	69		78	80
1753	65		79	80
1754	61	69	74	80
1755	67	80	74	80
1756	85	92	84	80
1757	98	103		107
1759	109	121		107
1760	121	129	130	
1762	100	100	100	100
1763	67	63	93	107
1764	83	81	91	93
1765	79	84	93	93
1766	79	88	93	93
1767	82	85	93	93
1768	81	90	93	93
1770	76	81	86	93
1772				93
1784	109	66	139	160
1785	82	57	130	133
1786	82	58	112	107
1787	80	60	93	107
1789				100
1790	77	59	93	120
1791	77	59	93	120
1792	95	70	95	113
1793	121	84	125	120
1794	255	161		
1795	218	117	216	
1796	264	131	209	180
1797	182	98	233	250
1798	246	140	223	250
1799	155	89	265	250
1800	209	113	233	250

Source: Business papers of Samuel Coates and John Reynell, Coates and Reynell Papers, 1751–1754; Clifford Papers, Correspondence, vol. 2, 1760–1762; Account Book, Folder: Brigantine *Elizabeth* Accounts, Richard Waln Collection; Ships and Shipping Folder, Etting Papers; Customs House Papers; Dutilh and Wachsmuth Papers, Miscellaneous Boxes 1726–1856 and 1704–1800; Thomas Mason's Journal, 1775, Miscellaneous Letters of Thomas and John Mason, Henry Pleasant's Papers; Journal of John and Peter Chevalier; Philip Benezet's Account with Sloop *Sally,* Dreer Collection; Thomas A. Biddle Shipbook, 1784–1792, all of the above at HSP; Business Records of Stephen Girard, APS; Donald R. Adams, Jr., "Wage Rates in Philadelphia, 1790–1830" (Ph.D. diss., University of Pennsylvania, 1967), 213.

Note: The years 1777–1782 are not included because the extreme volatility of wages makes the records unreliable for those years. Sources are not available for other years with missing values.

came down with a fever, they landed in the almshouse, and their families suffered. Mary Lewis and Mary Winger, wives of sailors on the frigate *City of Philadelphia* in 1800, ended up in the almshouse when unable to support themselves, the former because she was pregnant and the latter because she was ill. Even mariners' wives who had jobs struggled to provide for themselves and their children. When a constable picked up eight-year-old William Thomas for begging in the street, the boy explained that while his father "has been gone to sea" his mother "goes out washing of Cloaths for a livelihood . . . [and] leaves him at home to take care of his Brother." When his brother cried from hunger, William went soliciting bread.[71]

The pay of mariners responded to fluctuations in the city's economy in much the same fashion as that of laborers. The demand for sailors, and the significant role of wartime activities in shaping that demand, was a key factor determining their material comfort. Their wages were abnormally high during the French and Indian War (see Figure 15), partly because privateering attracted many men who hoped to strike it rich and left few able seamen in the city.[72] As shipping activity slackened during the early 1760s and again in the 1780s, so also did mariners' wages. The boom in the export and reexport trades during the 1790s raised seamen's wages after 1793.

Cordwainers and tailors formed the two largest groups of artisans, each accounting for about 5.6 percent of the taxable work force during the second half of the century. Although cordwainers were scattered throughout the tax structure, except at the very top, most found a place near the bottom of the economic scale. Forty percent were assessed the minimum tax in 1772.

More than 250 bills for shoes contained in the Pennsylvania Hospital records and merchants' papers permit construction of individual price series for a variety of shoes. Price relatives of each of these have been weighted equally to produce a retail price index for shoes (see Table 7).[73] This index does not accurately indicate cordwainers' wages since the costs of raw materials and labor are included in the price of shoes. However, this retail price index and a price index of raw materials can be employed to create an index of cordwainers' wages. According to a broadside issued during the Revolutionary War, the cost of raw materials in 1774 averaged 57 percent and labor 43

71. Daily Occurrences, Feb. 6, 1790; Jan. 18, 1793; Mar. 17 (quotation), Apr. 7, May 22, 1800; Aug. 29, 1801.
72. Included in the wills recorded in the city between 1755 and 1760 are those of many lower-class men who were going to sea on privateers; Will Book K and Will Book L, Wills, Philadelphia County Probate Records, 1683–1901, RW. See also Virginia D. Harrington, *New York Merchants on the Eve of the Revolution* (New York, 1935), 303–307.
73. Price series for slippers, "channel pumps," "dress shoes," and "ordinary" shoes for adult males, as well as for "Negroes shoes," boys' shoes and cobbling charges for "soaling" and "heel-taping," are constructed from Shippen Family Papers; Coates and Reynell Papers; Matron and Steward's Cash Books.

Table 7. Indices of shoe costs and cordwainers' wages for workmanship (base year = 1762), 1762–1800

Year	Retail prices of shoes	Wholesale prices of raw materials	Cordwainers' actual wages for workmanship	Cordwainers' real wages for workmanship
1762	100	100	100	100
1763	115			
1764	112			
1767	92			
1768	88			
1769	88			
1770	91	90	92	98
1771	96	90	104	109
1772	97	90	106	107
1774	96	96	96	100
1775	94	97	90	98
1776	181	133	243	201
1783	103	113	88	49
1784	100	110	86	52
1785	94	103	82	57
1786	91	113	62	44
1787	87	102	64	48
1788	89	99	77	63
1789	88	101	72	63
1790	89	113	58	44
1791	90	110	63	48
1792	91	107	75	55
1793	150	107	206	143
1794	115	110	122	77
1795	151	121	190	102
1796	117	93	149	74
1797	146	86	225	122
1798	136	103	178	101
1799	113	107	131	75
1800	124	108	144	78

Source: Bills, Receipts, and Accounts, Shippen Family Papers, vols. 28–30, 1754–1822, HSP; Business Papers of Samuel Coates and John Reynell, Coates and Reynell Papers, 1755–1767, HSP; Matron and Steward's Cash Books, Pennsylvania Hospital Records, APS.
Note: Records are unreliable or unavailable for years with missing data.

percent of the retail price of shoes. The Philadelphia wholesale price index of leather, hides, and sole leather developed by Anne Bezanson represents the cost of raw materials for shoes (Table 7).[74] Using the actual price of raw materials in 1774, Bezanson's wholesale price index, and the retail price index of shoes computed above, I have calculated an index of cordwainers'

74. *To the Inhabitants of Pennsylvania* . . . (Philadelphia, 1779), broadside, HSP, hereafter cited as *To the Inhabitants.* Bezanson et al., *Prices and Inflation,* 332–342; Bezanson et al., *Wholesale Prices in Philadelphia,* 1:385.

actual wages for their labor and, adjusting for the cost of the household budget, an index of their real wages (Table 7).[75]

Except for a large increase reflecting the rapid inflation of late 1776, cordwainers' actual and real wages remained stable during the years immediately preceding Independence (see Figure 16).[76] Real wages were markedly lower in 1783 than before the war and continued at about the same level until the early 1790s. They more than doubled in 1793 and remained relatively high for much of the rest of the period.

Though evidence is sparse, a few available sources permit rough approximations of the earnings of cordwainers. Their incomes can be estimated from information contained in their 1779 broadside and in the labor conspiracy trial of Philadelphia journeymen shoemakers in 1806. The broadside indicates that in 1774 a master cordwainer received 4.75s. for the craftmanship involved in each pair of shoes.[77] Journeymen testified at the trial that they produced about six pairs of common shoes per week.[78] A master thus might have earned 28.5s. weekly, or £74.1 in 1774, if fully employed. Masters collected an additional shilling on every pair made by their journeymen, so each journeyman might have contributed as much as £15.6 to his master's income in 1774.[79]

Master cordwainers enjoyed a relatively comfortable material position

75. The index of cordwainers' wages can be computed by either of two methods. The most direct technique is to calculate cordwainers' wages on a pair of shoes as the difference between the retail price of shoes and the cost of raw materials in each year. The cost of raw materials in a given year equals the product of its 1774 cost (6.25s.) and the price index of raw materials in that year (drawn from Bezanson's wholesale price index of sole leather, hides, and leather, adjusted to base year 1774). With the resulting series of cordwainers' wages, an index of their wages can be constructed and adjusted to base year 1762. The actual method employed, because it required relatively simple manipulation of index numbers, was to solve the following formula for each year:

$$I_W = \frac{I_P - .57I_M}{.43},$$

where I_W = index of cordwainers' wages, I_P = retail price index of shoes, and I_M = price index of raw materials.

76. See Table 7 and Table 8 for data, sources, and explanations of missing values in Figure 16.

77. *To the Inhabitants.*

78. Job Harrison testified that in 1799 he earned about 48.75s. ($6.50) per week making shoes for 9s. each. At this rate, he must have produced 5.4 shoes in a week of work. These shoes had linings and required slightly more time to make than common shoes, so the latter could probably be made at the rate of six shoes per week. Philadelphia's cordwainers apparently frequently observed the "holiday" of "Saint Monday" in the alehouse and thus probably averaged slightly more than one pair of common shoes per day. John R. Commons et al., eds., *A Documentary History of American Industrial Society*, vol. 3, *Labor Conspiracy Cases 1806–1842* (Cleveland, Ohio, 1910), 1:63, 73–74, 83–84, 121, 123–124; Eric Foner, *Tom Paine and Revolutionary America* (New York, 1976), 36.

79. In 1774 masters typically sold shoes for 11s., of which they paid 6.25s. in material costs and 3.75s. in journeymen's wages, leaving a profit of 1s.; *To the Inhabitants.*

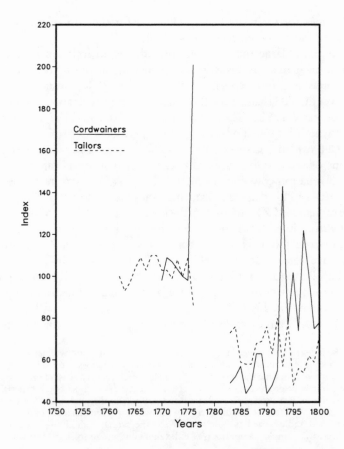

Figure 16. Indices of real wages for workmanship for cordwainers and tailors, 1762–1800

during most of the period. Food, rent, fuel, and clothing would have cost £62.9 in 1774. In that year a master, working without assistants, might have earned £74.1 if fully employed. Thus he would need to have been employed 85 percent of his possible working time to meet the cost of those four necessities. If he enjoyed the services of a journeyman or a few apprentices, the profits accrued from their labor would have covered his family's additional miscellaneous expenses. If he worked alone, however, earnings by his wife or children probably would have been required. His wife's contribution of £19.4 would have helped to provide the four necessities and some minor luxuries, with perhaps a bit left over for savings. The relatively favorable circumstances of master cordwainers deteriorated after the Revolution. The combined incomes of husband and wife, even if both were employed full-time, could not quite meet the cost of the four necessities.[80] Master cordwainers who hired journeymen, and the few who owned servants and slaves, were in the best position to survive the economic dislocations of the 1780s, but nearly all were forced to cut their living standards drastically until the early 1790s.

Journeymen cordwainers earned appreciably less than their masters. In 1774 each received 3.75*s.* for a pair of shoes, yielding £58.5 for a year of full employment. But, as they testified at their trial, work was seasonal, and winter was usually a slack period.[81] Although slightly better off than common laborers, journeymen shoemakers were hard pressed to meet the £64.3 cost of basic necessities during the early 1770s. The depression of the 1780s severely affected their material condition, not only by driving wages down but also by limiting the available work. Hugh Dugan, sent into the almshouse as a pauper in 1789, was one of many cordwainers forced to rely on public assistance.[82] Even during good times, journeymen made little money to spare. At their trial they declared that they each earned 45*s.* per week, or £117 annually during the late 1790s.[83] But their estimated family budgets during that period averaged £120 per year, so that their incomes barely matched the cost of the four necessities. As a result, a number of shoemakers, such as John and Esther Dougherty and their three children, spent time in a relief institution.[84]

Tailors and breech makers were the wealthiest of the four occupational groups considered in this chapter, but they still clustered near the bottom of the tax hierarchy. Assessors taxed 41 percent of them the minimum rate in 1772. But one-fourth of them, those who catered to the city's wealthy citizens, appeared in the top third of the tax structure. Tailors' bills scattered through merchants' papers and the Pennsylvania Hospital's records can be

80. The hard times of the 1780s are reflected in the "value" of cordwainers' occupations assessed by tax collectors in the 1783 and 1789 Provincial Tax Lists. In 1783, the occupations of 18 percent of cordwainers were assessed at £25 or less. By 1789, 40 percent of cordwainers were assessed that amount.

81. Commons et al., *Documentary History*, 3.1:114, 123–124. Work also fluctuated annually. The shoe market in 1769, for instance, was said to be "much overdone," and few jobs were then available (Thomas Clifford to Edward and William Gravena, May 23, 1773, Thomas Clifford Letter Book, Clifford Papers, 1767–1773).

82. Daily Occurrences, Feb. 18, 1789.

83. Because many journeymen were forced to perform "market work," which paid only half as much as "bespoke work," this probably was near a maximum; see Commons et al., *Documentary History*, 3.1:73–74, 86.

84. Daily Occurrences, Aug. 23, 1800.

used to determine their earnings.[85] These bills distinguish the charge for labor from the cost of materials and are sufficiently detailed to permit construction of individual series of wages for making a number of items of clothing.[86] Wage relatives for labor costs for sewing these articles have been weighted equally to create an index of tailors' actual wages; when this index is adjusted by the household budget, an index of real wages results (see Table 8).

Because the amount of available work fluctuated, the real wages of tailors do not translate exactly into their real incomes. But it is unlikely that wages varied inversely with demand for clothes. Real wages and real incomes should have been isomorphic, and changes in the former should be indicative of changes in the latter. Real wages varied little before the Revolutionary War (see Figure 16). This wealthiest of the four occupational groups was hard hit after the war as real wages fell 25–40 percent and remained at a low level during the 1790s.

Tailors' incomes and living standards can be roughly approximated from the few available sources. Naturally, a crucial determinant of a tailor's earnings was his status as either journeyman or master. Journeymen probably made up 40 or 50 percent of the tailors in the city during the second half of the century.[87] The masters belonging to the Taylors' Company limited each journeyman to a maximum of 4s. per day, which, assuming full employment, would have yielded £62.4 annually in the years immediately preceding the Revolutionary War.[88] Journeymen tailors thus had to work full-time at maximum wages to earn the £63 cost of essentials, but their job, like that of cordwainers, varied seasonally.[89] During the two decades following the war, their economic condition deteriorated seriously.

An appraisal of the incomes of master tailors is more tenuous than that for journeymen. The ledger of Joseph Graisbury records his average income from 1765 to 1769 at £182 per year, but he was one of the wealthiest tailors in the city.[90] His tax rate in 1767 exceeded the median tailor's assessment nearly fourfold, and he was even more exceptional in owning both his home and a slave. The majority of men in his occupation must have earned consid-

85. Shippen Family Papers; Cadwalader Collection; Coates and Reynell Papers; Hollingsworth Collection; Morris's Day Book; Ledger of Graisbury; Matron and Steward's Cash Books. Some tailors' bills were extensive, covering periods as long as two years of work.

86. Individual series of wages for making each of the following articles of clothing have been constructed: cloth and "surperfine" suits, cloth and silk breeches, cloth coats, damask and silk vests, Holland "draws," "ordinary" shirts and trousers, and "Negroes" cloth coats and breeches.

87. These estimates have been determined by the method described in n. 91 of this chapter and in chapter 5.

88. Minutes of the Taylors' Company.

89. Winter was invariably a slack season for Joseph Graisbury; see Ledger of Graisbury, passim.

90. Ibid.

Table 8. Indices of tailors' wages for workmanship (base year = 1762), 1762–1800

Year	Tailors' actual wages	Tailors' real wages
1762	100	100
1763	100	93
1764	99	97
1765	98	104
1766	98	109
1767	99	103
1768	99	110
1769	97	110
1770	97	103
1771	98	103
1772	98	99
1773	99	108
1774	96	100
1775	100	109
1776	104	86
1783	132	73
1784	124	76
1785	84	59
1786	82	58
1787	78	58
1788	84	68
1789	79	69
1790	100	76
1791	82	63
1792	109	80
1793	82	57
1794	123	78
1795	90	48
1796	112	56
1797	100	54
1798	110	62
1799	102	59
1800	134	72

Source: Bills, Receipts, and Accounts, Shippen Family Papers, vols. 28–30, 1754–1822; Incoming Correspondence: Bills and Receipts of John Cadwalader, Cadwalader Collection, Boxes 1–6, 12–14; Business Papers of Samuel Coates and John Reynell, Coates and Reynell Papers, 1755–1767; Business Papers of Levy Hollingsworth, Hollingsworth Collection, sec. 7: Bills, 1751–1789, and sec. 3: Invoices, 1764–1789; Samuel Morris's Day Book, 1755–1767; Ledger of Graisbury, 1759–1773, Forde and Reed Papers; all of the above at HSP. Matron and Steward's Cash Books, Pennsylvania Hospital Records, APS.

Note: Records are not reliable for the 1777–1782 period.

erably less than Graisbury, though still more than journeymen, perhaps on the order of £100 annually during the prewar years. This estimate is congruent with the appraisal of the incomes of master cordwainers. Masters in both crafts probably enjoyed similar living standards before Independence, but tailors' real wages plummeted during the 1780s and continued at a much lower plateau during the century's final decade.

Both shoemaking and tailoring were organized primarily on a small scale during the colonial period, and, on the eve of the Revolution, nearly half of these artisans worked as masters.[91] Most did not own shops; instead they toiled at home, mainly on "bespoke work," that is, shoes and clothes made to order for local customers. Masters invested in few unfree laborers; 7 percent owned servants and only three of them possessed a slave in 1772, although some directed a number of apprentices.[92]

The peculiar circumstances of cordwainers and tailors and their own actions affected their material conditions during the second half of the century. These artisans often defended their own economic interests. At times they supported all of their fellow mechanics who produced consumer goods, as in the "buy American" campaign begun in the days of the pre-Revolutionary nonimportation agreements, but more often they acted exclusively in behalf of their own specific craft. Cordwainers and tailors sometimes enjoyed considerable success in these ventures.

The wages of cordwainers and tailors were both high and stable during the final decade of the colonial era when compared to their pay during the post-Revolutionary period. To some degree this stemmed from the fact that relatively few of them lived in the city; both groups of craftsmen constituted a lower proportion of the work force in the 1770s than at any other time during the half century. But the high wages also reflected their ability to advance their own interests. Master cordwainers formed the Cordwainers' Fire Company during the 1750s. While ostensibly providing fire protection, it actually operated in many ways as a guild, issuing "certificates of character" to members leaving the city, denying membership to those who did not serve a "regular apprenticeship," and generally exerting more effort in controlling prices of raw materials and recovering runaway servants and apprentices than in extinguishing fires.[93] Not shy of politics, shoemakers successfully petitioned the Assembly in 1772 for a law to stop the monopolistic conduct of the suppliers of their raw materials.[94] Meanwhile, the Taylors' Company set

91. On the early history of shoemaking, see Paul G. Faler, *Mechanics and Manufacturers in the Early Industrial Revolution: Lynn, Massachusetts, 1780–1860* (Albany, N.Y., 1981), 1–27. While there are no records that indicate the total number of masters and journeymen in Philadelphia during this period, several sources give clues to the proportion of each. By identifying as many masters and journeymen as possible, and then determining their common and distinguishing characteristics, an approximation of their number can be obtained. For a complete explanation of the methodology, see chapter 5 and Thomas Smith, "Reconstructing Occupational Structures: The Case of Ambiguous Artisans," *Historical Methods Newsletter*, 8 (1975), 136–146.

92. These figures are calculated from the 1772 Provincial Tax List and the Account of Servants and Apprentices Bound before John Gibson, Dec. 5, 1772, to May 21, 1773, HSP.

93. Minutes of the Cordwainers' Fire Company, HSP.

94. Olton, *Artisans for Independence*, 21–22.

prices for their products and wages for their journeymen. The stability of wages during the late colonial period attests the apparent success of both of these organizations.

Tailors and cordwainers prospered from the increased domestic demand for clothes and shoes and the curtailment of these same imported goods during the Revolutionary War. The war spurred important changes in the organization of their crafts. Some of the masters seized the opportunities to supply the military on a large scale, thus becoming more involved in the distribution of their product and less directly engaged in its manufacture. By changing their occupational designations on tax lists to "merchant," "grocer," and "contractor," they signified the growing economic and social delineation between employers and employees within their crafts.

When British merchants dumped cheap manufactures on the American market following the Revolution, master cordwainers reacted not only by pressing the ruling Pennsylvania Constitutional party to pass protective legislation but also by resolving not to buy or sell any imported shoes or boots, "nor to mend, or suffer any of the same to be mended by any in our employ."[95] This declaration drew immediate support from journeymen shoemakers. The federal government rewarded their joint political activity by passing a protective tariff on shoes in 1789 and a higher one in 1790, laying the groundwork for the price and profit increases of the following decade.[96]

The demand for American-made shoes expanded during the 1790s. While protective tariffs enlarged the domestic market, European wars created a great international need for American footwear. As a result, the United States changed from a net importer of about eighty thousand pairs of shoes annually during the early 1790s to a net exporter of roughly fifty thousand pairs during the final years of the decade.[97] Cordwainers' wages responded accordingly, rising in 1793 and remaining on a high plateau thereafter. Masters and journeymen struggled with one another for the greater profits on their product, and each group formed an organization to further its own interests. Their conflict culminated in America's first labor conspiracy trial in 1806.[98] Tailors' products were not involved in the export market to the same degree and their wages remained depressed throughout the 1790s. Neither group, however, was able to exercise the same level of control over produc-

95. Ibid., 102–103.

96. Blanche E. Hazard, *Organization of the Boot and Shoe Industry in Massachusetts before 1875* (Cambridge, Mass., 1921), 39–40.

97. Adam Seybert, *Statistical Annals* . . . (New York, 1969; orig. 1818), 94–95, 100–101, 108, 160–161, 162–163.

98. For changes in shoemaking during this period, see Faler, *Mechanics and Manufacturers*, 1–27; Hazard, *Organization of the Boot and Shoe Industry*, 24–25; and Commons et al., *Documentary History*, 3.1:19–58.

tion in the 1780s and 1790s that they had enjoyed in the more limited environment of the pre-Revolutionary city.

Unskilled workers and journeymen artisans in the "lesser" crafts in Philadelphia often encountered very serious difficulties paying for their families' basic needs. Many, if not most, lived in poverty or on its edge. The severity of their struggle simply to maintain, or rise slightly above, the subsistence level depended to a great extent on the size and composition of their households. Unmarried, healthy males generally found it easy enough to earn a living wage. But most laboring Philadelphians were married and had at least two children, usually quite young. Because their employment opportunities were limited and their wages low, women and children rarely could earn their keep, but, as a supplement to the wages of the household head, their income was essential to the maintenance of the family. Only in the best of times, during the French and Indian War or during the late 1790s, could male heads of household in the four occupational groups earn enough money to pay for basic necessities. Those a step higher in the economic hierarchy, such as master cordwainers and tailors, who were able to profit from the labor of journeymen, apprentices, and in a few instances servants and slaves, enjoyed a more comfortable existence. However, in periods of depression, such as the early 1760s and the 1780s, they too faced serious hardships, and other members of their households had to contribute to the families' incomes.

The number of urban laboring people in colonial America was greater, and their economic plight more precarious, than sometimes has been assumed. It has been estimated that about one-third of the residents of eighteenth-century European cities were the laboring poor who frequently became destitute in times of crisis.[99] A similar proportion of Philadelphians, perhaps between one-fourth and one-third of the free population, experienced analogous conditions. Their material position was extremely vulnerable, and they were easily driven below the subsistence level by such ordinary occurrences as business cycles, seasonal unemployment, illness, injury, pregnancy or child-care requirements, and epidemics that disrupted the city's economy. As a result, private and public aid to the poor rose to unprecedented levels during the late colonial period and the 1780s, and increasingly not only the aged, infirm, widowed, and orphaned but able-bodied working men and women as well found themselves on the charity rolls.[100]

99. Jeffrey Kaplow, "The Culture of Poverty in Paris on the Eve of the Revolution," *International Review of Social History*, 12 (1967), 278–291. On the comparison of poverty in early America and in Great Britain, see Billy G. Smith, "Poverty and Economic Marginality in Eighteenth-Century America," *Proceedings of the APS*, 132 (1988), 85–118.

100. Smith, "Poverty and Economic Marginality," 96–100; Nash, "Poverty and Poor Relief"; Geib, "A History of Philadelphia, 1776–1789," 203–205.

Philadelphia's laboring people did not enjoy steadily increasing prosperity during the late colonial period. Indeed, they lived so near subsistence before the Revolutionary War that there appears to be no lower level from which they could have risen. The increasing wealth usually thought to have characterized the colonies in general and Philadelphia in particular during this period did not trickle down to the lower sort. If anything, the opposite occurred. Philadelphia's poor residents experienced relative prosperity during the late 1750s and early 1760s but generally suffered declining living standards from the end of the French and Indian War until Independence. For the city's laboring people, the Confederation era was a period of adversity that ended for many, although not all, only by the mid-1790s.

The material standards of Philadelphia's laboring people were spartan. The budgets constructed in this chapter are extremely lean ones: generally the data are estimates of minimal expenditures for four necessities and omit many essentials of a decent competency. If the lower sort met the costs of their budgets, they still lived very sparingly, even by contemporary standards, for they dined like prisoners, dressed in the same fashion as almshouse inmates, and crowded into cramped quarters. Any reduction in incomes or any increase in expenses meant significant sacrifices. Hard-pressed families ate more grains when necessary, doubled or tripled up in houses, went without essential clothing, shivered through winters without sufficient fuel, and forewent smallpox inoculation even though unable to flee the city in times of epidemics. Some undoubtedly were pushed into an illegitimate economy, stealing their necessary provisions; others turned to public and private charities; and many landed in relief institutions that often were little more than prisons for the poor. The specter of poverty and deprivation haunted their lives. If America was the best poor man's country for urban laboring people at the time (and that is a disputed question), it remained a world requiring daily vigilance to survive.

Chapter Five

Careers

FLAVIUS: Thou art a cobbler, art thou?
CITIZEN: Truly, sir, all that I live by is with the awl: I meddle with no
tradesman's matters, nor women's matters; but withal I am, indeed,
sir, a surgeon to old shoes; when they are in great danger, I recover
them. As proper men as ever trod upon neat's-leather have gone upon
my handiwork.
FLAVIUS: But wherefore art not in thy shop to-day? Why dost thou lead
these men about the streets?
CITIZEN: Truly, sir, to wear out their shoes, to get myself into more
work.

—William Shakespeare, *Julius Caesar*

MAGNUS MILLER, a young Philadelphia seaman, sailed on the three
voyages of the snow *Mary* to the Caribbean island of Antigua in 1755. He
earned £9 per cruise and an additional 3.5s. per day for unloading and
stowing the cargo, for a total income of about £30 that year. His promotion
to ship's mate the following year increased his income by a third. Taking
advantage of his greater wealth, Miller married and started a family; William
was born in 1761, and James four years later. Magnus's career proceeded
apace: by the late 1760s he became a ship's captain, purchased an indentured
servant, and paid taxes that placed him just below the median among taxpayers. During the next few years he secured more labor—a slave and
another servant—and moved into the richest third of the city's inhabitants, a
position that he never relinquished. Miller emerged from the Revolution as a
merchant rather than a sea captain. In the following decade he invested in a
house and several stores on the dock, a wagon and horses to haul goods,
another slave, gold plate, a rental dwelling valued at more than £1,000, and
two thousand acres of land in Pennsylvania's backcountry. In the early 1790s
Magnus assumed the title of gentleman. He established both of his sons as
merchants in the family business, enabling the eldest one to acquire a horse,

riding chair, and slave driver, all symbols of a genteel style of life. In 1795 Miller moved into an expensive house in an exclusive neighborhood several blocks away from the noise and congestion of his waterfront stores. His appointment as a warden of the city's port at the end of the century represented the apex of his career. When Miller died several years later, his sons and grandchildren successfully carried on the family business.[1]

The career of Andrew Dam took a different course. In 1769, at the age of forty-one, he migrated from Sweden to America. After brief stays with several of his kin in the Pennsylvania countryside, Dam moved, along with his brother, Peter, to Philadelphia. Peter died within several years, but Andrew continued to live in the city, working as both a mariner and a gardener. He took extended voyages to Sweden and China during the Revolution, returning to the Quaker City in the late 1780s. Although hardworking, Dam lived the rest of his life in modest circumstances, never acquiring any property. In the words of his minister, "being an industrious, complaisant man, and of good moral conduct, he was well esteemed and [had] employment sufficient for a pretty comfortable living, till the infirmities of old age obliged him to seek a retreat in the Bettering House for the last." Dam entered the almshouse in 1802; four years later he was buried in his brother's grave because he left no money for a plot of his own.[2]

These vignettes provide glimpses of the careers of two men who began their lives in an eighteenth-century American city as members of the laboring classes. While Magnus Miller realized substantial material and occupational advancement for himself and his family, Andrew Dam maintained only a decent competency at best, ending his days in the poorhouse. Which man, if either, most typifies the life experiences of the urban lower classes during the second half of the eighteenth century?

1. This vignette is constructed from information contained in the following records: Business Papers of Samuel Coates and John Reynell, 1755–1767, Coates and Reynell Papers, HSP; transcripts of the 1767 Tax Assessors' Reports, Van Pelt Library, University of Pennsylvania, Philadelphia; 1772, 1780, 1789, 1791, 1797, 1798, and 1800 Provincial Tax Lists, PCA, hereafter cited as Provincial Tax Lists; and the Philadelphia City Constables' Returns for 1775, PCA, hereafter cited as Constables' Returns; *Warantees of Land in the Several Counties of the State of Pennsylvania, 1730–1898, Pennsylvania Archives*, 3d Ser., (Harrisburg, Pa., 1898), 25:236, 245, 246, 735, 736, 738, hereafter cited as *Warantees of Land*; U.S. Bureau of the Census, *Heads of Families of the First Census of the United States Taken in the Year 1790: Pennsylvania* (Washington, D.C., 1908), 236; the U.S. Census for 1800, microfilm, reel no. 0363346, Mormon Genealogical Society, Salt Lake City, Utah. See also the following city directories: Francis White, *The Philadelphia Directory* (Philadelphia, 1785), 49; Clement Biddle, *The Philadelphia Directory* (Philadelphia, 1791), 89; Edmund Hogan, *The Prospect of Philadelphia* (Philadelphia, 1795), 116, 119; Cornelius William Stafford, *The Philadelphia Directory for 1797* (Philadelphia, 1797), 128; Stafford, *The Philadelphia Directory for 1801* (Philadelphia, 1801), 29, 51, 56; and Jane Aitken, *Census Directory for 1811* . . . (Philadelphia, 1811), 225.

2. The account of Dam's life is drawn from the Burial Records, Old Swedes Church, Gloria Dei, Oct. 21, 1806, GSP; and Index of Admissions and Discharges (to the Almshouse), 1785–1827, Guardians of the Poor, PCA.

Several decades ago, most historians, impressed by Benjamin Franklin's rags-to-riches success, the general scarcity of labor, and the lack of restrictions on individual initiative in the colonies, believed that opportunities abounded for urban laboring people to improve their position. David Montgomery asserted that "vertical mobility was . . . remarkable" in preindustrial cities. In Philadelphia itself, Sam Bass Warner, Jr., discovered "abundant opportunity" for advancement. Carl Bridenbaugh and Jessica Bridenbaugh characterized the city's social structure as "fluid," arguing that "it offered to individualism a degree of fair play seldom exceeded," where "men of ability and ambition could rise and flourish," and "a clever youngster, no matter what his breeding and antecedents, had a good chance to succeed." Charles Olton stated more guardedly that "the city's class barriers were not so high that there was no hope of hurdling them," and he claimed that "being born a mechanic could not be regarded as socially restrictive." Jackson Turner Main concurred that "in Philadelphia the chance to rise was indeed a good one." Main concluded that conditions in Revolutionary America generally were so favorable that "immigrants and native-born alike had reason to be confident about their future, and the few whites who failed were defeated not because of any external circumstance but because they lacked some essential quality."[3]

Successors to those historians contradicted their glowing evaluations of the opportunities open to urban laboring classes. Raymond A. Mohl, John K. Alexander, and Gary B. Nash demonstrated that poverty was more pervasive in American cities than scholars previously had believed. Nash extended the analysis, painting a dark tableau of the economic chances of many impoverished people after mid-century.[4] This more pessimistic view is now widely accepted, although hardly unquestioned. In a recent study of

3. David Montgomery, "The Working Classes of the Pre-Industrial American City, 1780–1830," *Labor History*, 9 (1968), 5, 7; Sam Bass Warner, Jr., *The Private City: Philadelphia in Three Periods of Its Growth* (Philadelphia, 1968), 9; Carl Bridenbaugh and Jessica Bridenbaugh, *Rebels and Gentlemen: Philadelphia in the Age of Franklin* (New York, 1942), 13–14, 26; Charles Olton, "Philadelphia's Mechanics in the First Decade of Revolution, 1765–1775," *Journal of American History*, 59 (1972–1973), 313–314; Jackson Turner Main, *The Social Structure of Revolutionary America* (Princeton, N.J., 1965), 194, 271–272.

4. Raymond A. Mohl, *Poverty in New York, 1783–1825* (New York, 1971); Mohl, "Poverty in Early America, a Reappraisal: The Case of Eighteenth-Century New York City," *New York History*, 50 (1969), 5–27; John K. Alexander, *Render Them Submissive: Responses to Poverty in Philadelphia, 1760–1800* (Amherst, Mass., 1980); Gary B. Nash, "Poverty and Poor Relief in Pre-Revolutionary Philadelphia," *WMQ*, 3d Ser., 33 (1976), 3–30; Nash, "Urban Wealth and Poverty in Pre-Revolutionary America," *Journal of Interdisciplinary History*, 6 (1976), 545–584; Nash, "Up from the Bottom in Franklin's Philadelphia," *Past and Present*, no. 77 (1977), 57–83; and Nash, *The Urban Crucible: Social Change, Political Consciousness, and the Origins of the American Revolution* (Cambridge, Mass., 1979). On the material conditions of laboring people in two smaller towns, see Lynne Withey, *Urban Growth in Colonial Rhode Island: Newport and Providence in the Eighteenth Century* (Albany, N.Y., 1984), 51–76, 123–136.

Philadelphia's merchants, Thomas M. Doerflinger has reasserted the neo-Whig position. In particular, he discovered that "entry into the merchant community was not inordinately difficult" even though, he cautioned, "it was far less easy to become actually wealthy."[5]

This chapter measures the economic and occupational experiences of hundreds of Philadelphia's lower classes during the second half of the eighteenth century. The focus again is on laborers, mariners, cordwainers, and tailors. Their career patterns are calibrated and the causes of the level of and fluctuations in material standards and mobility patterns are considered.

The careers of the city's males can be reconstructed from a series of tax lists. Assessors taxed working Philadelphians according to the "value" of their occupations (a crude income tax based on their estimated earnings) as well as the worth of their taxable goods. Three categories of taxpayers can be derived from these assessments. The first category, "propertyless taxpayers," is composed exclusively of men who owned no taxable assets *and* were assessed the minimum rate on their incomes. The second category, taxpayers of "minimum property or well-being," consists primarily of men who, in the judgment of assessors, fared slightly better than those at the lowest tax rate. Men levied moderate occupational valuations (and therefore earning a slightly higher income) accounted for the bulk of this group, even though most of them were without taxable assets. Approximately 20 percent of them also owned a few small items—a very inexpensive dwelling place or shop, a tiny, undeveloped piece of land, a cow, or an insignificant amount of silver or gold plate. The third category, men of "moderate property," includes individuals who possessed more substantial belongings—usually a house, an indentured servant, a slave, or some parcel of land yielding sizable rent. In addition, their earnings considerably exceeded the minimum. While assessments among this more affluent group varied considerably, their wealth was capped; few ranked among the top 20 percent of taxpayers.[6]

The majority of laborers, mariners, cordwainers, and tailors did not own taxable assets, nor did they earn more than minimal incomes in the judgment of assessors (see Table 9). About one-quarter of the taxpayers either possessed a small quantity of property or else paid slightly more than the lowest occupational rate. One out of every five owned sufficient belongings to qualify for the "moderate property" category. The propertyless proportion

5. Thomas M. Doerflinger, *A Vigorous Spirit of Enterprise: Merchants and Economic Development in Revolutionary Philadelphia* (Chapel Hill, N.C., 1986), 16, 17, 54–57.

6. The tax laws directed assessors to evaluate the occupations of taxpayers according to the incomes derived from those occupations in addition to specific items of property. James T. Mitchell and Henry Flanders, comps., *The Statutes at Large of Pennsylvania from 1682 to 1801*, 18 vols. (Philadelphia and Harrisburg, Pa., 1896–1911), 4:10–26, 5:207–212, 6:344–360, 8:96–116, 378–382, 9:443–448, 10:205–214, 11:454–486, 15:322–330.

Table 9. Tax assessments of laborers, mariners, cordwainers, and tailors, 1756–1798

		Assessment categories		
Tax list	N	Propertyless (%)	Minimum property (%)	Moderate property (%)
1756	424	19	58	22
1767	413	38	40	22
1772	722	69	19	12
1780	345	58	17	25
1789	565	75	9	16
1798	389	51	28	22
Average	2,858	52	28	20

Source: 1756 tax list in Hannah Benner Roach, comp., "Taxables in the City of Philadelphia, 1756," *Pennsylvania Genealogical Magazine,* 22 (1961), 3–41; 1767 Tax Assessors' Reports, Van Pelt Library, University of Pennsylvania, Philadelphia; 1772, 1780, 1789, and 1798 Provincial Tax Lists, PCA.

Note: Tax assessment categories are defined in the text. The 1756 tax list does not include unmarried men. The 1780 and 1798 data are based on a sample of 60 percent of all taxpayers, whereas the 1789 statistics are calculated from a sample of 80 percent of taxpayers.

was smallest at midcentury, expanded rapidly during the final decade of the colonial period, declined during the Revolutionary War, peaked again in 1789, and then shrank during the 1790s.

Stability of financial status was the most common characteristic of the four occupational groups when they were traced among tax lists.[7] Slightly more than half of the men remained in the same assessment category during any period (see Tables 10 and 11).[8] The majority of those in the lowest bracket did not improve their position from one tax list to the next; one of every four

7. Linking men among various records is always a difficult problem for mobility studies, and it is particularly acute for historians of the eighteenth century since surnames were spelled in a variety of ways. With the aid of Soundex—a mathematical code designed to adjust variant name spellings—and through experience, a researcher quickly learns to recognize correct matches. The geographic location of taxpayers often provided clues to their identification, but occupation and assessment obviously could not be used for identification purposes in the present analysis since they were the variables being measured. Duplicate names within the same tax roll were surprisingly few in number, and they, along with all common names, were discarded when people were being matched across lists. Mariners were easily identified in the various lists of ship's crews discussed later since a physical description of each man was included. For further discussion of the problems of record linkage, see Ian Winchester, "The Linkage of Historical Records by Man and Computer: Techniques and Problems," *Journal of Interdisciplinary History,* 1 (1970), 107–124.

8. In the matrices in Table 10, the rows correspond to the taxpayer's position on an initial tax list, the columns represent his position on the succeeding tax list, and the entries in the table denote the proportion of people who remained at the same level or moved from one category to another. In illustration, of the taxpayers who belonged in the lowest category in 1756 and who stayed in the city for the next eleven years, 40 percent ranked in the same category in 1767, 40 percent moved up one category, and 20 percent acquired sufficient property to be placed in the top bracket. Table 11 is a more concise organization of the same data.

Table 10. Laborers, mariners, cordwainers, and tailors: Short-term economic mobility, 1756–1798

		Assessment categories		
Initial status	N	Propertyless (%)	Minimum property (%)	Moderate property (%)
1756	87		1767	
Propertyless		40	40	20
Minimum property		25	38	37
Moderate property		16	16	68
1767	248		1772	
Propertyless		69	23	9
Minimum property		29	40	30
Moderate property		7	12	82
1772	125		1780	
Propertyless		57	21	22
Minimum property		32	36	32
Moderate property		3	0	97
1780	84		1789	
Propertyless		73	9	18
Minimum property		62	8	29
Moderate property		4	4	93
1789	129		1798	
Propertyless		41	30	28
Minimum property		25	25	50
Moderate property		12	24	64
Aggregate, 1756–1789	673		Aggregate, 1767–1798	
Propertyless		55	24	21
Minimum property		35	31	34
Moderate property		7	10	82

Source: 1756 tax list in Hannah Benner Roach, comp., "Taxables in the City of Philadelphia, 1756," *Pennsylvania Genealogical Magazine,* 22 (1961), 3–41; 1767 Tax Assessors' Reports, Van Pelt Library, University of Pennsylvania, Philadelphia; 1772, 1780, 1789, and 1798 Provincial Tax Lists, PCA.

of them managed to move up one step, and one in five acquired moderate property. Men ranked in the second category experienced a mixed fate: roughly a third remained in their original positions, a third lost ground, and another third improved their circumstances. Four of every five taxpayers in the wealthiest bracket maintained their situations.[9]

9. Rather than measure their economic mobility in relative terms, a technique commonly employed by social scientists, I established an absolute standard to assess the economic circumstances of laboring Philadelphians across their life cycle. To belong to a particular category or to

Table 11. Laborers, mariners, cordwainers, and tailors: Short-term economic mobility between assessment categories, 1756–1798

Time span	Stable (%)	Up 1 category (%)	Up 2 categories (%)	Down 1 category (%)	Down 2 categories (%)
1756–1767	47	26	2	20	5
1767–1772	62	20	4	12	2
1772–1780	62	18	11	8	1
1780–1789	61	12	7	19	1
1789–1798	44	26	20	7	2
Aggregate, 1756–1798	56	20	10	12	2

Source: 1756 tax list in Hannah Benner Roach, comp., "Taxables in the City of Philadelphia, 1756," *Pennsylvania Genealogical Magazine,* 22 (1961), 3–41; 1767 Tax Assessors' Reports, Van Pelt Library, University of Pennsylvania, Philadelphia; 1772, 1780, 1789, and 1798 Provincial Tax Lists, PCA.

That the wealth of these workers usually did not increase as they grew older further reveals their limited opportunities. The connection between the social age of householders (defined by the age of the oldest child living at home) and their taxable wealth was very weak. The chances that laboring Philadelphians would acquire a moderate amount of property or earn enough to move into a higher tax bracket did not improve significantly as they aged (see Table 12). Families in which the eldest child was older than ten, suggesting an age range of the midthirties to early forties for their fathers, were the most likely to own property. Yet nearly two-thirds of these adult males, presumably in their most economically productive years, remained without assets. Statistically, age accounted for less than 6 percent of the variation in taxable wealth among laborers, mariners, cordwainers, and tailors.[10] For most laboring Philadelphians, then, growing older did not mean growing wealthier.

---

move from one level to another during the years between tax lists meant that individuals experienced a certain set of material attributes. This formulation permits a more concrete measurement of the economic advance, stagnation, or decline experienced by laboring Philadelphians.

10. The 1775 Constables' Returns, which report the name of a householder and the age of the eldest child, permit the head of a family to be defined by social age. This characteristic should serve as an adequate proxy for actual age. Most importantly, social age specifies the stage in the life cycle of taxpayers. The most serious potential problem is that economic necessity probably forced poor Philadelphians to apprentice their children out of their households at a younger age than did the affluent. If so, then older, poorer householders were categorized in a younger social age bracket than is appropriate. This would artificially magnify the correlation between age and taxable wealth. I determined social age (and any connection between age and taxable wealth) by matching a sample of 50 percent of the 1775 Constables' Returns against the 1772 Provincial Tax List. The coefficient that measures the correlation between social age and taxable wealth is the $r = .235$ and $r^2 = .055$ at a significance level of $p < .00001$.

Table 12. Laborers, mariners, cordwainers, and tailors: 1772 tax assessment categories by 1775 social age groups

Age of eldest child (years)	N	Assessment categories		
		Propertyless (%)	Minimum property (%)	Moderate property (%)
0–5	103	85	11	4
6–10	116	69	21	10
11–15	90	68	13	19
16–24	61	61	21	18

Source: 1775 Constables' Returns; and 1772 Provincial Tax List, PCA. A sample of 50 percent of the constables' returns was matched against the tax list.

A few examples illustrate the careers these statistics represent. Some men followed Franklin's way to wealth, although their successes were more limited. Peter Dicks was a young, married tailor without taxable assets in 1756. During the next decade he acquired an indentured servant, one of the most valuable houses owned by anyone in his profession, and a high assessment on his earnings, all of which placed him among the city's wealthiest tailors. Purchasing another indentured servant, Dicks continued to enjoy his comparatively comfortable position with his wife and three children until the Revolution. Peter January was propertyless in 1767, although his status as a master cordwainer warranted a higher than average occupational valuation. Within the next eight years, January obtained the services of at least seven servants and two apprentices, rented a building sufficient to house them all, and organized a virtual shoe manufactory. Consequently, he was among the handful of artisans who changed their status to merchant on the 1780 tax roll.

But contrast their careers with those of Hugh Nelson, John Burns, Martin Shire, and George Bicherton. Assessors levied a higher than minimum tax on Hugh Nelson in 1767 because, even though without property, he earned more than most tailors. Within five years he lost his advantage, however, and paid the least possible tax. John Burns did not improve his taxable position during sixteen years' toil as a laborer; he and his family were still without possessions in 1772. Martin Shire, a married laborer in his early thirties, paid the minimum rate in 1767 and for the next thirteen years as well. George Bicherton was propertyless, earning a minimal income for a journeyman cordwainer in 1789. Nine years later his condition had not changed.

The vast majority of Philadelphia's laboring people were without property at any given point during the late eighteenth century. A few who resided in the city for a decade could expect to enjoy the same material success as Dicks or January, although generally on a more modest scale. Most, however, fared like Burns, Shire, and Bicherton; they were unable to acquire property or improve their economic status. The experiences of men who possessed a few assets or were assessed slightly above minimal occupational valuations varied widely during the years between tax lists, with their fortunes about evenly distributed among three groups: the economically successful men, such as Dicks and January; those whose slight edge slipped away, such as Nelson; and those who maintained the same position.

Affluent members of the four occupational groups generally fared well, although not all were so fortunate. John Stille, a master tailor, ranked among the wealthiest 10 percent of his profession in 1789, a position he preserved throughout the 1790s. Even though a riding chair and a slave slipped away during that decade, Stille still lived in relatively comfortable material surroundings. William Bell's experience was more unusual. As a twenty-eight-year-old tailor, he took up residence in Philadelphia after the British evacuated the city. By 1789, he had gained sufficient property to place him near the top of his profession, where he continued until the century's end. But his good fortune quickly evaporated; when his eyesight failed in 1801, Bell applied for admission to the almshouse as a pauper.[11]

Despite the experience of Bell, stability of condition was still an important characteristic of economic mobility even when measured over longer time periods than examined in Tables 10 and 11 (see Tables 13 and 14). At least 48 percent of laboring men remained at their initial economic levels over the long term (only 8 percent shy of that for short-term mobility). The mobility profile of the propertyless improved from the short term to the long term: one-third stayed propertyless, one-fifth acquired minimum property, and two-fifths acquired moderate property (Table 13). Workers who began with either minimum or moderate property had similar experiences over both the short and the long terms.

To summarize the major findings of this section on economic mobility, the majority, and frequently a substantial majority, of members of the four occupational groups were propertyless during the last half of the eighteenth century. Most of these men failed to acquire any taxable belongings within a decade, and while their chances of improving their economic position increased marginally with the length of their stay in the city, the odds were still against their obtaining property even after a decade and a half. One of every five individuals possessed moderate assets in the form of a house, lot, indentured servant, or slave. While this measure of economic security, once attained, was seldom relinquished, very rarely did any of these men amass true

11. The vignettes in this and the preceding paragraphs are drawn from the 1756, 1767, 1772, 1774, 1780, 1789, and 1798 tax lists discussed and cited in Appendix C, and from the Daily Occurrences Docket, Guardians of the Poor, May 30, 1801, PCA, hereafter cited as Daily Occurrences.

Table 13. Laborers, mariners, cordwainers, and tailors: Long-term economic mobility, 1756–1798

		Assessment categories		
Initial status	N	Propertyless (%)	Minimum property (%)	Moderate property (%)
1756	53		1772	
Propertyless		100	0	0
Minimum property		21	45	33
Moderate property		12	24	65
1767	55		1780	
Propertyless		39	39	22
Minimum property		33	11	56
Moderate property		0	5	95
1772	28		1789	
Propertyless		38	12	50
Minimum property		50	17	33
Moderate property		0	0	100
1780	18		1798	
Propertyless		17	0	83
Minimum property		33	50	17
Moderate property		17	17	67
Aggregate, 1756–1780	154		Aggregate, 1772–1798	
Propertyless		36	21	43
Minimum property		33	29	38
Moderate property		7	12	82

Source: 1756 tax list in Hannah Benner Roach, comp., "Taxables in the City of Philadelphia, 1756," *Pennsylvania Genealogical Magazine,* 22 (1961), 3–41; 1767 Tax Assessors' Reports, Van Pelt Library, University of Pennsylvania, Philadelphia; 1772, 1780, 1789, and 1798 Provincial Tax Lists, PCA.

riches, as defined by contemporary standards. Laboring men generally fared best during the late 1750s, early 1760s, and 1790s, when the smallest proportion of them were propertyless and the greatest advancement opportunities existed. Their chances for material improvement were most restricted (and the propertyless proportion the largest) from the mid-1760s until 1789.[12] That the economic prospects of workers did not significantly

12. One possible demographic explanation of these variations in mobility rates requires brief consideration. Differences in the age structure of the various cohorts could have created spurious changes in their career patterns. The apparent openness of the 1790s compared to the more restricted opportunities of the 1780s, for example, might be illusory if the cohort in 1789 was significantly younger than the one in 1780. However, the weak correlation between age and

Table 14. Laborers, mariners, cordwainers, and tailors: Long-term economic mobility between assessment categories, 1756–1798

Time span	Stable (%)	Up 1 category (%)	Up 2 categories (%)	Down 1 category (%)	Down 2 categories (%)
1756–1772	55	21	0	21	4
1767–1780	50	31	7	13	0
1772–1789	46	18	14	21	0
1780–1798	44	6	28	17	6
Aggregate, 1756–1798	48	21	11	17	2

Source: 1756 tax list in Hannah Benner Roach, comp., "Taxables in the City of Philadelphia, 1756," *Pennsylvania Genealogical Magazine,* 22 (1961), 3–41; 1767 Tax Assessors' Reports, Van Pelt Library, University of Pennsylvania, Philadelphia; 1772, 1780, 1789, and 1798 Provincial Tax Lists, PCA.

increase as they grew older reflects the limited ability of many laboring people to improve their economic condition.

This picture of the economic mobility of the lower sort is blurred in three important ways. First, it depicts only those people who resided in the city long enough to be recorded on at least two of the six selected tax lists. But how did the careers of the men who stayed in the city differ from those who left? This question can never be answered with certainty, but the attributes of the migrants and persisters provide clues. Approximately one-third of the laborers, mariners, cordwainers, and tailors who appeared on a tax list remained in the city a decade later. Even when adjusted for mortality, this persistence rate falls markedly below that of many contemporary American small towns and rural areas.[13] The greater inclination of citizens to leave the Quaker City strongly suggests that many of them found the prospects left something to be desired in comparison with other regions. Moreover, the rate of emigration of Philadelphia's taxpayers related inversely to their posi-

---

wealth discussed previously makes it highly unlikely that alterations in the age structure significantly affected mobility. And when the rates of economic mobility are controlled by the social age of taxpayers for the 1767–1772, 1772–1780, and 1780–1789 periods, the patterns are similar to those that emerge when mobility is not controlled by age. Following the methodology explained above, I used the social age of men on the 1775 Constables' Returns as a control for their economic mobility during the periods indicated.

13. Even if such a high proportion as 20 percent of adult males died each decade, Philadelphia's persistence rate of approximately 53 percent would still have been less than the 66–93 percent rate that characterized colonial American areas with smaller populations. Unfortunately, persistence rates for other early American cities are not available. These rates are presented in Douglas Lamar Jones, *Village and Seaport: Migration and Society in Eighteenth-Century Massachusetts* (Hanover, N.H., 1981), 111–113.

tions on the tax list: poor men moved more frequently than wealthier ones.[14] The previous analysis of the career patterns of the less-itinerant portion of the population thus very likely is skewed in favor of the most successful men.

Although it is impossible to ascertain the fate of all the migrants, it is unlikely that they would have been better prepared to achieve material success than those who stayed behind. In one respect, their success or failure is not essential to an assessment of conditions within the city itself, for those who remained were unable to or chose not to seize the opportunities available elsewhere. The residents most resistant to the pressures to migrate were those who had attained at least a modicum of financial success.[15] But those who were the most inclined to leave—the poor, the journeymen, and the unskilled—generally earned incomes far too low to permit the accumulation of savings for their own farms, particularly during the late colonial period when land prices outside the city rose rapidly. The objection often raised against the safety valve theory of the frontier applies here: transients rarely would have possessed either the capital or the skills necessary to take full advantage of the available land and opportunities that may have existed in other areas.[16]

Data on the experiences of a handful of migrants from Philadelphia support the argument. Forty-eight men in the four occupational groups who left the city during the late 1760s and 1770s were traced into eight of the surrounding counties.[17] About 50 percent of these people remained propertyless, assessed the lowest tax rate. Nearly 40 percent paid slightly above the minimum rate because of ownership of a cow, sheep, or horse. Five of the forty-eight were taxed a higher amount, three of them having acquired small

14. Allan Kulikoff discovered a similar relationship between economic status and emigration in Boston, in "The Progress of Inequality in Revolutionary Boston," *WMQ*, 3d Ser., 28 (1971), 402. See also Jones, *Village and Seaport*, 47–54; and Nash, *Urban Crucible*, 185–186. This contradicts speculation by Jeffrey G. Williamson and Peter H. Lindert that "those who migrated *from* the cities had, in all likelihood, more middling wealth and age than those who migrated *to* the cities. Emigrants to the hinterland presumably had enough wealth to start a farm"; *American Inequality: A Macroeconomic History* (New York, 1980), 29–30.

15. These statements are based on the persistence patterns of taxpayers among the 1756, 1767, 1772, 1780, 1789, and 1798 tax lists cited in Appendix C.

16. On the rising price of land, see James T. Lemon, *The Best Poor Man's Country: A Geographical Study of Early Southeastern Pennsylvania* (Baltimore, Md., 1972), 67–69; and Arthur L. Jensen, *The Maritime Commerce of Colonial Philadelphia* (Madison, Wis., 1963), 126–127. It is not possible here to consider all of the issues involved or to cite all of the relevant studies focused on the safety valve theory of the frontier, but see Carter Goodrich and Sol Davison, "The Wage Earner in the Westward Movement," *Political Science Quarterly*, 50 (1935), 161–185; 51 (1936), 61–110; and Fred A. Shannon, "A Post Mortem on the Labor Safety Valve Theory," *Agricultural History*, 19 (1945), 31–37. One recent study finds that "the frontier was not a safety valve," in John W. Adams and Alice Bee Kasakoff, "Wealth and Migration in Massachusetts and Maine: 1771–1798," *JEH*, 45 (1985), 367–368.

17. These men were traced using the index and tax lists published in *Warantees of Land*, vols. 11–29 (1898–1899).

parcels of land. The sample, although regrettably small, represents one of the only pieces of hard evidence about the fortunes of migrants. And it does not indicate any greater, and perhaps even a lesser, rate of material success for men who emigrated from the city.

A second problem with this picture of economic mobility is that it is linear, delineating the career patterns of laboring Philadelphians as either rising or not rising during a specific time frame. While this sketches the structure of opportunity, it obscures the cyclical reality of the lives of many eighteenth-century urban laboring people. Some bettered their position during favorable periods and then fell upon hard times that eradicated their previous gains. Such a pattern is nearly impossible to measure, but it is evident in the experiences of men such as Cadwalader Dickinson, Charles Jenkins, and John Campbell. A propertyless master cordwainer in 1767, Dickinson acquired a house and an indentured servant during the next five years but then lost everything during the economic dislocation of the Revolutionary War. Jenkins, a ship's mate, possessed a moderate amount of property in 1756. The depression at the end of the Seven Years' War apparently hit him hard, for when the tax collectors made their rounds in 1767, he owned hardly any assets. Jenkins recouped many of his losses, however, during the following five years. John Campbell led a still more dramatic rags-to-riches-to-rags career. Hobbled by a sore leg and too poor to maintain himself, Campbell languished in the almshouse in 1796. Within two years of his recovery, he bought a home and earned a relatively high income. But several years later, injured and penniless once again, he returned to the almshouse.[18]

A third problem with the image created by the statistical data is that a great many marginal men were excused or missed by tax assessors because of their poverty or geographic mobility. In Philadelphia, their numbers ranged as high as 20 percent of the tax-inscribed population, with most of the "missing" men belonging to the laboring classes.[19] The economic experiences of this portion of the lower sort are not evident in the above mobility analysis nor can they be calculated with precision, but they are nonetheless important to our understanding of the opportunities available to laboring men. Other sources are revealing about the fortunes of these people. At one time or another, as discussed in the next chapter, a great many of them suffered through unemployment and underemployment, illness, disease, and job-related injuries.[20]

Occupational mobility (measured by the transition from journeyman to master, the propensity of lesser artisans and unskilled workers to change

18. These men were traced using the 1756, 1767, 1772, and 1798 tax lists cited in Appendix C and by means of citations in Daily Occurrences.

19. See Appendix C.

20. Health problems are considered in chapter 2.

jobs, and the promotion from common seaman to ship's officer) was, for the lower sort, little better than economic mobility. Still, some members of the four occupational groups did enjoy advancement. For artisans, the transition from journeyman to master represented the most significant alteration in their work lives. Craft guilds of a European type designed to control that transition did not exist (as such) in America, although the Cordwainers' Fire Company and the Taylors' Company in Philadelphia assumed many of the functions of such organizations. Nevertheless, few legal or social impediments restricted a journeyman from becoming a master by setting up an independent business and selling directly to customers. Before opening a shop, a cordwainer or tailor had to be skilled in making shoes or clothes, although these lesser crafts, when compared to goldsmiths or clock makers, were considered relatively easy to master. The capital available to support such a venture undoubtedly was much more significant than legal or social factors in determining the ability of many journeymen to establish their independence. The tools necessary for shoemakers and tailors cost relatively little, but the initial investment required to establish a workplace, purchase raw materials, obtain a clientele, wait for weeks or months for customers' payments, and simultaneously support a family would have been substantial, far beyond the savings of most journeymen.

Benjamin Franklin's efforts to raise money for his own printing house are instructive. He entered into partnership with Hugh Meredith, an alcoholic with few printing skills, solely because Meredith's father agreed to finance the business. Subsequently, Franklin borrowed from his friends and even bargained for a marriage, providing the dowry was large enough to pay off his debt and fully establish himself as a master. Aware of the problems journeymen faced, Franklin provided two thousand pounds sterling in his will to be lent to young, married artisans in Boston and Philadelphia to enable them to set up their own shops.[21] These problems stung journeymen printers in the Quaker City, especially during the 1790s. An apprentice to Franklin's grandson reported their advice: "All the . . . Journay men tell [me] that I had not better learn the printing. . . . They say if they had money to set up independently they could make a fortune but without it, it is but a poor business."[22]

This complaint seems to apply to journeymen cordwainers and tailors as well as to printers. Tracing these artisans among tax lists reveals the limitations of their opportunities. Approximately one-third of cordwainers and tailors could be identified as journeymen, and another third as masters, with

21. L. Jesse Lemisch, ed., *Benjamin Franklin: The Autobiography and Other Writings* (New York, 1961), 63–68, 80; *Encouragement for Apprentices to be Sober . . .*, broadside, 1800, HSP; and Accounts Ledger, Franklin Legacy, 1791–1868, PCA.
22. Quoted in W. J. Rorabaugh, *The Craft Apprentice: From Franklin to the Machine Age in America* (New York, 1986), 29.

the status of the remainder unclear.[23] Maintenance of the same status was the most pervasive experience for these artisans over any given period (see Table 15).[24] At least 42 percent of journeymen remained employees, and 25 percent of them became masters during the years between tax lists. Assuming that the men of unknown status divided in a pattern identical to that of men with known status, the best estimate is that 61 percent of the journeymen continued in their initial situation, while 39 percent installed themselves as masters during any eight-year time period. Journeymen were most restricted in their mobility from the late 1760s through the Revolution but often achieved independence during the 1780s and 1790s. The position of master craftsman, once achieved, was relatively permanent. At least 75 percent, and likely closer to 85 percent, of masters retained their position between tax lists. The few who lost their status probably went broke and were forced once again to hire out to another craftsman.

Journeymen cordwainers and tailors may have fared somewhat better over the long term. Although the sample numbers are small, at least two-fifths of them became masters during any sixteen-year period, while one-fifth definitely remained in their dependent status (see Table 16). Once again, masters rarely relinquished their position. That so few cordwainers and tailors remained in the city for sixteen years, however, may indicate that some were discouraged by the prospects for further advancement.

Another criterion of occupational mobility among lesser artisans was their propensity to change jobs. Most cordwainers and tailors continued in the same line of employment throughout their residence in the city; only 9

23. Historians rarely have examined the transition from journeyman to master since records differentiating between masters and journeymen in any trade usually are nonexistent. But the status of most Philadelphia cordwainers and tailors can be determined from certain of their distinguishing traits. A number of masters and journeymen, for example, were identified from the Minutes of the Taylors' Company, Minutes of the Cordwainers' Fire Company, numerous advertisements in the *Pennsylvania Gazette* (Philadelphia), and bills submitted for work in the following collections: Bills, Receipts, and Accounts, Shippen Family Papers, vols. 28–30, 1754–1822; Business Papers of Samuel Coates and John Reynell, Coates and Reynell Papers, 1755–1767; Incoming Correspondence: Bills and Receipts of John Cadwalader, Cadwalader Collection, Boxes 1–6, 12–14; all of the preceding records are at HSP. Matching the men of known status to the tax rolls and constables' returns enabled the particular attributes of journeymen and masters to be isolated. The principal trait separating masters and journeymen was their tax assessment, since it was based not only on the taxable property owned but also on the value of the taxpayer's occupation. The occupation of a master was nearly always assessed at a substantially higher rate than that of a journeyman. Other qualities, such as the ownership of indentured servants, slaves, rental property, a house, the presence of a hired servant, the amount of house rent paid, and the status of the taxpayer as a tenant or household head, made it possible to distinguish between many masters and journeymen with some assurance. For a detailed explanation of this methodology, see Thomas Smith, "Reconstructing Occupational Structures: The Case of the Ambiguous Artisans," *Historical Methods Newsletter*, 8 (1975), 134–146.

24. Again, for the reasons discussed earlier, the data are biased, indicating greater opportunity than most laboring men actually enjoyed.

Table 15. Short-term occupational mobility of artisans, 1756–1798

		Status over time		
Initial status	N	Journeyman (%)	Master (%)	Unknown (%)
1756	32		1767	
Journeyman		23	38	38
Master		11	5	64
1767	116		1772	
Journeyman		61	36	3
Master		14	17	69
1772	65		1780	
Journeyman		43	35	22
Master		7	7	86
1780	41		1789	
Journeyman		31	23	46
Master		4	7	89
1789	54		1798	
Journeyman		26	21	53
Master		26	9	66
Aggregate, 1756–1789	308		Aggregate, 1767–1798	
Journeyman		42	32	27
Master		13	11	76

Source: 1756 tax list in Hannah Benner Roach, comp., "Taxables in the City of Philadelphia, 1756," *Pennsylvania Genealogical Magazine,* 22 (1961), 3–41; 1767 Tax Assessors' Reports, Van Pelt Library, University of Pennsylvania, Philadelphia; 1772, 1780, 1789, and 1798 Provincial Tax Lists, PCA.

percent assumed a new occupation each decade. The few masters who changed their occupational title followed the prevailing trend in many crafts, becoming merchants, shopkeepers, and grocers and thereby focusing on the distribution rather than the production of goods. Journeymen sometimes floated among a variety of less-skilled jobs when in need of employment, but they seldom moved permanently into other skilled occupations. After investing a substantial number of years in learning their craft, most artisans had few options but to continue in their line of work. Since most men in the lesser crafts never achieved the success enjoyed by many merchants, goldsmiths, carpenters, and the like, the trades to which boys initially were apprenticed dictated the limits of their future advancement.

Most unskilled workers functioned in that capacity throughout their lives.

Table 16. Long-term occupational mobility of artisans, 1756–1798

Initial status	N	Journeyman (%)	Master (%)	Unknown (%)
			Status over time	
1756	20		1772	
Journeyman		29	42	29
Master		0	92	8
1767	29		1780	
Journeyman		25	25	50
Master		5	86	10
1772	21		1789	
Journeyman		14	57	29
Master		0	91	7
1780	5		1798	
Journeyman		0	100	0
Master		0	75	25
Aggregate, 1756–1780	75		Aggregate, 1772–1798	
Journeyman		22	43	35
Master		2	88	10

Source: 1756 tax list in Hannah Benner Roach, comp., "Taxables in the City of Philadelphia, 1756," *Pennsylvania Genealogical Magazine,* 22 (1961), 3–41; 1767 Tax Assessors' Reports, Van Pelt Library, University of Pennsylvania, Philadelphia; 1772, 1780, 1789, and 1798 Provincial Tax Lists, PCA.

Even though 25 percent of laborers assumed a different occupation each decade, few of them developed new marketable skills. Instead, they worked as bricklayers, soldiers, draymen, painters, whitewashers, potato diggers, and bartenders. Their highest rate of occupational mobility occurred during the 1790s, when, according to the tax lists, 20 percent of laborers obtained skilled positions as mast makers, coopers, carpenters, and the like. Those able to learn a skill usually fared better materially. As is often the case, the higher rate of success may well have come to those men who were in the right place at the right time.

Occupational mobility among mariners was no better than it was among either laborers or journeymen cordwainers and tailors. The promotion of a common sailor to ship's officer was extremely rare. Among the 128 mariners examined, only George Craig successfully climbed the entire ladder from seaman to mate to captain, whereas Thomas Carew and Jacques LeBon were able to step one rung up to become mates. Many common seamen continued in their rank for considerable periods of time. John Smith sailed as a ship's hand for at least twenty-three years, and Thomas Loudon and Lawrence

Mahon for over four decades.[25] That the age structure of both common seamen and mates was virtually identical further supports this view of limited occupational mobility; if mariners generally won promotions after working a number of years as common seamen, then officers should have been older than sailors.[26]

Since ship captains seldom came from the ranks of common seamen, what was their origin? Most served as mates before assuming command. John Gantlet sailed to the West Indies as a mate on board the brigantine *Augustus*; the following year, at age twenty-one, he became master of that vessel. Twenty-one-year-old Samuel Loweth, formerly mate on the ship *Active*, became master of the brigantine *Favourite*. Mate Thomas Brown, twenty-four years old, left the brigantine *Tryphena* to take charge of the schooner *Sally* when its captain died.[27] The notable characteristics of these and other new masters was their youth and their failure to appear in the records as common sailors. Most likely, they had been apprenticed or sent as supercargoes by their fathers, often merchants or captains themselves, to learn the art and mystery not of an ordinary seaman but of the commander of a vessel. Such was the case for Silas Foster, Jr. Beginning at age thirteen, he served his apprenticeship on vessels that his father commanded and eventually became a captain himself. Laurence Anderson was another ship master who brought his son up to the same profession.[28] As ship captains, both Foster and Anderson were required to master the intricacies of seamanship, to be able to read and write, to solve complex mathematical problems, and to deal with merchants in buying and selling products at various ports of call. Common

25. Tax lists do not reveal much about the career patterns of merchant seamen, since most of them were at sea when assessors made their rounds. However, a sample of 128 mariners, randomly drawn from the crew lists of vessels clearing port, shows the low occupational mobility of sailors. These lists are part of the Maritime Records of the Port of Philadelphia, 1789–1860, LC, hereafter cited as Maritime Records. All crew members on ships clearing the port are listed in separate volumes for each year. For Craig, see 1799, p. 54; 1800, pp. 59, 112; and 1804, p. 272. For Carew, see 1798, p. 6; 1799, p. 36; 1800, p. 24; and 1802, p. 30. And for LeBon, see 1803, p. 143; 1804, pp. 18, 198; and 1805, pp. 19, 325. See also Daily Occurrences: entry on Smith, Aug. 24, 1801; entry on Loudon, Apr. 29, 1800; and entry on Mahon, Dec. 10, 1800.

26. The mean age of both mates and common seamen on vessels that cleared the port in 1803 was twenty-six years old. The breakdown of both groups into four age categories was very similar. This is based on an analysis of 304 crew members from a random sample of thirty-seven ships leaving Philadelphia, contained in the Ship's Crew Lists, Records of the Bureau of Customs, Record Group 36, NA, hereafter cited as Ship's Crew Lists. That many men served as common seamen for their entire lives is discussed by Marcus Rediker, "The Anglo-American Seaman as Collective Worker, 1700–1750," in Stephen Innes, ed., *Work and Labor in Early America* (Chapel Hill, N.C., 1988), 257–258.

27. Maritime Records: for Gantlet, see 1803, p. 35, and 1804, p. 132; for Loweth, see 1804, pp. 1, 174, 457; 1805, p. 244, and 1806, pp. 68, 170. Brown is recorded on the list of crew members on the brigantine *Tryphena*, in Ship's Crew Lists.

28. Foster appears in Maritime Records: 1804, pp. 29, 433; 1805, p. 135; and 1810, p. 44. Anderson is in Will Book K, p. 291, Wills, Philadelphia County Probate Records, 1683–1901, RW.

seamen ordinarily did not learn these skills, several of which were beyond the educational training of most mariners.

Once again, as in the case of lesser artisans and laborers, the craft that boys learned (or did not learn) to a large degree determined their future careers. The sons of fathers who possessed the means to apprentice them to a ship captain, a merchant house, or a master in a highly skilled craft and later to assist them in obtaining the capital necessary to establish their independence naturally enjoyed greater opportunities than available to common seamen for material and occupational rewards.

The Quaker City enjoyed the brightest economic record of any major American port during the second half of the eighteenth century, and its overall wealth increased markedly. Yet, as is evident in this and the preceding chapter, many laboring Philadelphians failed to improve their earnings, acquire property, escape their dependent positions within their crafts, or move up the economic and occupational ladders. What factors contributed to their material difficulties? What created the bursts of mobility and higher living standards in the early 1760s and the 1790s which bracketed decades of less promise? Epidemics, ill health, injuries, migration patterns, and business cycles have been considered previously. However, a brief review of changes in the economy in the context of migratory patterns is necessary to more fully explain the fluctuations in the circumstances of the lower sort.

Two important determinants of the conditions of the laboring classes were the availability of employment and the level of wages. These, in turn, were defined primarily by the demand for the services of the lower classes and the supply of their labor. The geographic flow of people affected the size of the labor pool, while cycles in the city's economy influenced the demand side of this equation.

As the economy spurted ahead during the late 1750s, the curtailment of overseas immigration, the vigorous recruitment of Pennsylvanians into the military, and the stampede of many poor men to sign aboard privateers limited the number of workers in the city. With a relatively small pool of unskilled laborers available in a booming economy, their chances for material and occupational advancement rose. These favorable conditions ended during the final years of the war, when most Philadelphians fared poorly. A new influx of Scotch-Irish and German migrants joined war veterans drifting into the city to enlarge the ranks of laboring men. As citizens with few skills scrambled after scarce jobs, city leaders complained about the "want of Employment, which was reducing a large number of residents to great straits."[29]

29. Anon., *Whereas the Number of Poor In and Around the City* . . . (Philadelphia, 1764), broadside, Library Company of Philadelphia.

The city emerged from its problems in the mid-1760s, but various factors once again disrupted the economy in the following years. At the same time a "labor surplus" developed as the proportion of laborers in the taxable work force doubled during the early 1770s. Employment opportunities and the wages of unskilled workers consequently declined, while their chances to acquire property deteriorated at the close of the colonial era. As one newspaper contributor in 1769 lamented, "mechanics . . . depending intirely on accidental employment, and having their families mostly idle, are generally poor."[30] During the next several years the economic predicament of immigrants and others at the bottom grew so severe that the Irish and English residents of Philadelphia founded three separate organizations to lend "advice and assistance" to their distressed national kinsmen. One of these organizations even appealed for aid in the British press.[31] Heavy European immigration accounted for the startling growth of urban laborers at the end of the colonial period.[32] Many migrants undoubtedly arrived as indentured servants to Philadelphia masters during the 1760s, achieved their freedom four or five years later, and then joined the ranks of an even greater number of new arrivals in search of employment.

Economic dislocation and depression characterized the city during much of the 1780s. Even though few immigrants settled in the city and many residents left, unskilled laborers continued to account for 7 percent of the tax-inscribed population during the 1780s, approximately the same proportion as in the early 1770s. As workers struggled to locate employment, public aid to the poor increased.[33] Unskilled workers and lesser artisans alike shared in the general prosperity of the mid-1790s, as they enjoyed higher wages and greater career opportunities. The proportional decline of laborers in the city, from 7 percent of the taxable work force in 1789 to 5 percent in 1798, further contributed to improvements in their condition.

Seasonal employment, low wages, and changing labor relations also influenced the level and variations in the material standards and the mobility opportunities of the lower sort. Like workers in all preindustrial societies, Philadelphia's laborers and artisans endured periodic slack times of unemployment because weather, the length of daylight, vacillating consumer demand, the erratic delivery of raw materials, and the seasonal dependencies of agriculture all affected their jobs. Freezing temperatures, for example, left mariners without berths when ice-filled harbors closed, forced shoemakers to

30. *Pennsylvania Chronicle, and Universal Advertiser* (Philadelphia), Mar. 27, 1769.
31. Bridenbaugh and Bridenbaugh, *Rebels and Gentlemen*, 239–240.
32. Gary B. Nash, "Slaves and Slaveowners in Colonial Philadelphia," *WMQ*, 3d Ser., 30 (1973), 233.
33. George W. Geib, "A History of Philadelphia, 1776–1789" (Ph.D. diss., Univ. of Wisconsin, 1969), 203–205.

quit their benches when their waxes hardened, and slowed or halted the activity of men who built houses and ships. The city's laboring people undoubtedly were familiar with "cucumber time," as eighteenth-century English tailors referred to the colder months when they could afford little other dietary fare. Newspapers and broadsides characterized winter as a season when the city had "little occasion . . . for the labour of the Poor," and when "for want of Employment, many . . . are reduced to great Straits and rendered burthensome to their neighbors."[34] As one resident noted, "collections (time immemorial) have been made *every* winter . . . for the poor."[35] The cyclical nature of employment is evident in the increase in the number of ship arrivals in the city's port each spring and their decline each fall. Periodic variations in the cost of living corresponded to the seasonality of employment. During winter, firewood prices doubled or tripled, and the range of foodstuffs available in the markets narrowed, restricting the options of the lower sort to live within their food budgets. That the number of applicants for poor relief generally rose during late autumn and fell in early spring demonstrates the impact of seasonal economic fluctuations on the financial conditions of laboring people.[36]

Many laboring men simply earned too little to maintain a family, even when fully employed. James Ross's wife and three children entered the almshouse because, as a "Drummer of Marines," his "pay and rations are not sufficient to support himself and family, who are in a distressed condition, suffering for want of the necessities of life." As a construction worker at the Schuylkill bridge, Charles Johnson could not "provide and take sufficient care" of his wife and son.[37] Another Philadelphian with a large family complained that "I have strove all in my power and find that I cannot support them . . . I could point out a great number in similar circumstances with myself, and I am sure some of them in a more deplorable condition, if possible."[38]

The slow transformation in labor relations among artisans, involving the gradual erosion of a paternalistic structure and its replacement by a wage labor system during the course of the eighteenth century, shifted many of the risks and some of the rewards from masters to journeymen. Early in the century masters routinely hired journeymen for long periods, reimbursing them with both a wage and "found," the latter consisting of meals and occasionally lodging. This guaranteed workers a measure of financial security

34. *Pennsylvania Packet, and Daily Advertiser* (Philadelphia), Dec. 12, 1787; *Whereas the Number of Poor In and around the City.*

35. *Independent Gazeteer; or, the Chronicle of Freedom* (Philadelphia), Dec. 12, 1785.

36. Billy G. Smith, "Poverty and Economic Marginality in Eighteenth-Century America," *Proceedings of the APS*, 132 (1988), 96–108.

37. Daily Occurrences: entry on Ross, Dec. 21, 1802; entry on Johnson, Mar. 8, 1803.

38. *Pennsylvania Packet, and Daily Advertiser* (Philadelphia), Oct. 20, 1784.

by ensuring their employment for weeks or months; protecting their pay from deductions during days of injury, illness, or inactivity; and minimizing their vulnerability to increases in the cost of living. But by the end of the colonial era, most employees depended entirely on wages, and they bore the full responsibility of the vagaries of the economy and their own personal fortunes. Some individuals gained from this arrangement, and others lost. During the boom times of the 1790s, for example, high wages and the easy availability of capital enabled half of the journeymen shoemakers to establish their own shops. However, the general economic problems in the decade preceding the Revolution restricted the financial resources accessible to journeymen. One result was that as few as one out of every ten cordwainers and tailors became masters during that decade.[39]

What expectations of material achievement could Philadelphia's laboring men realistically entertain? The career patterns of the four occupational groups analyzed in this chapter provide solid answers to this question. Mariners, laborers, cordwainers, and tailors composed between a third and a half of the city's free adult males. Most of them congregated near the bottom of the tax-inscribed population, although they surely enjoyed better material conditions and greater career prospects than the lowest substratum of males whose impoverishment prevented them even from paying taxes. Members of these four groups stood virtually no chance of rising from the bottom to the top of the socioeconomic hierarchy. To become a merchant, a member of a profession, or a ship captain was also very difficult, although within the grasp of a few.

If the virtues of Poor Richard did not guarantee riches to most laboring men, did they at least ensure that these workers could achieve a measure of economic security, acquire property, improve their incomes, or obtain skilled positions? The findings of this analysis suggest that many of the lower sort encountered serious problems fulfilling even these modest goals. A large number of laborers, mariners, cordwainers, and tailors not only were trapped permanently at the bottom, but, as the previous chapter demonstrated, they led economically precarious lives that sometimes forced them to seek public and private relief. Moreover, the majority began and ended their careers in the city as propertyless individuals without, in the judgment of the tax assessors, having bettered their physical circumstances. One of every five of the propertyless obtained assets within eight or nine years, and the chances of

39. On changing labor relations, see Nash, *Urban Crucible*, 258–261; Sharon V. Salinger, "Artisans, Journeymen, and the Transformation of Labor in Late Eighteenth-Century Philadelphia," *WMQ*, 3d Ser., 40 (1983), 62–84; and Salinger, *"To Serve Well and Faithfully": Labor and Indentured Servants in Pennsylvania, 1682–1800* (Cambridge, England, 1987), 137–171.

improving their lot increased only marginally if they remained in the city an additional decade. Some families made strides during good times, only to slip backward in periods of hardship. Most unskilled urban workers—who in Franklin's terms were "bred to country work" or "brought up to no business"—found themselves unable to learn and practice a marketable skill or trade.[40] Migrants from the city may not have fared much better, and perhaps not even as well, as those who remained behind. The weak correlation between wealth and age confirms the restricted nature of economic mobility.

Still, a considerable number of laboring men enjoyed important fiscal and occupational advances. At least one of every three of the lower sort improved his income or acquired taxable assets during his stay in the city. And as many as four of every ten journeymen shoemakers and tailors may have become independent each decade. Meanwhile, master craftsmen and property owners tenaciously held on to their positions.

What features distinguished those who advanced from those who did not? Franklin's professed values undoubtedly had some importance: hard work and frugality played a role, although perhaps not the dominant one. Thomas M. Doerflinger recently has argued that "it was not very difficult to enter Philadelphia's merchant community if one had contacts, capital, or experience."[41] But these attributes prevented the vast majority of laboring people from bettering their circumstances or participating in the city's most lucrative occupational endeavor. The development of a marketable skill was a key ingredient to achieving modest success, yet it was beyond the control of many boys who either were apprenticed to masters in lesser-skilled occupations or were never put out to learn the mystery of any craft. Laborers and mariners frequently could not compensate for a handicap that generally was not of their own making. Nor did journeymen shoemakers and tailors automatically become masters after learning the intricacies of their trade; that transition depended heavily on the availability of capital. Some were able to save the required amount, but most must have depended on loans from others to set up their own shops. In all of these calculations, the vicissitudes of fortune assumed great significance. Epidemics, illnesses, injuries, unemployment, political unrest, and fluctuations both in the flow of migrants and in the economy numbered among the primary factors that differentiated masters and property owners from almshouse inmates.

The experiences of the four occupational groups fluctuated during the second half of the century. Periods of high or increasing inequality and propertylessness in the city, particularly during the late 1760s through the

40. Lemisch, *Benjamin Franklin*, 65.
41. Doerflinger, *Vigorous Spirit of Enterprise*, 57.

1780s, generally coincided with cycles of relatively restricted economic and occupational mobility. Similarly, periods when the gap between rich and poor and the proportion of the propertyless in the city were the smallest—the late 1750s, early 1760s, and 1790s—were also times of comparatively high mobility for the lower sort. That a parallel relationship existed between greater inequality and lesser mobility for laboring people does not necessarily imply that the former caused the latter, but it is suggestive.

The portrait limned by these findings differs fundamentally from the more optimistic portrayals of the conditions and prospects of the early American urban lower classes. In Philadelphia, the most prosperous American city during the late eighteenth century, the material circumstances of the lower sort were considerably worse, their position at the bottom more permanent, and their chances to achieve the most modest economic goals substantially more limited than scholars sometimes have assumed. The increasing wealth thought to have characterized America in general and the Quaker City in particular during much of this period did not trickle down to many laboring men. Indeed, most struggled not to sail ahead but to remain afloat.

Chapter Six

Migration, Housing, and Poverty

For, in the first place, things are no better in Pennsylvania. However hard one may have had to work in his native land, conditions are bound to be equally tough or even tougher in the new country.
—Gottlieb Mittelberger, *Journey to Pennsylvania*, 1756

JAMES BROWN, a weaver by trade, was born in Ireland in the middle of the eighteenth century. During the late 1760s, probably spurred by problems in that country's linen manufacturing, he decided to migrate to America. Choosing the middle colonies, he disembarked at Philadelphia and then traveled on to Staystown, a small village outside Lancaster, Pennsylvania. Within a few years Brown moved again, this time to Danbury, where he became a "foreman in the first [linen] factory in Connecticut." There he selected young Rachel Sherwood, age sixteen, as his bride, and on Christmas Day, 1774, the local Presbyterian minister pronounced them husband and wife in her father's house. Together they lived in the "weave shop," where he continued to work until the outbreak of the Revolution. Shortly thereafter, the British attacked Danbury and, because of its potential value to the Patriot cause, burned the factory. James and Rachel promptly set out on the long horseback ride to Staystown, where he knew he could "live by his trade of weaving." On one of his trips to Lancaster "to buy some necessaries," James met a recruiting agent who, no doubt tapping Brown's anger over his treatment at the hands of the British soldiers, convinced him to join the war effort. But first he needed to provide for his pregnant wife, so they moved to Philadelphia where she could live with friends. Soon after James's enlistment as a private in the First Pennsylvania Regiment, Rachel gave birth to their first son, William, named after James's army captain. With her husband intermittently at war during the next five years, Rachel cared for their child and earned wages making rifle cartridges and soldier's clothing.[1]

1. The quotations and vignette about Brown and Sherwood here and in the following paragraph are from Petitions for Revolutionary War Pensions, W15877, NA, hereafter cited as Revolutionary War Pensions.

The Browns continued to share a small house in one of the city's alleys for a short time after the war and then returned to Danbury, where James resumed his previous job in the factory. All told, they produced twelve children before James died in Ontario County, New York, in 1815. Rachel lived nearly thirty more years, relying primarily on her own resources and her children's support. Her brother Andrew, a "wealthy man who lived at his care" in New York City, died in 1830, leaving Rachel the substantial sum of four thousand dollars. But when a Mrs. Strong absconded with the inheritance, Rachel applied for a pension as the destitute widow of a Revolutionary War veteran. The small amount she received helped defray her expenses until her death in 1844.

Such is the story of the lives of an "ordinary" American man and woman during the late eighteenth and early nineteenth centuries. Their tale is distinct from thousands of others in part because it can be told in even this amount of detail. James Brown was a weaver, a member of the lower sort, a Revolutionary War soldier, a brief resident of Philadelphia. Rachel Brown was a wife and mother who worked hard to hold her household together during and after the war years and struggled with poverty during her old age. Their migration in search of subsistence, their occupation of a small home in a back street, and their occasional struggle with poverty make them representative of many in their class.

Earlier chapters have set the physical, demographic, and economic conditions of the city and its laboring people. This chapter examines various other aspects of the lives of the lower sort. Specifically, it addresses three questions: What were their geographic and social backgrounds? How did they adapt to the city in terms of the houses in which they lived, and in what ways did urban residential patterns change over time? Who fell into poverty, and how did they cope with their dilemmas?

Geographic mobility marked the lives of the great majority of Philadelphia's laboring inhabitants. During the decades preceding the Revolution, most poor Philadelphians had migrated to the city from Germany, Ireland, and England. The Scotch Irish and Irish continued to arrive during the final fifteen years of the century, albeit in smaller numbers, while wealthy French refugees and their slaves swelled the migration stream during the 1790s. As the tide of overseas migration subsided between the third and fourth quarters of the century, many of the city's new settlers flowed in from the surrounding countryside and states. The proportion of Philadelphia's laboring people who were born in America increased correspondingly. Of the city's mariners who swore their allegiance to Pennsylvania around 1790, for example, 80 percent were foreign born.[2] But by the turn of the century

2. Data on one hundred men who took an oath of allegiance to the state of Pennsylvania are

these figures were reversed: over 80 percent of seamen who lived and sailed out of Philadelphia were born in the United States.[3] While these two sets of records are not strictly comparable, they reflect the changing places of origin of the city's poor, a shift that began during the closing years of the century.

Still, during the 1790s, when records designating the birthplaces of some laboring people are first available, few of the lower sort were born in the city itself. Of fifty laborers, mariners, cordwainers, and tailors whose places of birth were indicated when they entered the almshouse, only five were native Philadelphians. Cordwainer John Chatham and laborer John Williams may have been "Old Denizens born." But John Dougherty and Mageor Richards, fellow Knights of St. Crispin, migrated to the city from Delaware, while laborer Jesse Scott moved from nearby Chester County. Shoemaker Thomas Kelby, tailor Anthony Dawson, and laborer Patrick Coyle all were natives of Ireland. The likelihood that mariners were migrants was greater still. All together, 90 percent of the fifty admittees to the almshouse were born outside the city, and two-thirds of them hailed from overseas, primarily from Ireland.[4] While these figures do not represent exact proportions of the native and the foreign born among all of the lower sort, they suggest that during the 1790s, as throughout the second half of the century, most laboring Philadelphians came from outside the city, many of them from abroad.

Most of the city's laboring people shared not only a common migratory experience but also similar social and economic backgrounds. The best available data describe the origins of merchant seamen. For decades the romantic picture drawn by Samuel Eliot Morison dominated our image of eighteenth-century sailors: They were primarily "adventure-seeking boys" incited by their wanderlust and the high wages paid seamen to abandon temporarily the tediousness of farm chores for the excitement of life at sea. After a few years before the mast, most returned to their senses and to their homes, purchased farms with their saved earnings, and settled down with local maids. The "old salt," according to Morison, was nearly nonexistent. The few men who remained at sea for extended periods did so only out of

---

available in John B. Linn and William H. Egle, eds., *Pennsylvania Archives*, 2d ser., 12 vols. (Harrisburg, Pa., 1875), 3:66–97.

3. This is based on my analysis of 304 crew members who served on a random sample of thirty-seven ships leaving Philadelphia in 1803, as recorded in Ship's Crew Lists, Records of the Bureau of Customs, Record Group 36, NA, hereafter cited as Ship's Crew Lists.

4. These figures are based on the admissions to the almshouse between Aug. 13, 1790 and Dec. 18, 1805, as indicated in the Daily Occurrences Docket, Guardians of the Poor, PCA, hereafter cited as Daily Occurrences. John Chatham was admitted June 16, 1800; John Williams on June 30, 1801; Jesse Scott and Thomas Kelby on Apr. 7, 1800; Anthony Dawson on June 6, 1800; and Patrick Coyle on July 6, 1801. Selections from these records are available in Billy G. Smith and Cynthia Shelton, eds., "The Daily Occurrence Docket of the Philadelphia Almshouse, 1800," *PH*, 52 (1985), 86–116; and Smith and Shelton, eds., "The Daily Occurrence Docket of the Philadelphia Almshouse: Selected Entries, 1800–1804," ibid., 183–205.

Table 17. Nativity of Philadelphia mariners, 1803

Mariners	N	American born (%)	Foreign born (%)	Philadelphia born (%)
All	285	84.6	15.4	8.1
Common seamen	118	89.0	11.0	4.2
Masters	31	83.9	16.1	12.9

Source: A sample of thirty-seven ships leaving Philadelphia in 1803 from the Ship's Crew Lists, Records of the Bureau of Customs, Record Group 36, NA.

hopes for rum or for promotion to ship's captain, objectives that they usually achieved.[5] Jesse Lemisch questioned this characterization of early American mariners twenty years ago, and Marcus Reddiker more recently again revised the image.[6] The evidence about Philadelphia's merchant seamen brings Morison's portrayal into even greater doubt.

Ethnically and racially, Philadelphia's merchant marines were a hetero-geneous lot, among the most mixed conglomerations of people in their world. Whites from each of the American states, the British Isles, and nearly every European country, blacks from Africa, the West Indies, and various parts of North America, and a sprinkling of South Americans and Asians jostled with one another on vessels that plied the Atlantic. A sample of 148 mariners who wed in Philadelphia during the 1790s indicates that the parents of only one in ten had last resided in the Quaker City. The parental residence of another third was divided equally among New England, the mid-Atlantic states, and the Upper South. The parents of slightly more than half lived abroad: one-third in England or Ireland and the remainder in various European countries, the West Indies, and Nova Scotia.[7] The birth-places of a sample of nearly 300 mariners appearing in the crew lists of ships clearing the port of Philadelphia at the turn of the century corroborate these findings (see Table 17). Fewer than 10 percent of the sailors were Phila-delphia natives. Michael Burke, the son of a cordwainer, was born in the city shortly after the Revolution began, and he continued to live and work there

5. Samuel Eliot Morison, *The Maritime History of Massachusetts* (Boston, 1921), 105–107, 111.

6. Jesse Lemisch, "Jack Tar in the Streets: Merchant Seamen in the Politics of Revolution-ary America," *WMQ*, 3d Ser., 25 (1968), 371–372; Marcus Rediker, *Between the Devil and the Deep Blue Sea* (Cambridge, England, 1987).

7. The rector at Gloria Dei, Old Swedes Church, recorded the last known residence of the brides and grooms that he married in the Marriage Records, GSP, hereafter cited as Marriage Records, Old Swedes Church. Of the 148 mariners he wed between 1793 and 1800, 10 percent of their parents had most recently lived in Philadelphia, 12 percent in the Mid-Atlantic states, 11 percent in New England, 11 percent in the Upper South, 34 percent in England or Ireland, 19 percent in Europe, and 1 percent each in the West Indies and Nova Scotia.

for several decades.[8] Belonging to the more numerous group of seamen whose birthplace was abroad, James Hunter was born in Shakespeare's Walk, four miles outside London. He shipped to the Pennsylvania capital in 1784 and sailed out of it for the next sixteen years.[9] William Taylor and Dennis McDonald represented yet another group. Born in Bucks County, Pennsylvania in 1766, Taylor moved to Philadelphia in the same year as James Hunter, married, and worked out of the port for at least the next two decades. McDonald was a native of Baltimore and the son of a bricklayer. At about age twenty he left for Philadelphia and served as a crewman on ships sailing from that port during the 1790s.[10]

Rather than coming fresh from the farm, the majority of mariners appear to have been born and raised in urban areas. Over half of the seamen who applied for protective certificates during the 1790s listed Philadelphia, Boston, New York, or Baltimore as their birthplaces, and a good many others hailed from smaller towns such as Salem, Massachusetts and Richmond, Virginia.[11] That so few identified agricultural areas as their places of birth is surprising since only about 10 percent of all Americans resided in urban areas at that time. Foreign-born mariners came from similar backgrounds: most who swore allegiance to Pennsylvania were born in sizable cities. Englishmen often came from London, Liverpool, and Suffolk; Irishmen from Cork, Londonderry, and Belfast; and Europeans from Marseilles, Nantes, Rotterdam, and Hamburg.[12]

Most people did not hold the life of a common mariner in high esteem. As Samuel Johnson observed, "No man will be a sailor who has contrivance enough to get himself into a jail; for being in a ship is being in jail with the chance of being drowned. A man in jail has more room, better food, and commonly better company." And young Benjamin Franklin appalled his father, a humble tallow chandler, by expressing interest in a career at sea.[13] Given these attitudes, why did sailors select their occupation?

The family backgrounds of mariners hint at their motivations. Of the seventy-seven seamen who gave information about their parents' occupa-

8. Seamen's Protective Certificate Applications, Collector of Customs for the Port of Philadelphia, Records of the Bureau of Customs, 1798, Record Group 36, NA, hereafter cited as Protective Certificate Applications.

9. Daily Occurrences, Sept. 12, 1800.

10. Protective Certificate Applications, 1798.

11. Based on my analysis of 132 mariners who applied for protective certificates between 1796 and 1800; Protective Certificate Applications.

12. Linn and Egle, *Pennsylvania Archives*, 3:66–97. Ira Dye reached the same conclusion regarding the urban origin of most Philadelphia seamen in his analysis of their protective certificates between 1796 and 1803 and from 1812 to 1815, in "Early American Merchant Seafarers," *Proceedings of the APS*, 120 (1976), 339–340.

13. L. Jesse Lemisch, ed., *Benjamin Franklin: The Autobiography and Other Writings* (New York, 1961), 26–27.

Table 18. Occupations of fathers of Philadelphia mariners

Occupation	N	Foreign born (%)	American born (%)	All mariners (%)
Farmer	16	22.0	18.5	20.8
Merchant	11	16.0	11.1	14.3
Mariner	20	30.0	18.5	26.0
Unskilled	6	8.0	7.4	7.8
Artisan	24	24.0	44.4	31.2

Source: Seamen's Protective Certificate Applications, Records of the Bureau of Customs, 1796–1800, Record Group 36, NA. Information on the men who took the oath of allegiance to Pennsylvania is contained in John B. Linn and William H. Egle, eds., *Pennsylvania Archives,* 2d ser., 12 vols. (Harrisburg, Pa., 1875), 3:66–97.

tional status in either the oaths of allegiance or the petitions for protective certificates, the fathers of only one in five were farmers (see Table 18). Most worked in occupations associated with towns and cities. Typical were Robert Taylor, the son of a cordwainer; Daniel Ace, the child of a laborer; and William Ewes, the offspring of a ship master.[14] The fathers of these seamen generally earned their livings as mariners, unskilled workers, or artisans. Men engaged in these urban occupations usually did not own farmlands to pass along to their sons or to hold them near home. Nor, perhaps, did many of these fathers envision that their sons' futures lay in working the land. The employment options for many laboring Philadelphians from urban, landless families had been limited. If fortunate, they might have learned a craft. Otherwise, each may well have faced a lifetime of toil as a mariner or a casual laborer. The necessity of earning a living probably was much more significant than romantic notions about life at sea in most sailors' decisions to sign on for ocean voyages.[15]

The geographic origins of mariners who left farms for a life on board ship provide additional clues about the economic imperative of their migrations. John Perkins was born in 1775 on his father's farm in Norwich, Connecticut. Two decades later, when his father died, John and his friend Christopher Potts moved to Philadelphia and began to work as ship's crewmen.[16] Nearly all of the city's seamen who came from rural areas migrated from coastal regions, and their numbers increased over time. Only a handful of men found their way to the Pennsylvania capital from the frontier.[17] Why did the

14. Linn and Egle, *Pennsylvania Archives,* 3:79–80, 91; Protective Certificate Applications, 1798.

15. Ira Dye argued convincingly that most very young, white seafarers were not runaways but went to sea with the consent of their parents, in "Early American Merchant Seafarers," 343.

16. Protective Certificate Applications, 1798.

17. Dye, "Early American Merchant Seafarers," 340.

promise of maritime employment appeal more to men from the countryside of Pennsylvania, New Jersey, New York, Maryland, and even New England than it did to frontiersmen? As population pressure in coastal areas increased throughout the century, and as chances for young men to acquire land diminished correspondingly, farm boys responded more enthusiastically to opportunities in the Quaker City.[18] Compared to the necessity of earning a wage, the quest for adventure probably played a minor role in instigating rural men to move to urban areas.

If the motivations of men who manned the ocean vessels differed from those depicted by Morison, so did the courses of their careers. A few undoubtedly went to the sea from farms, saved their wages, and then returned home to buy land. But a sizable core of mariners, although never promoted to mate or captain, spent a considerable portion of their lives as crewmen, forming a type of permanent deep-sea proletariat. Based on the petitions for seamen's protective certificates, Ira Dye has estimated that at the turn of the century Philadelphia's mariners served before the mast for an average of seven years each.[19] The small proportion of "landsmen" (first-time sailors) among the crews lends support to this estimate, suggesting that it may even err on the conservative side.[20] Thomas Loudon, John Smith, and John Quail, who shipped out of Philadelphia for between two and four decades apiece, counted among the "old salts" who formed the backbone of the city's merchant marines.[21]

A great many seamen were African-Americans, especially during the 1790s when they accounted for as many as one of every five crewmen. Three-quarters of the vessels clearing the port contained at least one black crewman, frequently the cook, the lowest paid of all hands except the cabin boy.[22] A few ships, such as the schooner *Harriet* bound for St. Croix in 1799, were manned entirely by slave laborers overseen by a white master and mate.[23] The great majority of black mariners, however, were either manumitted or escaped slaves or the sons of free women.

Like their white fellow workers, most African-American seamen had mi-

18. For a discussion of the increasing population density in the countryside surrounding Philadelphia, see James T. Lemon, *The Best Poor Man's Country* (Baltimore, Md., 1972), 93.

19. Dye, "Early American Merchant Seafarers," 338–339. See also Marcus Rediker, "The Anglo-American Seaman as Collective Worker, 1700–1750," in Stephen Innes, ed., *Work and Labor in Early America* (Chapel Hill, N.C., 1988), 257–258.

20. Maritime Records of the Port of Philadelphia, 1789–1860, LC, hereafter cited as Maritime Records. The crew members on ships clearing the port of Philadelphia between the late 1790s and 1860 are listed in these volumes.

21. Daily Occurrences, Apr. 29, 1800; Aug. 24, 1801; and Aug. 29, 1801.

22. On the Ship's Crew Lists, 1803, 24 percent of seamen were black. Blacks accounted for 12 percent of men who applied for a seamen's protective certificate during the late 1790s and 18 percent of applicants during the War of 1812; Protective Certificate Applications.

23. Maritime Records, 1799.

grated to the city. Of the more than fifty black sailors for whom information is available at the turn of the century, only five were native Philadelphians. But unlike their white counterparts, blacks generally came from rural backgrounds. The city attracted most from the hinterlands or adjacent states, while a smaller number moved from the Upper South and New England.[24] Thus, Alexander Giles migrated to the Pennsylvania capital from Kent County, Delaware, where he was born the son of a free black man during the Revolution.[25] Isaac Smith was born a slave in Bucks County, Pennsylvania, sold to William Smith, and manumitted at age twenty-one during the Revolutionary War. He moved to Philadelphia shortly thereafter and sailed out of the port for the rest of the century. Both Randal Shepherd and James Phillips were born free, and they migrated to the city during the 1790s. The child of a free black laborer in Virginia, Shepherd trekked north and began to ship as a seaman when he was eleven. Phillips was born of a free black mother and a white father outside Philadelphia, and at age twenty-seven he saw a maritime occupation as one of the ways he could make a living.[26] A few blacks were born on foreign soil, in the West Indies, Africa, or Portugal, and ended up in Philadelphia by various means. John Aires arrived by a circuitous route. A native of Guinea, he was "in infancy kidnapped by White Ruffians and carried to St. Croix," where he was sold to a Swedish merchant. Granted his freedom at age eighteen, he worked for four years as a sailor out of the West Indies until shipwrecked in 1788. Captain Weekes of Philadelphia saved Aires and brought him to the Quaker City, where he remained at least through the early 1790s.[27]

The chance that black mariners would rise above the rank of common seaman hardly existed: no blacks (except Paul Cuffee) commanded ships or served as officers. Even so, black sailors remained at their jobs for longer periods than did their white counterparts; over 38 percent of the former and only 25 percent of the latter were more than thirty years old.[28] Black males in

24. Fifteen black mariners who shipped out of Philadelphia in 1798 applied for a seamen's protective certificate. Three of them were born in the city, three in the hinterlands, six in the upper South, and two in New England; Protective Certificate Applications. The birthplaces of forty-one black seamen were identified on a random sample of thirty-seven ships sailing from Philadelphia in 1803. Two of them were born in the city, four in the Pennsylvania countryside, eight in New Jersey and Delaware, three in New York, four in New England, thirteen in the upper South, and one each in the West Indies, Guinea, and Portugal; Ship's Crew Lists. See also Gary B. Nash, *Forging Freedom: The Formation of Philadelphia's Black Community, 1720–1840* (Cambridge, Mass., 1988), 134–171.

25. Protective Certificate Applications, 1798.

26. Ibid.

27. Linn and Egle, *Pennsylvania Archives*, 3:91. Ira Dye found similarities in the backgrounds of black seamen, in "Early American Merchant Seafarers," 348–353.

28. Based on my analysis of the Ship's Crew Lists. The extraordinary life of Paul Cuffee is discussed by Sheldon H. Harris, *Paul Cuffee, Black America and the African Return* (New York, 1972).

most agricultural areas had little hope of creating an independent life for themselves as farmers or landowners. Life at sea was an option that many black men, frustrated by racial prejudice and without capital or perhaps even the requisite farming skills, could not afford to pass up. Their opportunities for advancement within the maritime ranks may have been nonexistent, but blacks nonetheless continued to work as mariners since so few other alternatives were available.[29]

This evidence, although rudimentary, suggests a profile of Philadelphia's sailors. Nearly all were migrants. Fleeing racial prejudice, isolation, and the difficulty of life in many agricultural regions, free blacks appeared increasingly among ship's crews after the Revolution; by 1800 they accounted for one out of every five seaman. Relatively few white sailors hailed from the rural countryside, and hardly any from the frontier. Most were the sons of men engaged in nonfarming pursuits in cities and small towns. They possessed few skills, little capital, minimal support from their families, and no promise of a family farm when they came of age. Both whites and blacks often took to the sea because their opportunities at home were limited and their futures bleak. Once in Philadelphia they found that employment as a merchant marine was one way they could earn a living. And many, although aware that the chance for promotion was small, remained at sea for the greater part of their lives.

While information about the background of other laboring people is not as plentiful, it is evident that most men of the lower classes migrated to the city. Among a sample of 406 men married during the 1790s in one church that served laboring people predominantly, the parents of only 20 percent had recently lived in Philadelphia. The parents of another 25 percent resided in various parts of the United States, while slightly more than half of the grooms indicated that their parents were in a foreign country. As would be expected, since single women usually moved less frequently than unmarried men, the brides came preponderantly from America: 43 percent of their parents last lived in Philadelphia, 26 percent in other areas of the union, and 30 percent abroad. Migration thus was an experience shared by the great majority of laboring men and a significant, but lower, proportion of women among the lower classes.[30]

Locating adequate housing constituted one of the first chores laboring people faced after moving to the city. Most crowded into narrow wooden

---

29. Gary B. Nash, "Forging Freedom: The Emancipation Experience in the Northern Seaport Cities, 1775–1820," in Ira Berlin and Ronald Hoffman, eds., *Slavery and Freedom in the Age of the American Revolution* (Charlottesville, Va., 1983), 8.

30. This sample of 406 marriages is drawn from the Marriage Records, Old Swedes Church, 1793, 1794, 1799, and 1800.

Plate 8. Wood-framed houses of laboring people, 726–728 South Front Street, Philadelphia, ca. 1750. Photograph courtesy of Robert Blair St. George.

structures. Typical is Philip Mager, a tailor with a wife and four children, who leased a two-story wooden tenement twelve feet wide and eighteen feet long. Mariner Richard Crips and his family rented a single-story dwelling, eleven feet by fourteen feet, in the northern suburbs. In his two-story wooden box, eighteen feet square, in Harmony Alley, tailor William Smith may have found himself in even more cramped quarters. Like many others in his class, Smith did not have a separate kitchen, so his wife prepared meals in the fireplace, not only for their three children but also for two boarders.[31]

31. These conditions are reconstructed from descriptions of dwellings contained in the U.S. Direct Tax of 1798: South Ward, 26, Form A, reel 2, frame 169; and East Northern Liberties, 43, Form A, reel 3, frames 51, 122, PCA. Occupational information is from Cornelius William

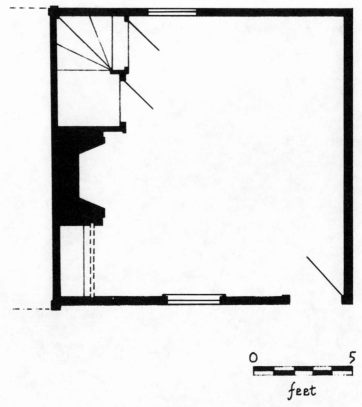

Plate 9. Plan of a single-room house constructed by Robert Moffatt, a waterman, at 33½ Catherine Street, Southwark, Philadelphia, ca. 1790. Drawing courtesy of Robert Blair St. George after the original in the Historic American Building Survey.

Many families saved on expenses by doubling up in houses. Laborer Martin Summers and his family, for example, resided with cordwainer Henry Birkey, his spouse, and three children and divided the rent. With his wife and four young children, Christian Fight shared his abode and lease with fellow shoemaker Christian Nail and his family.[32] Laboring families often took in single men as lodgers. Francis Ravenhill and John Haynes, for instance, lived with laborer George Claypole, his wife, and two children, while William Norman boarded with widow Greenway and her three off-

---

Stafford, *The Philadelphia Directory for 1797* (Philadelphia, 1797), 51, 122, 169. Information on family composition is in the U.S. Census Office, *Return of the Whole Number of Persons within the Several Districts of the United States: Second Census* (Washington, D.C., 1800), reel 8, frames 74, 134; and reel 9, frame 90.
    32. Constables' Returns, 1775, North Ward, PCA.

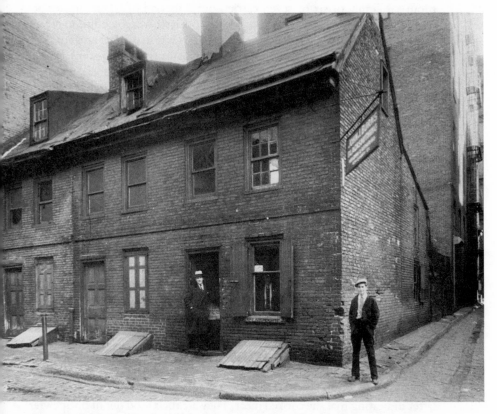

Plate 10. Brick rental units of laboring people, 530–534 Quarry Street, Northern Liberties, Philadelphia, ca. 1760–1780. Photograph courtesy of Robert Blair St. George.

spring.[33] A number of unmarried mariners and laborers roomed in the wooden boarding houses along the Delaware River in the northern part of the city. By contrast to these conditions, wealthier citizens frequently occupied three-story brick houses of comparable width but two or three times as long, with such outbuildings as kitchens, washhouses, and stables. Many owned two-story brick kitchens of a size equal to or greater than most of the dwellings of the lower sort.[34]

In these small confines, often within a room measuring less than two hundred square feet (the approximate size of a modern American living

33. Ibid., 1767, Upper Delaware Ward.
34. Based on the descriptions of houses in U.S. Direct Tax of 1798, High Street Ward, 1, Form A, reel 1, PCA; and in Thomas M. Doerflinger, *A Vigorous Spirit of Enterprise: Merchants and Economic Development in Revolutionary Philadelphia* (Chapel Hill, N.C., 1986), 20–36.

room), a family of six or seven carried out a myriad of commonplace activities, from preparing food to procreating. Such crowded conditions meant that laboring people did not undertake specific tasks in distinct areas of their home, nor did they experience much individual privacy. To some extent, however, a great many poor men and women used their social space in specialized ways. For example, home and work lives were separated for most mariners, stevedores, construction workers, day laborers, journeymen artisans, washerwomen, nurses, and domestic servants, who regularly left their homes to pursue their livelihood.

Laboring Philadelphians provisioned their rooms sparingly. Benjamin Rush, a doctor who worked among the poor, described his visits to their homes during the early 1790s: "Often have I ascended the upper story of these huts by a ladder, and many hundred times have been obliged to rest my weary limbs upon the bedside of the sick (from the want of chairs)."[35] The 1775 inventory of the estate of Jacob Barr, one of the wealthiest laborers in the city, provides a glimpse of the material home life that affluent laboring people must have led.[36] Jacob, his wife Margaret, and their four young daughters resided in a single room containing less than eight pounds (Pennsylvania currency) worth of furniture. They owned two beds, their most valuable possessions, suggesting that Jacob and Margaret slept with their youngest child while the other three daughters occupied the other bed. A chest and table, both made of cheap pine wood, and two old chairs were the only other large items in the room. The parents probably sat in the chairs and the daughters on the chest or floor. Margaret prepared food with an earthen pot, sauce pan, skillet, tea kettle, coffeepot, and a spit and a "flesh iron," the latter indicating that she cooked meat. They ate their food out of one pewter plate and six pitchers, but they did not own any cutlery. Thus they must have drunk stews and soups from the pitchers, and used their hands both to tear apart meat and bread and to eat out of the saucepan and skillet. Their few amenities consisted of a pair of "coarse" sheets, a tablecloth, two rugs, a Bible and several other books, and a "looking glass." But they lacked several items that would have made their lives more pleasant and that routinely appeared in somewhat wealthier households, goods such as candles, spoons, and chamber pots.[37]

35. George W. Corner, ed., *The Autobiography of Benjamin Rush* (Princeton, N.J., 1948), 84.

36. According to the 1772 Provincial Tax List, PCA (hereafter cited as Provincial Tax List), Jacob Barr belonged to the richest decile of laborers. His will is in Will Book Q, p. 117, Wills, Philadelphia County Probate Records, 1683–1901, RW. His estate was inventoried on Mar. 27, 1775, no. 99, Philadelphia County Probate Records, Wills and Inventories of Estate, RW. In addition, Barr's possessions exceed those of most other laboring people for whom inventories of their estates exist.

37. For the ordinary and luxury items owned by inhabitants in other areas of early America, see the excellent studies by Gloria L. Main, "The Standard of Living in Southern New England, 1640–1773," *WMQ*, 3d Ser., 45 (1988), 124–134; and Lois Green Carr and Lorena S. Walsh, "The Standard of Living in the Colonial Chesapeake," ibid., 135–159.

Table 19. Residential segregation in Philadelphia, 1772–1798

Tax bracket (%)	Index of dissimilarity		
	1772	1789	1798
1–20	9.4	21.1	24.8
21–40	14.7	21.2	27.0
41–60	9.0	13.3	19.2
61–80	6.4	8.6	24.8
81–100	11.3	11.5	22.4

Source: 1772, 1789, and 1798 Provincial Tax Lists, PCA.

The quarters occupied by laboring people grew more cramped as real estate values escalated during the second half of the century. Because Philadelphia was a city where all but the richest citizens relied on walking, the greatest monetary worth was attached to property near the main market and primary business section in the center of town. As a consequence, residential segregation by economic categories began to take shape. During those five decades, residents behaved as if Philadelphia rotated on an axis running through the eastern end of High Street in the middle of the city. The laws of motion affected the various classes differentially: centrifugal force dispersed poor folk to the perimeter, while centripetal force propelled wealthier ones to the core. By 1800 laborers and mariners congregated in the northern, southern, and western areas of the city, while most of the rich concentrated around several of the eastern blocks of High Street near the Delaware River. The outline of the classic preindustrial urban residential pattern—concentric rings radiating from a nucleus of wealthy people through bands of successively poorer ones—became recognizable in the Pennsylvania capital by century's end. Yet this configuration did not completely crystallize. While the lower sort dominated Philadelphia's periphery and suburbs, many of them continued to inhabit the center city region, crowding primarily into cheap shelter in alleys, courts, and lanes and leaving the major thoroughfares to the middling and better sort of citizens.[38]

38. Other scholars have found somewhat similar residential patterns emerging in Philadelphia. See Richard G. Miller, *Philadelphia—The Federalist City: A Study of Urban Politics, 1789–1810* (Port Washington, N.Y., 1976), 6–12; Norman J. Johnston, "Caste and Class of the Urban Form of Historic Philadelphia," *Journal of the American Institute of Planners,* 32 (1966), 334–350; and Thomas Samuel Gentry, Jr., "Specialized Residential and Business Districts: Philadelphia in an Age of Change, 1785–1800" (Master's thesis, Montana State University, 1988). According to Doerflinger, few merchants lived on minor lanes or in alleys, in *Vigorous Spirit of Enterprise,* 40. The spatial patterns of preindustrial cities are discussed by Gideon Sjoberg, *The Preindustrial City, Past and Present* (Glencoe, Ill., 1960), 95–102; Allan Pred, *Urban Growth and the Circulation of Information: The U.S. System of Cities, 1790–1840* (Cambridge, Mass., 1973); and Betsy Blackmar, "Re-walking the 'Walking City': Housing and Property Relations in New York City, 1780–1840," *Radical History Review,* 21 (1979), 131–148.

A statistical analysis of Philadelphia's residential pattern reveals the extent of these changes in the housing arrangements of the lower sort during the last quarter of the century. The "index of dissimilarity" measures the degree to which a group of people clustered in specific areas of the city.[39] In Table 19, the larger the index number, the greater the residential segregation. The residential segregation of every group of taxpayers, particularly the poorest 40 percent, increased between 1772 and 1798. The bottom 40 percent of taxpayers spread relatively evenly throughout the city on the eve of the Revolution, but many of them moved to areas more exclusively composed of low-rent housing during the next quarter century. The poorest shifted in two directions: to the riverfront sections of Upper and Lower Delaware wards and to the eastern midcity region of Middle ward (see Appendix G). The 21-to-40 percent bracket clustered in greater numbers in the city's northern and southern extremities of Mulberry and Dock wards. The pace of residential segregation accelerated during the 1790s, especially among wealthy taxpayers. As poor Philadelphians congregated in the southern and northern perimeters, affluent families found housing in the center city.[40] The lines of demarcation between the homes of the poor and those of the rich that were evident before the Revolution became more distinct by 1789, and segregation grew more apparent during the last decade of the century.

During the second half of the century, laboring Philadelphians gradually moved to more crowded as well as more homogeneous neighborhoods than previously inhabited, at least in terms of the economic characteristics of residents. The ratio of taxpayers to houses increased in the poor wards between 1750 and 1790.[41] In Mulberry ward, one of the poorest in the city, the number of houses rose at an annual rate of 2.5 percent, while taxpayers expanded by 3.1 percent each year. Simultaneously, both houses and taxpayers grew at the same pace (.4 percent annually) in Walnut ward, an area of

39. The index of dissimilarity measures the average deviation within wards of the percentage of a specific group from its mean percentage in the total population. For the method of construction of the index, see Karl E. and Alma F. Taeuber, *Negroes in Cities: Residential Segregation and Neighborhood Change* (Chicago, 1965), 235–237. A further discussion of the meaning of the index is in Sam Bass Warner, Jr., *The Private City: Philadelphia in Three Periods of Its Growth* (Philadelphia, 1968), 226–227.

40. See Appendix G. Doerflinger discovered that merchants moved inland, away from the waterfront during this period, in *Vigorous Spirit of Enterprise*, 40.

41. Between 1772 and 1789 the population density of most wards in the middle of the city remained relatively constant, but the population density of wards on the fringes of the city, where most of the lower sort lived, generally increased. Thus, the number of taxpayers per house grew by nearly one-half in Mulberry ward, one-third in Lower Delaware ward, and three-fourths in Upper Delaware ward. The numbers of houses are given in John F. Watson, *Annals of Philadelphia, and Pennsylvania, in the Olden Times* . . . , 3 vols. (Philadelphia, 1881), 2:404–407. The number of taxables in 1772 and 1789 are from counts of the 1772 and 1789 Provincial Tax Lists. See Appendix B.

affluence.[42] Judged by the increasing population density, the quality of life in lower-class neighborhoods must have deteriorated. Compared to earlier conditions, a greater number of confined streets, more small alleys, and houses built closer together meant more cramped quarters, increasingly unsanitary conditions, and higher incidences of disease.

Eighteenth-century Philadelphia enjoyed a reputation for civic-minded projects—many of them initiated or inspired by Benjamin Franklin—that created clean, paved streets lined with brick footpaths, public water pumps and oil lamps, and regular patrols by constables. Some of the major avenues exhibited these attributes, but they were uncommon elsewhere in the city. The municipal government spent relatively little money physically developing and providing services to poor neighborhoods on the fringes of town or in the alleyways. In laboring-class neighborhoods streets generally went unpaved, watchmen made rounds sporadically, scavengers appeared infrequently, and mounds of garbage fed a multitude of pigs, chickens, dogs, rats, and vermin.[43]

Laboring people often lived a hand-to-mouth existence, struggling to maximize their family income and to cut the cost of basic necessities. Diseases, epidemics, injuries, business cycles, political turmoil, wars, and seasonal unemployment could create times of personal financial crisis for the lower sort. Although most managed to make ends meet without regular outside assistance, a considerable number at some point during their residence in the city found themselves mired in poverty, occasionally pushed below the subsistence level. What were their circumstances and how did they respond during periods of difficulty?

Poor Philadelphians sometimes resorted to an illegitimate economy, occasionally stealing essential provisions. During the 1790s, robberies accounted for as much as 80 percent of crimes, committed primarily by African-American and Irish immigrants, the poorest residents in the city. They frequently pilfered such items as a pair of shoes, a coat, a pound of meat or

42. Mulberry ward contained 488 and 1,343 houses in 1749 and 1790, respectively, and 309 and 1,372 taxpayers in 1741 and 1789, respectively. During the same years, houses in Walnut ward increased from 104 to 125, and taxpayers grew from 98 to 102. The number of houses in 1749 and taxables in 1741 are given in Watson, *Annals of Philadelphia*, 2:404–407, 3:236. The number of houses in 1790 is from Benjamin Davies, *Some Account of the City of Philadelphia* . . . (Philadelphia, 1794), 17. Taxables in 1789 are from my analysis of the 1789 Provincial Tax List.

43. John K. Alexander, *Render Them Submissive: Responses to Poverty in Philadelphia, 1760–1800* (Amherst, Mass., 1980), 19–24. On pigs rooting in the streets, see J. P. Briscot De Warville, *New Travels in the United States of America, 1788*, ed. and trans. Durand Escheverria and Mara Soceanu (Cambridge, Mass, 1964), 201. Streets in poor neighborhoods are described in Kenneth Roberts and Anna M. Roberts, eds., *Moreau de St. Mery's American Journey* [1793–1798] (Garden City, N.Y., 1947), 260.

sugar, or a chicken, indicating their pressing need for the necessities of life.[44] Barney Mullin numbered among many mariners who cheated their employers out of wages, although his circumstances may not have been monetarily desperate. After signing on with "the Captain of a Schooner going to the West Indies," Mullin "received a months-pay advance." But "instead of going on board according to agreement, he secreted himself upon the top of a Stack of Chimnies of a three Story House in Callowhill Street, to avoid Sailing in said Schooner." He celebrated his deception a bit too enthusiastically, however, and "tired and groggy, he laid himself across the Chimnies, on his belly, [and] went fast to sleep." At "about two of the Clock he fell from the top of said Chimnies into the street; and was taken to his Lodgings . . . in a Mutilated condition."[45]

Families in dire financial straits sometimes bound out their young children, who, because they usually could not earn their keep, posed an economic burden on the household. Shoemaker William Niles apprenticed his eight-year-old son to a fellow cordwainer, while Edward Burman, a laborer, indentured his boy when he was but ten. The Overseers of the Poor often bound out the offspring of impoverished families, as was the case for one of the three children of James Barry and his wife.[46]

When their attempts to balance their household budget failed, laboring families turned to kin, friends, and the community for support. The almshouse released mariner Richard Crosby, a rheumatic sailor, when he "met with a Friend who offered him some light employment which he Hopes he may be able to stand." Most almshouse inmates, such as shoemakers John Sherridan and John Chatham, entered the institution "destitute of friends," suggesting that during times of financial distress poor Philadelphians would, if possible, depend first on friends for aid.[47] But in a city populated with immigrants who had left relatives and friends far behind, and where the inhabitants were highly mobile, laboring folk must have had few others on whom they could rely. Moreover, friends and neighbors could contribute only so much during extended periods of unemployment or illness.

A host of private organizations aided people suffering misfortune. Various ethnic groups founded such philanthropic associations as the Deutsche

44. These crimes are evident in G. S. Rowe and Billy G. Smith, "The Prisoners for Trial Docket for Philadelphia County, 1795," *PH*, 53 (1986), 289–319. Also see Alexander, *Render Them Submissive*, 127–128.

45. Daily Occurrences, Sept. 18, 1801. Similar cases appear in Rowe and Smith, "Prisoners for Trial Docket."

46. Niles and Burman appear in The Account of Servants and Apprentices Bound before John Gibson, Dec. 5, 1772 to May 21, 1773, HSP. The entry on Barry is in Daily Occurrences, Nov. 2, 1792. See also Indentures, 1751–1797, Guardians of the Poor, PCA.

47. Daily Occurrences: entry on Crosby, May 28, 1796; entries on Sherridan and Chatham, June 3, June 16, 1800, respectively.

Gesellschaft von Pennsylvanien, the Society of the Sons of St. George, the Friendly Sons of St. Patrick, and the Sons of King Tammany to assist poor citizens.[48] Many religious denominations likewise solicited funds and their ministers regularly preached "charity sermons" for the distressed.[49] After many attempts to establish a permanent system for providing cheap firewood, a privately financed endowment was created in 1793 to supply fuel to the needy. And at the end of the century, private financing opened the first soup kitchens for the poor.[50]

Philadelphians in need could petition for two types of public aid. An outrelief system provided food, clothing, fuel, and other essentials and allowed the recipients to live in their own houses. Thus, when Samuel Cryndal and his family—new arrivals without kin or friends in the city—fell on hard times, they initially subsisted "on only what Charitable Well disposed People pleased to give" them. Eventually, though, Cryndal was "obliged to apply to the Overseers of the City, for wood to keep Himself and his Family from Perishing in the Cold."[51] The outrelief program functioned throughout the second half of the century, reaching its peak during the yellow fever epidemic of 1793 when the evacuation of the city disrupted the economy and threw many people out of work. During the last half alone of October 1793, public officials distributed over 4,000 loaves of bread, 500 fowls, 5 calves, 50 sheep, 5 carts of vegetables, 150 cords of wood, and 1,750 dollars to nearly 2,000 families, or about 25 percent of the residents remaining in the city.[52]

Only complete destitution could convince some people to apply for institutional relief. A few, such as the Sorrees, a "poor modest family," were too proud to accept charity and "rather than apply for relief would suffer accordingly."[53] Many individuals forewent assistance for long periods rather than endure the prisonlike atmosphere of the almshouse and workhouse. Some parents resisted in order to protect their children. Disregarding Isabella Johnson's objections, for example, the Guardians of the Poor indentured her three-year-old daughter because Isabella was pregnant, abandoned by her husband, and destitute. When Johnson discovered her daughter's master in the city and seized her child "by force," the authorities jailed her and bound her child to a farmer in Delaware, far from Isabella's reach.[54]

48. Gary B. Nash, "Poverty and Poor Relief in Pre-Revolutionary Philadelphia," *WMQ*, 3d Ser., 33 (1976), 23–24.
49. See, for example, *Independent Gazette* (Philadelphia), Dec. 12, 1785.
50. Alexander, *Render Them Submissive*, 198–199.
51. Records of Pennsylvania's Revolutionary Governments, Clemency File, 1775–1790, Record Group 27, roll 37, frames 1242–1243, PHMC, hereafter cited as Clemency File.
52. *Federal Gazette, and Philadelphia Daily Advertiser* (Philadelphia), Nov. 2, 1793.
53. Minutes, Overseers of the Poor, Jan. 25, 1773, PCA, hereafter cited as Minutes.
54. Daily Occurrences, Aug. 16, Nov. 3, 1800.

We can learn a great deal about people who sought relief from a rich collection of late eighteenth-century institutional records. These registers act as a camera, the shutter opening and closing as the clerks made notations to expose brief glimpses of the lives of indigents as they entered the almshouse, received medical care at the hospital or dispensary, applied for outrelief from the Overseers, or fell into the hands of the watchmen. To begin to understand the variety of experiences of the poor, we need to categorize and examine a number of individual cases.[55]

While ostensibly designed to serve the needs of the elderly, widowed, orphaned, and infirm primarily, the turn-of-the-century almshouse contained relatively few inmates belonging to the first three categories (see Table 20).[56] Slightly more than half of the admittees suffered some ailment. However, many if not most applicants feigned sickness to qualify for the almshouse since the Guardians of the Poor generally did not accept unemployment as sufficient grounds to grant admission. "Sore legs" thus reached epidemic proportions among many able-bodied people who were without work, a charade recognized by both the paupers and the managers.[57] New adult inmates divided equally between the sexes. Nearly one-third of the women were pregnant or afflicted with venereal disease, many of them prostitutes who found ready employment in a port city filled with itinerant men. Another 6 percent of adult females, deserted or physically abused by their husbands, could not earn a living wage. Because the Guardians often indentured them before they reached the almshouse, children accounted for only one-fifth of the admittees. Nearly 40 percent of minors were orphaned, abandoned, or committed when their parents were jailed; one-third accompanied their mother or father into the institution, and 15 percent required assistance because their parents could not support them.[58]

55. The following picture of the needy is sketched primarily from descriptions of individuals who found refuge in the almshouse, workhouse, or hospital. People who avoided these establishments, who required only limited or temporary help, or who generally maintained their health are underrepresented in the surviving records. See also Billy G. Smith, "Poverty and Economic Marginality in Eighteenth-Century America," *Proceedings of the APS*, 132 (1988), 85–118; and Priscilla Ferguson Clement, *Welfare and the Poor in the Nineteenth-Century City: Philadelphia, 1800–1854* (London, 1985).

56. This differs with James A. Henretta's view that "many of the 'poor' in the colonial ports consisted . . . of the old, the young, and the widowed," in "Wealth and Social Structure," in Jack P. Greene and J. R. Pole, eds., *Colonial British America: Essays in the New History of the Early Modern Era* (Baltimore, Md., 1984), 278.

57. Comments by the almshouse clerks indicate that they were cognizant of this subterfuge. Robert Nesbit, Jr., "a notorious, worthless chap," according to the clerk, joined many other admittees with the "usual" complaint of "sore legs"; Daily Occurrences, Nov. 18, 1800. See also Raymond A. Mohl, *Poverty in New York, 1783–1825* (New York, 1971), 82.

58. My analyses of a sample of 1,400 inmates who appeared in an index of the almshouse between 1796 and 1803, and of a sample of 564 inmates recorded in the censuses of the almshouse taken between 1807 and 1810, reveal similar demographic patterns in the division between the sexes and in the proportion of adults and children. See Admissions and Discharges,

Table 20. Admittees to Philadelphia's almshouse, 1800–1801

Reason for admittance	Adult men (%)	Adult women (%)	Children (%)	Total (%)
Old	5.9	8.3		5.7
Sick	66.2	38.0		43.1
Venereal disease	9.0	16.1		10.2
Alcoholic	3.6	3.9		3.1
Deranged	9.0	2.4		4.8
Poor, destitute	3.2	8.8		4.8
Pregnant		13.7		5.4
Physically abused		1.0	2.1	.8
Deserted by husband		4.9		1.9
Deserted by parents			12.6	2.3
Orphan			10.5	1.9
To be bound out			2.1	.4
Parents cannot support			14.7	2.7
Committed with parents			32.6	5.9
Parents in jail			16.8	3.1
Miscellaneous	3.2	2.9	8.4	4.0

Source: Daily Occurrences Docket, June 20, 1800 to June 20, 1801, Guardians of the Poor, PCA.

Note: These tabulations include 895 individuals (380 adult men, 352 adult women, and 163 children) who entered the almshouse between June 20, 1800 and June 20, 1801.

Even if scenes of massive misery did not afflict Philadelphia as they did London and Paris, many indigents in the Pennsylvania capital experienced appalling conditions by any standards, lacking adequate food, clothing, and shelter to prevent their physical deterioration and premature demise. In 1776 the almshouse managers disclosed that "most" of the unfortunates admitted during the past year were "naked, helpless and emaciated with Poverty and Disease to such a Degree, that some have died in a few Days after their Admission."[59] Thomas Peters was one of many who arrived at the almshouse "in a naked, starved and ragged condition, and running away with Vermin, insomuch that they stript him and shaved his head and put clean clothes on him." Elizabeth Deford suffered from venereal disease "and almost deprivation of the use of limbs by being exposed to a Street lodging in the night, not having the wherewith to lay her head."[60] She died from her afflictions. "Having no place of abode and living for some time past in the Stables," Nancy, a black woman, was charged with vagrancy.[61] The watch-

Index, 1785–1827, Guardians of the Poor, PCA, hereafter cited as Admissions and Discharges; and Almshouse Census, 1807–1810, Guardians of the Poor, PCA.

59. *Pennsylvania Gazette* (Philadelphia), May 29, 1776.
60. Daily Occurrences, Nov. 20, Aug. 28, 1800.
61. Vagrancy Docket, Dec. 30, 1796, PCA, hereafter cited as Vagrancy Docket.

men carried John Griffin, a laborer in the city for twenty-seven years, to the almshouse in a cart since he "has had no nourishment for this week past, slept at night in any hole or corner he could creep to, . . . not being able to walk, and being very dirty and swarming with bodily vermin."[62]

"Old age" accounted for relatively few institutionalized paupers since it did not automatically qualify a person for relief. William Wooten migrated from England when he was seventy-eight and then spent the next seven years "striving to make a living by picking and gathering of rags." Not until he was "feeble and unable to contribute towards his support by that or any other way of employment" did the managers allow him in the house.[63] Alice Edleston, aged and destitute, solicited alms at the main city market. But her aggressive approach, "cursing and abusing those who refuse her charity," drew her a jail term rather than community support.[64]

Having slipped below the subsistence level, many laboring people found it nearly impossible to climb out of the abyss of poverty. Thus, John Barret, a baker, was "in and out [of the almshouse] as often as the number of his fingers and toes."[65] When shoemaker John Cribbin died an indigent in the almshouse, he followed the tradition established by his father and older brother.[66] And Mary Gallagher, her daughter, and grandchildren all entered the almshouse at some point during their lives.[67]

Women of the lower classes suffered similar hardships as men, and, as in modern America, they undoubtedly endured poverty more often. Twice as many females as males applied to the Overseers of the Poor for aid during the years preceding the Revolution.[68] If their spouse died, left, grew ill, landed in jail, or took jobs in other areas, married women and widows carried an enormous economic burden, especially if they had young children. When her spouse succumbed to yellow fever, Sarah Campbell washed clothes to make ends meet. But within two years Campbell and her three children sought refuge in the almshouse, "the Mother not being able to support herself and the Children." The Guardians of the Poor apprenticed Sarah's six-year-old daughter to learn housewifery in a household in New Jersey, and her eight-year-old son to a cordwainer in the Northern Liberties. Sarah and her youngest child were discharged at the year's end, but they intermittently

62. Daily Occurrences, June 6, 1801.
63. Daily Occurrences, July 17, 1800.
64. Prisoners for Trial Docket, Philadelphia County Prison, 1798, p. 42, PCA.
65. Daily Occurrences, Dec. 12, 1800.
66. Burial Records, Dec. 17, 1825, Old Swedes Church, Gloria Dei, GSP, hereafter cited as Burial Records, Old Swedes Church.
67. Daily Occurrences, Sept. 21, 1804.
68. Minutes, 1768–1774. Since the almshouse adult inmates were equally divided by gender at the end of the century, it appears that the Overseers more readily institutionalized men than women.

received aid for the next decade and a half. Deserted by her husband, Elizabeth McIntire, forty years old, was "not capable to provide for herself."[69] While her husband was at sea, Jane Riley's infant died for want of milk, "the mother being obliged to hire herself out as a wet nurse, and to put him out."[70]

Single women often fared little better. Two sisters, Susannah and Sarah Ward, successfully ran a grocery in Philadelphia for a decade and a half.[71] But most other women were not so fortunate. After working for seventeen years as a maid in the city, Rosannah Where found that she could no longer make ends meet. Ann Bright, apparently in complete despair, agreed to bind herself out for three years of indentured service. When Matthias Clay, a member of Congress, impregnated Mary Berry but refused to take responsibility for his deed, she had little choice when her "lying in" period arrived but to apply to the almshouse.[72]

Many new arrivals, not fully recovered from the ocean voyage, turned to immigrant aid societies for immediate help. Few suffered disasters worse than the Edwards family, who landed from Wales in 1800. When her husband failed to survive the New World diseases, Bridget, "destitute of the means of supporting herself" and her four daughters, eventually took refuge in the almshouse. Within a month, one daughter died and the Overseers indentured her four-year-old twins. Edwards and her infant gained their freedom half a year later.[73] Still, while overseas and rural migrants appear in the vagrancy dockets and hospital registries, new arrivals did not constitute the major portion of the institutionalized poor. At the turn of the century, almshouse inmates who had not been born in Philadelphia had resided in the city for an average of eleven years.[74]

Like others in their circumstances, Henry and Ruth Kendah developed a

69. Daily Occurrences: entries on Campbell, Nov. 1, Dec. 8, 16, 1800; entry on McIntire, Dec. 23, 1803. Many women apprenticed their children at young ages because they could not support them. See Indentures, 1751–1797, and Indenture Papers and Bonds, 1795–1799, Guardians of the Poor, PCA.

70. Burial Records, Old Swedes Church, July 16, 1802.

71. The Wards appear in Francis White, *The Philadelphia Directory* (Philadelphia, 1785); Clement Biddle, *The Philadelphia Directory* (Philadelphia, 1791); Cornelius William Stafford, *The Philadelphia Directory for 1800* (Philadelphia, 1800); the U.S. Bureau of the Census, *Heads of Families of the First Census of the United States Taken in the Year 1790: Pennsylvania* (Washington, D.C., 1908); and the U.S. Census Office, *Return of the Whole Number of Persons within the Several Districts of the United States: Second Census* (Washington, D.C., 1800).

72. Daily Occurrences: entry on Where, Oct. 8, 1800; entry on Bright, June 2, 1790; and entry on Berry, Oct. 6, 1800.

73. Daily Occurrences, Nov. 29, 1800; Jan. 5, 8, 1801; Admissions and Discharges, 1801.

74. This is based on my analysis of new admissions to the institution during 1800 and 1801. That immigration did not play the predominant role in creating poverty is evident in Philadelphia in the 1740s and 1750s, when thousands of Germans arrived in the city but the level of indigence remained relatively low.

welfare strategy that combined seasonal employment and public aid. "Frequent Customers" of Philadelphia's almshouse, according to the clerk, Henry and Ruth were

> most Notorious Strolling Ramblers generally known from Boston to Baltimore. . . . They appear to have scarce any Necessary Cloathing. But are very artful in appearances, frequently leaving their cloathes & other property at different places through the Country & though they may have Money, came here in such wretched plight & swarming with Vermin so as immediately to extort clothing. They are both lame & both subject to Fits, of which they frequently avail themselves, in appearance, which with their wretched plight extorts Commiseration and Charity.[75]

The lower sort could exercise one final option in their attempt to earn a decent living: they could migrate in search of employment. John and Esther Dougherty and their three children moved to the city from Logtown, Delaware, in 1799 so that John might practice his craft of shoemaking. Within six months, however, he was on the road again, this time in search of employment in New York City, while his family languished in the almshouse. Daniel Seaman was a native Philadelphian, but he roamed for over twenty years, laboring in New York and other states before finally returning to the Quaker City.[76]

The petitions for Revolutionary War pensions provide clues to the fate of many itinerant members of the four occupational groups. Rarely did they remain in Philadelphia for their entire lives. Only one petitioner, John Abel, resided in the city when he applied for his pension in the nineteenth century. He stayed there until his death in 1833. Others radiated out of Philadelphia in various directions. Weaver James Brown, whose story begins this chapter, returned to Connecticut after the Revolution and then moved to Ontario County, New York, before his death in 1815. John Hutchinson died in the same New York county as Brown after first having lived in York County, Pennsylvania. Mariner Daniel McDonald followed a southern route. Born in Scotland in 1757, he migrated to Philadelphia before the Revolution, fought in the war, lived in the city until 1795 when he again enlisted in the army, was discharged in Georgia, and finally settled in South Carolina. After a brief southern excursion, William Miller, a tailor, headed west. He joined the Revolutionary army in Philadelphia at the beginning of the war. Miller was about to quit after five years' service, but, stirred by a speech delivered by General Anthony Wayne, he reenlisted for the duration. After the war he moved to Virginia, where he married Rebecca, and then on to Kentucky in

75. Daily Occurrences, July 28, 1789.
76. Daily Occurrences, Aug. 23, Nov. 10, 1800.

the early 1790s. Miller's widow continued the westward migration after his death in 1811, and she subsequently filed for a pension as the widow of a Revolutionary War soldier from Park County, Indiana. Laborer John Murphy could not decide which direction to go, so first he moved east, to Trenton, New Jersey, then west, to Bucks County, Pennsylvania, where he died a poor farmhand.[77]

Many poor Philadelphians must have paid a severe price for their peripatetic existence, especially since surrounded by a society that placed considerable value on family, neighbors, and community. The stories of three cordwainers who left the city illustrate the impact of their itinerant experience on their lives. John Smith trekked steadily south, first to Baltimore and then to Virginia. By 1820, he, like many other of his Revolutionary War compatriots, found himself "in reduced circumstances, and . . . in need of the assistance of his country for support." John McKinney and Jacob Hood faced similar predicaments. Half a century after he fought for his country's independence, McKinney's assets totaled $160 and his debts nearly twice that amount. He filed for a pension not simply because "by reason of age and infirmities I am not able to pursue [my] occupation," but also because his "wife had long since been dead and my children have all left me," so he had no other means of support. In 1825 Jacob Hood lived in East Tennessee without a wife, children, or kin of any kind, and, aside from his wearing apparel, he had "nothing earthly over which to claim ownership." "I am," he lamented, "cast among strangers," a burden to those who knew him not. The condition of Smith, McKinney, and Hood reflects not only the poverty but also the isolation that surely marked the lives of many of those who left Philadelphia as well as of others who stayed behind in an immigrant city filled with strangers.[78]

Transience marked the lives of most laboring Philadelphians. Many laborers moved with the seasons to take advantage of changing employment opportunities; some journeymen and lesser artisans tramped in an orbit connecting cities, towns, villages, and the countryside to make and peddle their wares; and mariners sailed from port to port to earn their living. Job opportunities and the chance to earn a decent competency attracted many of the lower sort to the Quaker City from urban and sometimes rural areas of Europe and America. They frequently fled backgrounds of near poverty,

77. These vignettes are based on the following Revolutionary War Pensions: John Abel, R9; James Brown, W15879; James Hutchinson, S44945; Daniel McDonald, S9426; William Miller, W9539; and John Murphy, W3290.

78. Revolutionary War Pensions: John Smith, S38380; John McKinney, S41858; and Jacob Hood, S38841.

families who could not provide security in the form of land or jobs, and futures with little promise. After the Revolution, blacks, envisioning the city primarily as a refuge, joined the migration stream. Escaped slaves hoped to blend in with the growing African-American population in Philadelphia, while many free blacks sought to trade the racial prejudice and limited prospects of the countryside for opportunities to make a living and build a community with others of their race.

Once having moved to the city, laboring families discovered themselves quartered spartanly. They often packed into one or two small rooms and shared houses with boarders and other families. They usually owned few home furnishings and hardly any conveniences or luxuries. At midcentury, they rented shelter in streets and alleys spread throughout the city. But during the next fifty years, poor citizens were increasingly relegated to areas of high population density on the city's fringes—the most crowded, odoriferous, unsightly, and unsanitary neighborhoods. Still, residential patterns did not completely assume the partition of housing by class evident in modern American urban centers. Eighteenth-century Philadelphians instead recognized a different segregation model. At the end of the century, most poor people inhabited blocks on the urban periphery, but they continued to live, albeit in smaller numbers, in the alleys and lanes behind grand houses in the center of the city. Meanwhile, the most affluent citizens occupied homes lining the major downtown avenues. Growing residential segregation thus matched increasing inequality in the distribution of wealth during the second half of the century.

Many migrants undoubtedly enjoyed considerable material success, and, given their austere background, even modest accomplishments might have satisfied most. But the efforts of a great many other lesser-skilled Philadelphians met with frustration and failure. They adopted a variety of strategies to cope with their inability to sustain themselves. A few stole what they needed, some parents apprenticed their children prematurely, and others appealed to their kin and friends for support.

People in distress also turned to private and public welfare in great number. In 1772, for example, one-quarter of the city's mariners, laborers, sawyers, and carters, one-sixth of the cordwainers, and one-eighth of the tailors, weavers, and breech makers received poor relief. This group of laboring people comprised the major proportion of the impoverished throughout the later part of the century.[79] Fearing the stigma attached to poverty and a loss of control over their lives, men and women often shied

79. Smith, "Poverty and Economic Marginality," 96–99; Alexander, *Render Them Submissive*, 11–25; Gary B. Nash, "Up from the Bottom in Franklin's Philadelphia," *Past and Present*, no. 77 (1977), 57–83; and Gary B. Nash, Billy G. Smith, and Dirk Hoerder, "Laboring Americans and the American Revolution," *Labor History*, 24 (1983), 421–425, 434–439.

away from public aid until their circumstances became desperate. Those who applied for outrelief may have fared best since they continued to maintain much of their independence. Still, the poor law forced such paupers to wear a "P" sewn on their clothing to designate their dependent status. Many in penury strenuously resisted entering the almshouse or workhouse, realizing that such actions entailed relinquishing authority over their lives to the officials in charge of the institution.[80]

For numerous migrants, Philadelphia represented but one stop among many in their continuous search for subsistence. Some, especially those who became mired in poverty, must have experienced the feelings of isolation and atomization that often accompany itinerancy and big-city life. Others must have despaired at finding themselves, like Jacob Hood, "cast among strangers" in an immigrant port populated by newcomers. Having abandoned their parents, siblings, communities, and networks of kin and friends, they entered a city that contained few relatives or acquaintances and found housing in neighborhoods where residents constantly moved in and out. Fear of urban life may have intensified their sense of unease. John Edgworth, for example, came to Philadelphia "unacquainted with the wiles and Cunning of such Rogues as are about it," and he naturally suspected a citizenry who were "all Strangers."[81] Some newcomers, particularly those from urban backgrounds, must have adjusted quickly, and they may even have enjoyed the anonymity of city life. But a great many others may have continued to feel like misfits in a city where the "sense of community" valued by most early Americans was difficult to establish.

80. The relevant poor laws are in James T. Mitchell and Henry Flanders, comps., *The Statutes at Large of Pennsylvania from 1682 to 1801*, 18 vols. (Philadelphia and Harrisburg, Pa., 1896–1911), 3:224–225, 8:95. On the resistance of urban women even to labor in an institutional environment, see Gary B. Nash, "The Failure of Female Factory Labor in Colonial Boston," *Labor History*, 20 (1979), 165–188.

81. Clemency File, 1775–1790, Record Group 27, roll 38, frame 642.

Chapter Seven

Family Lives

Divorce [in Philadelphia] is obtained with scandalous ease. From this alone one can judge the extent of loose habits.
—Moreau de St. Mery, 1798

Abraham Smith . . . formerly Slave to a certain Widow Smith well known in this City . . . contracted for the Purchase of his Freedom; and afterwards by Purchase redeemed his Wife from Slavery . . . and brought up a Family of Children.
—Testimony on Abraham Smith,
Pennsylvania Abolition Society, 1787

THE UNCERTAINTY AND INSTABILITY that marked the material existence of laboring Philadelphians extended to their family lives as well, influencing the size and composition of their households and the nature of their intimate interpersonal relationships. Many historians have argued that during the eighteenth century family life in America began a long period of transition from a "traditional" form often associated with agrarian societies to a "modern" configuration more characteristic of industrialized nations.[1] Thus, the concerns of the individual waxed as the needs of their family waned, relationships based on "love" gradually supplanted the authoritarian power exercised by many males over their households, some couples started to curtail their fertility, and women, confined to the home, increasingly became the primary parents who cared for and socialized the children. Poor Philadelphians of the late eighteenth century commonly lived in ways that resembled modern more than traditional families, but their lives still do not

1. The vast literature on this subject is synthesized in Robert V. Wells, *Revolutions in Americans' Lives* (Westport, Conn., 1982); and Wells, *Uncle Sam's Family* (Albany, N.Y., 1985). See also Daniel Blake Smith, "The Study of the Family in Early America: Trends, Problems, and Prospects," *WMQ*, 3d Ser., 39 (1982), 3–28. Lawrence Stone finds these changes occurred earlier in England, primarily among the upper classes, in *The Family, Sex, and Marriage in England, 1500–1800* (New York, 1977).

fit neatly into either of these two categories. Instead they developed structures and relationships that reflected their own prevailing circumstances and needs.

This chapter examines two areas of the family experiences of white laboring people. Initially, the size and composition of their households are analyzed and described with a sizable amount of quantifiable data. The nature of interpersonal relations among family members, a much more elusive topic addressed by fewer extant records, is next considered. The family lives of free blacks are then discussed.

Three important factors that helped shape the family lives of laboring Philadelphians warrant brief review. First, the great majority of these workers had migrated to the city, leaving most kin behind. Second, high birth and death rates, an age structure skewed toward the young (particularly those in their child-bearing years), and an unbalanced gender ratio characterized the Quaker City. In 1800, the first date for which figures are available, more than a third of free whites were younger than sixteen, and half were between sixteen and forty-four years old. At the same time, men outnumbered women by eleven to ten in the latter age bracket.[2] The city's age and gender imbalances undoubtedly were even more skewed when itinerants disembarked at the docks in large numbers during the closing decades of the colonial era.[3] Third, since the earnings of all members of laboring families were needed to make ends meet, men could not exercise complete economic leverage over their wives and children.

Before forming families, young adults rarely established their own households. Between 12 and 20 percent of the city's males were unmarried at any one time, many of whom boarded with families who needed the rent to supplement their income.[4] Surprisingly few journeymen resided in the homes of their masters, reducing their employer's control over their private

<hr/>

2. These figures are from the U.S. Census Office, *Return of the Whole Number of Persons within the Several Districts of the United States: Second Census* (Washington, D.C., 1800), hereafter cited as *Second Census*.

3. Since much of the migration to Philadelphia was comprised of family groups, the surplus of males over females in the city did not grow excessively large, as it did, for example, in the seventeenth-century Chesapeake region. Most German migrants, for instance, traveled as families during the pre-Revolutionary period. See Ralph Beaver Strassburger and William John Hinke, *Pennsylvania German Pioneers: A Publication of the Original Lists of Arrivals in the Port of Philadelphia from 1727 to 1808*, Pennsylvania-German Society Publications nos. 42–44 (Norristown, Pa., 1934); and Marianne Wokeck, "The Flow and the Composition of German Immigration to Philadelphia, 1727–1775," *PMHB*, 105 (1981), 249–278.

4. Single men were identified from the special tax they paid in five different years during this period. The 1756 tax list was published by Hannah Benner Roach, comp., "Taxables in the City of Philadelphia, 1756," *Pennsylvania Genealogical Magazine*, 22 (1961), 3–41; also see 1772, 1780, 1789, and 1798 Provincial Tax Lists, PCA, hereafter cited as Provincial Tax List.

lives.[5] Nor were many tenants relatives of the family with whom they lived.[6] Many mariners and laborers roomed in the boarding houses and inns along the Delaware River in the city's northern district.[7] Most single young women lived and worked as servants in the households of others, caring for children and performing the myriad tasks associated with the home. The one major exception, prostitutes, occupied brothels, taverns, inns, boarding houses, and, on occasion, stables, outbuildings, and the nooks and crannies of various courts and alleyways.

A considerable number of people, not unlike their modern counterparts, chose to cohabitate without a formal ceremony. Although Anna Magdalena was born to Jacob Ench and Catherine Hahn in 1766, they did not marry for another year and a half.[8] And when Mr. Dealth, a sailor, and his intended bride asked the rector at Gloria Dei to perform their nuptials, they requested a marriage certificate dated three years earlier since they "had lived together a good while." As evident from the registry of Gloria Dei, such cases were far from rare.[9]

Young unmarried Philadelphians frequently determined their own sexual behavior and selected their own marriage partners, at times rejecting the prescriptions of their parents and society. Between a third and a fifth of all lower-class women conceived a child before going to the altar, a figure well above that for most contemporary areas.[10] Gloria Dei's minister complained

5. Only 20 percent of journeymen cordwainers and tailors lived with members of their own craft in 1775; based on my analysis of a sample of 50 percent of the Constables' Returns, 1775, PCA, hereafter cited as Constables' Returns.

6. To the extent that kinship is indicated by identical last names, very few tenants recorded on the Constables' Returns for 1775 were related to the household head. Households generally contained only nuclear families' members and unrelated boarders.

7. John F. Watson, *Annals of Philadelphia, and Pennsylvania, in the Olden Time . . .* , 3 vols. (Philadelphia, 1881), 1:446; and my analysis of residential patterns revealed in various city directories, including Francis White, *The Philadelphia Directory* (Philadelphia, 1785); Edmund Hogan, *The Prospect of Philadelphia and Check on the Next Directory* (Philadelphia, 1795); and Cornelius William Stafford, *The Philadelphia Directory for 1801* (Philadelphia, 1801).

8. Birth and Burial Records, St. Michael's Church, GSP. Susan E. Klepp kindly provided this information.

9. Marriage Records and Records of Remarkable Occurrences, Old Swedes Church, Gloria Dei, March 31, 1805, GSP, hereafter cited as Marriage Records and Remarkable Occurrences, Old Swedes Church. Excerpts from these records indicating that a significant number of people lived together without marriage are available in Susan E. Klepp and Billy G. Smith, eds., "The Records of Gloria Dei Church: Marriages and 'Remarkable Occurrences,' 1794–1806," *PH*, 53 (1986), 125–151. On the struggle between parents and children about the marriage decision, see Daniel Scott Smith, "Parental Power and Marriage Patterns: An Analysis of Historical Trends in Hingham, Massachusetts," *Journal of Marriage and the Family*, 35 (1973), 419–428.

10. Susan Edith Klepp, "Philadelphia in Transition: A Demographic History of the City and Its Occupational Groups, 1720–1830" (Ph.D. diss., University of Pennsylvania, 1980), 87–93. See also John D'Emilio and Estelle B. Freedman, *Intimate Matters: A History of Sexuality in America* (New York, 1988), 39–40; Daniel Scott Smith, "The Dating of the American Sexual Revolution: Evidence and Interpretation," in Michael Gordon, ed., *The American Family in*

repeatedly about the great number of "young girls" who insisted "on their capacity and right of choosing [spouses] for themselves."[11] One couple, denied marriage because the woman had no certificate from her father, "thought it very odd, as many others, having no idea of parental authority."[12] Another couple threatened that if refused "they would bed without the nuptial ceremony."[13] When the minister declined the petition of an applicant who lacked his mother's consent, the man retorted angrily that "he was his own master and could, if he chose, kill himself to-morrow."[14] On another occasion a shoemaker, turned away because he did not possess his freedom papers, left with a "miff, saying he was free and independent. . . . If one or two other clergymen refuse," noted the pastor, "he will probably either quit the woman, or live with her without wedlock."[15] Others evinced contempt, occasionally tinged with class consciousness, for marriage laws. When Gloria Dei's minister turned away a man who lacked evidence of his freedom, the intended "bride's sister abused me for this hardship to the poor, tho' I told her similar precaution is taken with people of all conditions."[16]

As young adults acted independently, they sometimes had to confront problems resulting from their behavior. One prospective groom acknowledged his "premature connection with the bride, for whose reputation he expressed great anxiety." Another man whose intended wife was visibly pregnant pleaded desperately that "he must try and get married this night to save the girl's reputation." Some men were more concerned with their own well-being: an Irish lad requested "to be joined to a young woman, with whom he had a child, and in consequence thereof was threatened with imprisonment by her father." "Bastards," one French visitor noted, "are extremely common in Philadelphia."[17] Of course, pregnant young women faced the greatest ordeal, coping as best they could. Eighteen-year-old Elizabeth Fitzpatrick fled to Philadelphia from her father's home in New Jersey, and, despondent over her situation, "took a poisonous draft and plunged

---

Social-Historical Perspective, 2d ed. (New York, 1980), 426–438; and Daniel Scott Smith and Michael S. Hindus, "Premarital Pregnancy in America, 1640–1971: An Overview and Interpretation," *Journal of Interdisciplinary History*, 5 (1975), 537–550.

11. Marriage Records and Remarkable Occurrences, Old Swedes Church, July 29, 1797. Moreau de St. Mery likewise noted that Philadelphia women "invariably make their own choice of suitor, and the parents raise no objection because that's the custom of the country," in Kenneth Roberts and Anna M. Roberts, eds., *Moreau de St. Mery's American Journey* [1793–1798] (Garden City, N.Y., 1947), 283.

12. Marriage Records and Remarkable Occurrences, Old Swedes Church, July 15, 1805.

13. Ibid., Mar. 31, 1805.

14. Ibid., Aug. 10, 1806.

15. Ibid., Nov. 8, 1806.

16. Ibid., Apr. 3, 1795.

17. Ibid., Apr. 12, 13, 1800, and July 15, 1795; Roberts and Roberts, *St. Mery's American Journey*, 293.

into the Delaware River" in a futile attempt to end her life. Christiana Candle sought refuge in the Quaker City from the nearby countryside for the same reason, subsequently giving birth while an almshouse inmate. Like many others, Candle must have encountered considerable difficulties earning a living, caring for her child, and eventually finding a husband.[18] Mary Catherine, overwhelmed by the attendant problems, abandoned her baby. A great many others undoubtedly used various means to terminate their pregnancies, while some, such as Mary Hansbury, Lucy Low, and Sarah Moser, served prison terms for murdering or concealing the deaths of their bastard children.[19]

Many young adults enjoyed the freedom to control their sexuality, to live together, and to choose their own mates because their parents were either dead or lived far away. Of the nearly five hundred individuals whose first marriages were recorded by the rector of Gloria Dei in 1793 and 1794, 37 percent did not have a living parent, and the fathers and mothers of another 20 percent resided abroad. Among these newlyweds only 18 percent had both parents living on American soil, and some of them were too far away to guide their children's behavior.[20] Moreover, poor urban residents often lacked material resources, especially in the form of land, to provide them much economic leverage over their heirs. That so few parents even attended their children's weddings further suggests their inability to exercise much authority in matrimonial affairs.[21]

Once living together, legally or not, laboring people established small households during the late colonial period and considerably larger ones after the Revolution. Laborers, mariners, cordwainers, and tailors generally lived with only four or five people in the mid-1770s, but with between six and eight persons during the 1790s. During these decades, the number of children at home changed little: households contained an average of 2.1 children in 1775, 2.4 in 1790, and 2.5 in 1800.[22] The lessening of migration to the

18. Daily Occurrences Docket, July 13, Aug. 4, 1800, Guardians of the Poor, PCA, hereafter cited as Daily Occurrences.

19. Hansbury is recorded in Prisoners for Trial Docket, Philadelphia County Prison, 1792, p. 33, PCA, hereafter cited as Prisoners for Trial Docket. Low and Moser entries are in Prison Sentence Docket, Philadelphia County Prison, 1799, 1800, respectively, PCA.

20. The Gloria Dei minister recorded information about the parents of 476 brides and grooms married for the first time in 1793 or 1794. Of the 321 newlyweds whose parents had lived in America, the fathers of 96, the mothers of 26, and both parents of 111 had died; 88 brides and grooms had both parents alive. Marriage Records and Remarkable Occurrences, Old Swedes Church.

21. It was very rare for parents to attend the weddings in Gloria Dei during the 1790s; ibid.

22. The statistics here are based on my analysis of a sample of 50 percent of the Constables' Returns, 1775; a sample of 60 percent of the 1790 census of the city and its northern and southern suburbs, in U.S. Bureau of the Census, *Heads of Families of the First Census of the United States Taken in the Year 1790: Pennsylvania* (Washington, D.C., 1908); and a sample of 50 percent of the 1800 census of the city, in *Second Census*. I identified the occupations and

city in the last quarter of the century and the consequent increase in the ages of most Philadelphia couples probably explain this slight growth of children residing with their parents. Tenants accounted primarily for the large households. In 1775 approximately one out of every five laboring families took in a boarder.[23] But as the population expanded, exerting pressure on available housing near the center city, by 1800 most lower-class households found it necessary to share their dwelling with two or three lodgers.

In 1775 the households of laborers, mariners, cordwainers, and tailors were smaller than those of Philadelphians in general. The former group contained an average of 4.5 individuals and the latter 5.2, with servants and slaves in affluent households accounting for most of the difference. The household size of all residents increased dramatically during the last quarter of the century, typically numbering 7 members by 1800. As poor people increasingly rented space to boarders, household size among the four occupational groups grew even more quickly, measuring 7.5 at the time of the second national census. Throughout these decades, the average number of children per family did not vary among classes; slightly more than two children lived in the typical household regardless of the economic status of the household head.[24]

These data relate information about the structure of "typical" households at any point in time, but equally important from the perspective of laboring people were their changing experiences throughout their lives as their families underwent a reproductive cycle of growth and decline. Theoretically, the first child of an average Philadelphia couple arrived within a year and a half after their marriage, and a new baby was born every 24 to 36 months for the next fifteen or twenty years. But there was a good deal of variation from this norm. Most laboring women probably delivered only four or five children in the course of their lives. While a few elite Philadelphians began to curtail their fertility at the end of the century, conscious planning did not affect the family size of lower-class citizens.[25] Instead, breast feeding limited

---

economic ranking of household heads in the *Second Census* by matching them against a sample of 60 percent of the 1798 Provincial Tax List. Laborers, mariners, cordwainers, and tailors had an average household size of 4.5 in 1775, 5.9 in 1790, and 7.5 in 1800. The number of boys younger than sixteen years in each family was doubled in order to estimate the number of girls and thereby compute the mean number of children per household in 1790 and 1800. The composition of households among the bottom 40 percent of taxpayers in 1800 resembled very closely that of the four occupational groups. Because the 1775 Constables' Returns probably underrecorded the city's inhabitants, the growth in household size and in the number of tenants per household may not have been as dramatic during the final decades of the century as these data suggest.

23. This ratio is from my analysis of a sample of 50 percent of the 1775 Constables' Returns.

24. I calculated the figures on household size and structure for all Philadelphians from the same sources and by the same method described in n. 22, this chapter.

25. Klepp, "Philadelphia in Transition," 172–183.

the fecundity of new mothers, accounting for the extended interval between births, while an elevated mortality rate shortened the lives of many laboring women (and their husbands) before their fertile years had ended. Poor mothers consequently bore fewer children than wealthier mothers.[26]

These experiences helped shape the expectations of young adults about their future family lives. Women would bear a large number of children, and couples would spend most of their lives raising their progeny. Since as many as forty years might pass between the birth of the first child and the departure from home of the last, few parents would ever escape the burdens of child care. Often one spouse would die, leaving the other alone to hold the family together, a particular hardship for women with limited prospects of earning much money. Not infrequently the demise of both parents left young children to fend for themselves or to be bound out by the Guardians of the Poor. Many husbands and wives did not survive to influence the decisions of their children as they matured. Thus, young adults, freed by the death of their parents, often made important life decisions independently. Since half of their children died before reaching adulthood, laboring couples who lived to an old age had only two or three of their descendants alive to support them, and the duration of their dependency usually was short.

In addition to these issues of the size and composition of households and the family's development, there are questions about the intimate interpersonal relations among laboring people. How did they view their loved ones? Who was important in their families and how did they exercise power? What roles did friends, immediate family, and other kin play in their lives? Evidence is scant, but the wills of laborers, mariners, cordwainers, and tailors provide valuable insights into these matters. Many among the lower sort left their only personal recorded statements about their lives in these documents. The process of writing a will offered a final opportunity for individuals to deal with their family and friends, at least in an economic sense, as they dispersed their material goods. And in a preindustrial world of limited resources, especially among people for whom even a few articles of clothing contained great value, inheritance could be crucial. By parceling out property, leaving instructions for child rearing, and providing for their spouses, testators expressed their conceptions of and feelings about their relatives and friends. The types of provisions that people made thus reflect the nature of their relationships with other humans.

26. On the average birth interval and number of children per family, see ibid., 184, 206–207. Another indication of the small number of children born into poor families is that laborers, mariners, cordwainers, and tailors who died during the second half of the century specified an average of 1.9 surviving children in their wills. This figure is based on the information contained in a random sample of 136 wills left by members of the four occupational groups between 1750 and 1800, in Wills, Philadelphia County Probate Records, 1683–1901, RW, hereafter cited as Wills.

The testation patterns, based on an analysis of 136 wills written by laborers, mariners, cordwainers, and tailors during the second half of the century, verify that laboring people depended little on relatives other than their nuclear families.[27] Similar to other immigrant areas where most kinsfolk were left behind, poor Philadelphians cited very few nonnuclear kin in their wills; more than three-quarters of testators mentioned no relatives other than their wives and children.[28] Rarely did dying men note parents (in only 4 percent of wills); fewer than one in five left property to siblings, nephews, or nieces; and less than 10 percent indicated the existence of grandchildren.

Hardly any married men recognized friends in their wills. Of the testators with minor children, only 3 percent left any property to friends, a figure much lower, for example, than in the more stable rural counties of Virginia.[29] Of course, the limited material possessions of most poor Philadelphians precluded them from leaving much to their friends. But that so few wills even mention friends suggests that in an immigrant city close and dependable friendships were difficult to establish. Since single men frequently had no relatives living in the city, they often bequeathed their goods to the person with whom they boarded. Laborer Thomas Pitt bestowed his estate to Margaret Peelin "at whose house I now dwell . . . as a token of my gratitude for her tender care and services."[30] Many merchant seamen wrote wills to permit nonrelations to claim their wages or privateering prizes if they died during a voyage. Mariner Joseph Gray gave the right "to sue and recover by Sea or Land any such Sums of money" owed him to Pat Carr, a Philadelphia yeoman.[31] Some, such as Feliz Jordan, left their prizes to their "friend Margaret Bale of the said City, Tavernkeeper."[32] As evident from the marriages contracted in Gloria Dei, many sailors married immediately before leaving on a voyage, in part to legitimize their sweethearts' claims on their

27. The analysis of wills discussed here is drawn from the information contained in the random sample of 136 wills described in n. 26.

28. Of course, the proportion of wills in which nonnuclear kin are mentioned is not an exact gauge of their presence in Philadelphia. The reliability of such a measurement may vary over time or from place to place. Comparing the data from wills with those from reconstituted families in one seventeenth-century, preponderantly immigrant county in Maryland, Lois Green Carr and Lorena S. Walsh found the number of kin indicated in wills was fairly accurate for immigrants but somewhat low for native men, in "The Planter's Wife: The Experience of White Women in Seventeenth-Century Maryland," *WMQ*, 3d Ser., 34 (1977), 565. My analysis of the 1775 Constables' Returns presented previously supports the conclusion, based on data from wills, that few nonnuclear kin lived in the city.

29. In eighteenth-century York and Albemarle counties, 8 percent of testators who left minor children bequeathed property to a friend, in Daniel Blake Smith, *Inside the Great House: Planter Family Life in Eighteenth-Century Chesapeake Society* (Ithaca, 1980), 237–241.

30. Will Book X, p. 446, Wills.

31. Will Book P, p. 351, Wills.

32. Will Book S, p. 144, Wills.

earnings. Others apparently sold for small amounts the claims to their estates. James Wilson, a clerk at the Sheriff's office, was named heir by a host of seamen, five of whom sailed on the Continental Ship *Saratoga* in 1780, and he must have collected a tidy sum when they were all lost at sea.[33]

The central concern expressed in the wills of most laboring men was for the welfare of their wives and children, and wills thus shed the most light on the nature of nuclear family relations. That many women enjoyed positions of considerable authority, trust, and responsibility in lower-class households is evident in their husband's wills. Three of every four testators made their wives executors of their estates, responsible for paying debts and preserving the property. A few men appointed friends or their sons to aid their spouses in overseeing the estates. Thomas Rodgers, a ship captain, named a friend and his brother-in-law to sell his possessions, invest the money in land securities, and pay the interest to his wife.[34] But such cases were rare since most men trusted the financial judgment of their marriage partners. Nearly half of the testators named their spouses as sole executors of their estates, a pattern similar, for instance, to seventeenth-century Maryland where women were accorded a prominent social position. Moreover, poor Philadelphians dispersed their goods to their widows in at least as generous a fashion as did men in that early Chesapeake region.[35] While 20 percent of the city's four occupational groups left their wives only one-third of their estates, the dower required by law, most men left them much more. In the absence of children, testators generally bestowed all of their property to their spouses.

Laboring men trusted their wives to care for their offspring according to the spouses' best judgment. John Beck's concern for the welfare of his four children, several of whom were from his previous marriage, caused him to nominate two friends to help his wife raise them, making sure, for example, that his daughter Catherine would receive the tea table and server "when she goes to housekeeping."[36] And mariner Robert Fagen explicitly instructed his widow to return with their five children to Paris where his brother Christopher could "attend to their education."[37] But these instances were highly unusual; the great majority of testators accorded their wives the sole responsibility for their children's upbringing.

Recognizing the problems attendant to these child-rearing duties, most laboring males gave the major portion of their estates to their widows to help with their own and their children's maintenance. Of the testators with children, 25 percent bequeathed all their possessions to their wives. Joseph

33. Will Book U, pp. 25, 75–81, Wills.
34. Will Book P, pp. 293–294, Wills.
35. Carr and Walsh, "Planter's Wife," 555–557.
36. Will Book U, pp. 282–286, Wills.
37. Ibid., 273–274.

Tatem, a tailor, left his property to his wife Mary "for her support and the support of the children during her widowhood."[38] Another tailor, Amos Bell, likewise gave his goods to his wife Elizabeth "for the bringing up of my beloved Children while in their Minority." To increase her economic authority, Amos encouraged Elizabeth to use her discretion to divide the residue, if any remained, among their descendants when they reached their age of majority.[39] Mariners George Correy and John Taber articulated the high regard that many laboring men apparently had for their wives' ability to manage the finances and raise the children. "Placing great confidence in her goodness," Correy left his entire estate to his wife "upon this especial Trust and Confidence that she my Said wife Elizabeth shall and will out of the Same Educate, maintain, Cloath and bring up my only son George in a decent manner until he shall arrive to a lawful age."[40] Taber left only five shillings each to his four children and the remainder of his estate to his wife Rebecca. It was "not for want of affection for my said Children that their Legacies are so small," he explained, "but that I can well confide in my said Wife's Prudence & Love for them and that she will maintain & Educate them & Provide for them to ye utmost of her Power."[41] Specific instructions on managing the estate or raising the children were absent from the wills of most laboring Philadelphians, who instead relied primarily on the wisdom of their wives.

It is not surprising that lower-class men placed so much confidence in their wives' ability since women bore a great deal of the daily burden of maintaining low-income households. Women were intimately involved in the economic affairs of most laboring families. Benjamin Franklin described his wife as "a good and faithful helpmate [who] assisted me much by attending the shop."[42] The spouses of most craftsmen helped their husbands make and sell items, and the wives of many laboring men regularly toiled at various tasks to earn money for their family's welfare. All of this, of course, was in addition to their domestic chores. Furthermore, laborers and journeymen daily left their wives to care for the home as they pursed their jobs, while mariners and other workers were absent for weeks or months sailing on a vessel or engaged in seasonal employment. While they were away, their wives shouldered the family responsibilities, managing the budgets and the children, purchasing necessities, and coping with household problems. Unlike many of their more affluent sisters who were "protected" by fathers, husbands, and servants,

38. Will Book X, p. 20, Wills.
39. Will Book U, pp. 320–321, Wills.
40. Will Book S, p. 177, Wills.
41. Will Book L, pp. 531–532, Wills.
42. L. Jesse Lemisch, ed., *Benjamin Franklin: The Autobiography and Other Writings* (New York, 1961), 81.

poor women were not shielded from the activities essential to everyday life. Their experience in this sphere provided their husbands ample reason to trust their competence.[43]

Yet the power and trust commanded by women in poor households should not be exaggerated, nor should it be assumed that the reality of daily life caused husbands and wives to view themselves as "equals." In the hierarchical structure of eighteenth-century American society, even during the height of Revolutionary demands for political and social equality for all white *men*, Philadelphians found it hard to conceive of a similar equality between the sexes. Males expected their spouses to acquiesce to their desires in most matters, and they sometimes punished their wives in their wills when their expectations had not been fulfilled. Because of his displeasure with his wife's behavior, mariner Edward Colley left his entire estate to his ten-year-old daughter.[44] "It is my full will & pleasure," laborer Jacob Barr wrote, "that my wife Margret Barr shale have & fully paid to her for her Share of Legacys or any Claim to my Estate one English Half Crown . . . & the Reason of So Small a donation to her bequeathed is on the Loose & Scandelous behavour from her Since our Marridge."[45]

John Williams, drafting his will after signing up for a berth on board a ship, specified his objections to his wife's conduct. He gave her only the possessions she brought to the marriage because

> my wife Ann, was, at the time of my inter-marriage with her possessed in her own Right of certain Monies Goods Chattels and personal Estate of a considerable value which she the said Ann, some short time after intermarriage did secretly privately and in a surreptitous manner without my knowledge . . . take away By means of which I am deprived of that Interest and Property which such Marriage gave me, and by Law I was entitled unto. And Whereas she . . . by her evil demeanor hath deprived me of that . . . Help and Comfort, the Principal and, for which Marriage was ordained. And hath pursued and followed her own Will & desire no ways obedient to, or observant of, my lawfall and reasonable demands will or desire. Whereby she hath broke the Commands of the Law of God and violated that Solemn vow which she made in contracting matrimony.[46]

Legally, Williams was correct: women merged with men when they married, and wives were expected to relinquish their property and decision making to

43. The financial experiences of women in laboring families apparently differed markedly from that of the wealthier women portrayed by Mary Beth Norton, "Eighteenth-Century American Women in Peace and War: The Case of the Loyalists," *WMQ*, 3d Ser., 33 (1976), 386–409.

44. Will Book X, pp. 471–472, Wills.

45. Philadelphia County Probate Records, Wills and Inventories of Estate, 1775, no. 99, RW.

46. Will Book K, pp. 11–12, Wills.

their husbands.[47] For his wife to manage her own possessions or follow her own desires, Williams interpreted as a breach of man's and God's commandments. Poor women thus may have exercised considerable power within the politics of family life, but their position ultimately was circumscribed and certainly far from one of total equality with their husbands. Still, as the wills indicate, the wives of laboring men enjoyed a great deal of responsibility and authority relative to many of their contemporaries.[48]

Even though laboring men could rely on the judgment of their wives, they understandably remained anxious about their children's prospects after their own deaths. Some testators tried to guide their descendants' futures, thereby providing us with insights about their expectations. A handful of fathers, mostly better-off craftsmen, directed that their sons receive formal education. Master cordwainer John Jackson ordered that his boy be kept in school until his fourteenth birthday.[49] Another shoemaker, Peter Sefference, wanted his son George to be "well educated and instructed in the English and German Languages and if he chuses in the Latin and French."[50] Tailor Christian Grassold, perhaps a Deist, left his books to his grandson, advising "all possible care to keep his mind free from all Superstition & prejudice and to send him to the English School, and after he will be able to read & write to send him to the Academy there to be instructed in all good & useful Sciences, but particularly & afore all the rest in the Philosophie."[51] However, few among the lower classes believed that their sons could or should receive this type of training.

Many laborers, mariners, cordwainers, and tailors were oriented to urban rather than rural life. A significant number of them had migrated to Philadelphia from towns and cities, few owned land, and others probably knew or cared little about farming. They felt that their sons should be taught a craft rather than how to work the land. Thus, tailor David Seyferhold wanted his wife to raise their seven children "until they shall be fit to bind out and learn a trade."[52] And Henry Nagel charged his wife Barbara to "educate & bring up

47. In *Commentaries on the Laws of England*, 3 vols. (Oxford, 1765–1769), 1:442, Sir William Blackstone articulated the legal subordination of wives: "By marriage, the husband and wife are one person in law; that is, the very being or legal existence of the woman is suspended during the marriage, or at least is incorporated and consolidated into that of the husband; under whose wing, protection, and cover, she performs everything." For a discussion of this issue, see Marylynn Salmon, "Equality or Submersion?" in Carol Ruth Berkin and Mary Beth Norton, eds., *Women of America* (Boston, 1979), 93–98.
48. On the family position of most contemporary women, see Wells, *Revolutions in Americans' Lives*, 49–68; Linda K. Kerber, *Women of the Republic: Intellect and Ideology in Revolutionary America* (Chapel Hill, N.C., 1980), 115–184; and Mary Beth Norton, *Liberty's Daughters: The Revolutionary Experience of American Women, 1750–1800* (Boston, 1980), 3–124.
49. Will Book K, p. 72, Wills.
50. Will Book U, pp. 129–131, Wills.
51. Will Book L, pp. 264–265, Wills.
52. Will Book P, p. 401, Wills.

my [five] minor children until they respectively arrive to the age of fourteen years and fit to learn a Trade."[53]

Laboring men afforded their sons considerable freedom to select their occupations, even encouraging their independent decision making, in part because they were unable to offer their male offspring a secure future in any profession. After George Sefference's education, he was to be bound to a "Conveyance or such other business or trade as he shall make Choice of."[54] Concerned about his children's future contentment, Robert Fagan enjoined his brother to "fix them in such line of as May promise most for their Interest and Happiness."[55] Judging from the wills, few cordwainers or tailors taught their skills to their sons; perhaps fathers hoped they would learn a more lucrative trade. Indications of how daughters should be instructed are rare, the unspoken assumption almost certainly being that they would marry and perform the varied functions of wives and mothers. Like most parents, John Beck expected that his daughter would "go to housekeeping,"[56] and, of course, the overwhelming majority of girls apprenticed in Philadelphia were tutored in the art and mystery of housewifery.[57]

In terms of inheritance, laboring men treated their children in an equitable fashion. Nearly every laborer, mariner, cordwainer, and tailor who left property to their children divided it equally among them regardless of age or gender. Such a pattern differs significantly from traditions that give preference to the eldest son or to boys over girls, and parity in the transmission of property suggests something about the parents' perceptions of their children. Although sons and daughters undoubtedly were not viewed as complete equals, the behavior of laboring couples must have engendered feelings of respect and undercut hierarchical attitudes among their children.

The reality of daily life thus contributed to the growth of affection and the development of companionate families for many laboring people.[58] The essential contributions of women and children to the household economy helped foster a sense of importance among them. The spouses of mariners and other migrant workers bore the sole responsibility for sustaining their families during their husbands' extended absences, adding to their esteem. Adolescents and young adults enjoyed considerable independence in making important life decisions. Since most laboring families were immigrants living in a city filled with strangers, they could rely on few kin or friends for aid.

53. Will Book X, pp. 463–464, Wills.
54. Will Book U, pp. 282–286, Wills.
55. Ibid., 273–274.
56. Ibid., 282–286.
57. Indentures, 1751–1797, and Indenture Papers and Bonds, 1795–1799, Guardians of the Poor, PCA.
58. The best description of the development of the companionate family is in Stone, *Family, Sex, and Marriage*, 217–299, 407–428.

Such isolation necessarily must have encouraged internal bonding within many families.

Yet even with the development of companionate family relationships among many laboring Philadelphians, family lives were not without negative aspects. Conflict, ranging from verbal arguments to physical abuse, undoubtedly had always marred domestic tranquility, exacerbated in part by the economic plight of laboring people and the tensions that their material shortages created. But the level of violence among family members during the late eighteenth century is impressive; the names of offenders are recorded on prison lists, relief rolls, and divorce suits. Although impossible to measure accurately, discord may well have increased as new values fostering substantial independence for women and children clashed with more traditional views sanctioning the strong authority of the male household head. Esther Marrow and her child thus sought refuge in the almshouse because of "a little domestic Strife" with her husband.[59] But more serious charges of wife beating were lodged against shoemakers Joseph Cressman and John Young, tailor John Cline, and laborer Charles Curry.[60] Constables apprehended others repeatedly for the same crime: Patrick McGlaughlin, James Campbell, James Scott, and Daniel Call were all picked up twice, each within several months of their previous offense. Frederick Sleiker went to jail at least four times during the mid-1790s for mistreating his spouse. The nature of many assaults indicates the intensity of the rage involved. Michael Digney "beat his wife and young child insomuch that the Neighbours were apprehensive that murder might ensue," while James Hunter, aided by his lover Joanna Deleany, inflicted such injuries on his spouse "that her life is despaired of."[61]

Elizabeth Clandenin's suit for divorce from the "bed and board" of her husband, John, on the grounds of his "brutal and barbarous behaviour towards her," provides a graphic description of the type of violence that sometimes occurred. John abused his wife throughout their eight years of marriage, finally forcing her and the children to leave him. In her deposition, Mary Jones, a neighbor, described one incident when she entered the Clandenin's home and found "Elizabeth lying on the floor and the said John with one hand in her hair and the other to her throat and to all appearances likely

59. Daily Occurrences, Oct. 22, 1789.
60. Prisoners for Trial Docket: entry on Cressman, 1800, p. 136; entry on Young, 1792, p. 42; entry on Cline, 1799, p. 91; and entry on Curry, 1800, p. 116. The occupations of the first three men are indicated in Cornelius William Stafford, *The Philadelphia Directory for 1800* (Philadelphia, 1800); and Curry's occupation is recorded in Cornelius William Stafford, *The Philadelphia Directory for 1797* (Philadelphia, 1797).
61. Prisoners for Trial Docket: entries on McGlaughlin, 1791, pp. 8, 11, 15; entries on Campbell, 1791, p. 3, 1792, p. 18; entries on Scott, 1800, p. 142, 1801, p. 6; entries on Call, 1800, pp. 143, 199; entries on Sleiker, 1792, pp. 18, 25, 28, 1798, p. 60; entry on Digney, 1800, p. 29 (quotation); and entry on Hunter and Deleany, 1791, p. 16 (quotation).

to strangle her." With "much difficulty," Mary freed Elizabeth and stopped John from hitting her with a hammer. Hearing a noise at the Clandenin home on another occasion, Mary "ran over to the house and saw John beating his wife in great fury with his horsewhip, holding her at the same time by the petticoat to prevent her from running away." When a nearby waggoner rescued Elizabeth, Mary took her home, where she saw Elizabeth's "back raised in large blisters by the violence of the blows received and her face strongly marked with one end of the whip." John threatened to kill his wife if she returned. According to Mary, over the years John had "turned Elizabeth out of doors upwards of thirty times" and "manifested a continuance of barbarous and brutal usage, beating, kicking" and otherwise treating his wife "with the most inhuman violence." In his defense, John accused Elizabeth of striking him "in the face with an oven swab." Recognizing that John's behavior went beyond the acceptable ways in which men should discipline their wives, the court granted Elizabeth a divorce and an alimony of twelve pounds annually.[62]

Elizabeth's nimbleness with the oven mop demonstrates that women were not always passive victims. One couple asked the Gloria Dei rector for a divorce since the husband often got drunk and beat the wife and she retaliated by slashing him with her "cutting tongue."[63] Other wives attacked their spouses physically. Catherine Houshel, Charlotte Beam, Rodah Church, Elizabeth Evans, and Mary Foggy all were arrested for assaulting their mates.[64] Cordwainer Alexander McArthur complained that his wife, Sarah, endangered his life by "Cruel and barbarous Treatment." Specifically, Sarah had "run at and endeavoured to Strike [him] with Sharp Forks and thrown Bottles, hammers and other dangerous weapons at [his] head."[65]

Parents and children also inflicted pain on one another. As in any society, some adults, sick or unable to cope with their problems, took out their frustrations on their offspring. William Miller's mother was confined to the workhouse when she "cruelly whipped" him. She commonly left her two young children "confined in the house alone without any victuals and naked." John Deimert, a chairmaker, chained his sons "at night by the neck and heels in a cellar where [he] worked. They were left alone to sleep on chips and shavings. The father striped the boys naked so their shirts would not wear out from the chips." Deimert served two days in jail and his sons were bound out.[66] The Guardians of the Poor likewise indentured eight-year-old

62. Records of the Supreme Court, Divorce Papers, Clandenin v. Clandenin, Record Group 33, PHMC, hereafter cited as Divorce Papers.

63. Marriage Records and Remarkable Occurrences, Old Swedes Church, Nov. 30, 1795.

64. Prisoners for Trial Docket: entry on Houshel, 1791, p. 12; entry on Beam, 1798, p. 54; entry on Church, 1800, p. 138; entry on Evans, 1799, p. 87; and entry on Foggy, 1792, p. 27.

65. Divorce Papers, McArthur v. McArthur.

66. Minutes, Overseers of the Poor, Aug. 27, Sept. 8, 10, 1768, PCA.

William Blake to protect him from his mother's beatings during her alcoholic bouts.[67] Demonstrating that turnabout was fair play, William Kensler went to prison for assaulting his mother, while William Troutwine twice suffered incarceration for threatening his father and family.[68]

As affection became the primary cementing agent between husbands and wives, and the social support of marriage offered by neighbors, kin, and the community declined, families occasionally underwent considerable strain. Spouses who did not find emotional fulfillment within marriage sometimes pursued the numerous opportunities for other intimate relationships available in the anonymity of American cities. Poor Philadelphians thus engaged in adultery, desertion, divorce, and bigamy on a wide scale. Although advocating strict public morality in his autobiography, Benjamin Franklin casually noted several cases of desertion and bigamy, his own wife having previously wed a man who already was married.[69] When tailor John Lux was "caught on top of Laurence Connor's wife with his Breeches down, and her clothes up," their behavior was not that uncommon. Indeed, the constables may not even have arrested Lux except for his threat to burn down Connor's house.[70]

Mariner Elijah Banes sued his wife for divorce because of adultery and desertion. After five years of marriage, while Elijah was at sea, Mary Banes moved in with merchant Richard Duffield "because she loved the said Duffield a great deal better than she did" her husband. Reminding us that sexual intercourse was not necessarily a very private affair in the eighteenth century, two witnesses testified that they had "very often seen" Richard and Mary together in bed where they "acted towards each other as man and wife."[71] Catherine Clements likewise deserted her husband, a cordwainer, choosing instead to keep a "common bawdy House." His appeal for her to return home met Catherine's icy reply "that she would be damned to Hell, if ever she lived with him again."[72] The case of Catharine Lauer illustrates the fluidity of many relationships. She initially married William Cuniers in 1777. When he moved to South Carolina, she wed Casper Iseloan, who already had a wife. Some time later, Catherine took William Kenley as her husband. Kenley, enraged when he discovered Catherine's past, successfully petitioned for a divorce in 1797.[73]

67. Daily Occurrences, Aug. 18, 1800.

68. Prisoners for Trial Docket: entry on Kensler, 1800, p. 58; entries on Troutwine, 1791, p. 16, 1792, p. 30.

69. Lemisch, *Benjamin Franklin*, 53, 64.

70. Prisoners for Trial Docket, 1792, p. 25. Lux was black and Connor and his wife were white, possibly adding to the tensions between the two neighbors. See also Stafford, *Philadelphia Directory for 1797*.

71. Divorce Papers, Banes v. Banes.

72. Ibid., Clements v. Clements.

73. "Divorces Granted by the Supreme Court of Pennsylvania from December, 1785, Until 1801," *Pennsylvania Genealogical Magazine*, 1 (1898), 427.

Although hundreds of individuals filed for divorce after 1785 when the Pennsylvania legislature enacted a more lenient law, poor Philadelphians, some of whom complained about the "impossibilities of procuring legal divorce because of [their] poverty," generally elected to end their marriages simply by leaving or driving their spouses from their homes.[74] Of course, economic cooperation between spouses added to the incentive for couples to remain together, especially for women who enjoyed limited material opportunities. But bigamy still was widespread as people established serial relationships or sometimes even maintained more than one partner at a time. While her husband was living in New York, Mary White pretended to be a widow in order to wed Philip Land, by whom she was pregnant.[75] The aunt of Mary Sanky warned Gloria Dei's rector that "the hussy intended new marriage in her husband's absence."[76] Richard deserted Hesther Hill to cohabitate with two "Lewd Women."[77] And, as the Reverend Collin complained, some "New England men, as well as other Americans not seldom have 2 or more wives by getting married in diverse places."[78] Such conditions caused Collin to moan about "the licentious manners which in this part of America, and especially in Philadelphia, are evidently striking, and which in matrimonial affairs are so pernicious."[79]

The family life of black Philadelphians differed significantly from that of white laboring people during the late eighteenth century. The primary story concerning the city's African-American inhabitants is one of struggle, survival, and eventually a modicum of success in the face of enslavement and racism. Like all black Americans at the time, those in the City of Brotherly Love, as the anthropologists Sidney Mintz and Richard Price remind us, were "required to engineer styles of life that might be preserved in the face of terrible outrage."[80] And slavery in Philadelphia did thwart the family lives of its victims, severely limiting their opportunities to form lasting relationships, reside with their loved ones, raise their children, and even reproduce.[81] As a

74. Marriage Records and Remarkable Occurrences, Old Swedes Church, Apr. 20, 1795. Men often advertised in newspapers for their wives who had absconded. See, for example, *Pennsylvania Gazette* (Philadelphia), Feb. 24, 1757, and Sept. 11, 1766. On changes in the Pennsylvania divorce laws, see Thomas R. Meehan, "'Not Made Out of Levity': Evolution of Divorce in Early Pennsylvania," *PMHB*, 12 (1968), 441–464.

75. Marriage Records and Remarkable Occurrences, Old Swedes Church, Jan. 24, 1794.

76. Ibid., Oct. 1, 1804.

77. Prisoners for Trial Docket, 1792, p. 24; and Vagrancy Docket, Mar. 2, 1792, PCA.

78. Marriage Records and Remarkable Occurrences, Old Swedes Church, July 2, 1800.

79. Ibid., Jan. 1795.

80. Sidney W. Mintz and Richard Price, "An Anthropological Approach to the Study of Afro-American History," MS, 1974, pp. 12–13, as quoted in Herbert G. Gutman, *The Black Family in Slavery and Freedom, 1750–1925* (New York, 1976), 353.

81. On the family lives of slaves, see Billy G. Smith, "Black Family Life in Philadelphia from Slavery to Freedom, 1750–1800," in Catherine Hutchins, ed., *Shaping a National Culture: The*

community of African-Americans emerged in the city during the post-Revolutionary decades, free blacks enjoyed considerably greater success than had slaves in forming families and establishing intimate personal relationships. Since the focus of this book is on unbound laboring people, the following discussion centers on family life among the city's free blacks after the Revolution.

Slaves constituted the vast majority of the urban African-American population during the pre-Revolutionary period, but, after Pennsylvania's gradual emancipation law passed in 1780, the number of people held in bondage declined and the number of free blacks increased rapidly.[82] Free African-Americans had never been very numerous during the colonial era; only about 200 or 300 inhabited the city in 1775. But as emancipated and escaped slaves flocked to Philadelphia during and after the Revolution, their population expanded to roughly 1,000 by 1783, to 1,849 in 1790, then nearly tripled to 6,083 during the next decade. Simultaneously, the number of slaves dwindled to 301 by 1790 and to 55 at the century's close.[83]

Many newly freed slaves married and started families shortly after they arrived in the Quaker City. Four times as many blacks wed in the city's churches during the 1780s than in the decade before the war: some were ex-slaves legalizing unions that had not been recognized under slavery; others

Philadelphia Experience, 1750–1800, forthcoming. For different perspectives, see Gary B. Nash, *Forging Freedom: The Formation of Philadelphia's Black Community, 1720–1840* (Cambridge, Mass., 1988), 14–15, 36, 81–82; and Susan E. Klepp, "Black Mortality in Early Philadelphia, 1722–1859" (Paper presented at the Meeting of the Social Science History Association, Chicago, November 1988).

82. Approximately one thousand slaves lived in the city in 1750, and their numbers increased during the Seven Years' War, reaching about seventeen hundred by the early 1760s. Slave imports declined during the next decade, and the African-American population dwindled to fewer than seven hundred by the eve of the Revolution. For the years before 1767, the number of slaves is estimated by multiplying the black proportion of total burials in the city by the population. Figures after 1767 are more reliable since they are counted from various tax lists and constables' returns. The proportion of black burials and the number of slaves on the tax lists are in Gary B. Nash, "Slaves and Slaveowners in Colonial Philadelphia," *WMQ*, 3d Ser., 30 (1973), 231, 237. Jean R. Soderlund employs a similar approach to estimate that fifteen hundred blacks lived in Philadelphia at midcentury, in *Quakers and Slavery: A Divided Spirit* (Princeton, N.J., 1985), 55–65, 81. I counted the number of slaves on the 1775 Constables' Returns.

83. Nash, "Slaves and Slaveowners," 237; Nash, "Forging Freedom: The Emancipation Experience in the Northern Seaport Cities, 1775–1820," in Ira Berlin and Ronald Hoffman, eds., *Slavery and Freedom in the Age of the American Revolution* (Charlottesville, Va., 1983), 5; Nash, *Forging Freedom*, 38; Susan E. Klepp, "The Demographic Characteristics of Philadelphia, 1788–1801: Zachariah Poulson's Bills of Mortality," *PH*, 53 (1986), 204. The federal censuses for 1790 and 1800 tabulate free blacks and slaves in urban Philadelphia; see *Return of the Whole Number of Persons within the Several Districts of the United States . . .* (Philadelphia, 1791); and U.S. Census Office, *Return of the Whole Number of Persons within the Several Districts of the United States . . .* (Washington, D.C., 1801). The free black population of New York City grew equally rapidly after the Revolution, but its slave population expanded as well; Shane White, "'We Dwell in Safety and Pursue Our Honest Callings': Free Blacks in New York City, 1783–1810," *Journal of American History*, 75 (1988), 448–451.

found new partners among the increasing urban population of African-Americans. Not surprisingly, since blacks had to delay marrying until their terms of bondage were complete, most married at a later age than their white counterparts. In Gloria Dei, the church for which such records are available, the average age of black men and women on their wedding day was 27.5 and 26.0 years, respectively, as compared to 23.5 and 20.0 for white males and females.[84]

Still, at only a dozen annually, the number of marriages in white churches remained small. Although repeatedly encouraged by white members of Abolition Societies to wed legally, most free blacks ignored such conventional rituals, choosing instead to follow their own customs or simply to move in with one another.[85] Thus, Ann Hayman lived with Philip Hayman for three years and even assumed his last name, although they never took vows in a church. Having children out of official wedlock probably was not uncommon among black women. Elizabeth Thompson, a "single" woman, took refuge in the almshouse when she became pregnant; she had given birth to another child two years earlier. A black sailor impregnated Maria Harris, also unmarried. Cudjo Desire and Elizabeth Murray brought their sixteen-month-old infant to Gloria Dei Church when they decided to wed.[86]

The first task undertaken by many newly freed blacks was to liberate their loved ones from slavery so that they could live as families. Attle Waters, a laborer, borrowed thirty pounds from Robert Wharton to purchase the freedom of his wife and daughter. Waters agreed to bind himself as a servant to Wharton for thirteen months to pay off the debt. Abraham Smith, a whitewasher, bought himself and, subsequently, his wife out of bondage. Pollidore convinced twenty-three people to loan him funds to save his wife from being sold to a buyer in Maryland.[87]

The high fertility of Philadelphia's blacks after the Revolution attests their

84. Between 1765 and 1779, 56 black couples (an average of about 4 per year) married in the city's churches; 84 couples, or approximately 12 annually, wed between 1779 and 1786. See Soderlund, *Quakers and Slavery*, 81; Nash, *Forging Freedom*, 75–76. The mean ages of brides and grooms were calculated from Marriage Records, Old Swedes Church, 1793–1805. I thank Susan E. Klepp for this data.

85. In 1796, for example, the Convention of Deputies from the Abolition Societies of the United States advised blacks about the "moral and religious necessity of having your marriages legally performed"; broadside, Jan. 6, 1796, Cox, Parrish, and Wharton Papers, vol. 14, p. 52, HSP.

86. Examination of Paupers, vol. 1826–1831, Guardians of the Poor, PCA. Hayman and Thompson appear in vol. 1826–1831, pp. 95–96 and 29, respectively. Harris is in vol. 1822–1825, p. 4. The episodes noted here all occurred during the 1790s. Many other unmarried black women with children are recorded in the Daily Occurrences; see Billy G. Smith and Cynthia Shelton, "The Daily Occurrence Docket of the Philadelphia Almshouse, 1800," *PH*, 52 (1985), 86–116. Desire and Murray are in Marriage Records, Old Swedes Church, Nov. 22, 1800.

87. Pennsylvania Abolition Society Papers, HSP: Waters and Pollidore records in Box 3A, Smith records in Box 3B.

success in establishing viable family lives. Their crude birth rates averaged about forty-five per thousand, slightly higher than that of the white population and more than twice the rates among slaves before the Revolution.[88]

Most free blacks succeeded in creating and maintaining family ties; about 80 percent of them resided with at least one other African-American during the century's final decade. But many continued to live under the supervision of whites: 50 percent dwelled in white households in 1790, and 64 percent a decade later. Both rising rents, which forced people to share their living arrangements, and the indenturing of hundreds of French West Indian slaves imported to Philadelphia accounted for the increase of blacks in white households. During this decade the vast majority of African-Americans who lived on their own probably resided in family groups, since 96 percent lived with at least two others of their race. Women headed these households in about 15 percent of the cases, approximately the same proportion as existed among whites. Still, by the end of the century, a majority of blacks lived in households controlled by whites—a few as slaves, more as servants, and most as boarders or domestics who occupied a room or floor of a home. And nearly 66 percent of those in white households shared their quarters with at least one other black person. Even though the relationships among blacks in any of the households were not recorded, the statistical evidence strongly suggests the formation of black family units.[89]

Recreating the inner workings of black families from the extant records is nearly impossible. But the monetary problems common to most blacks undoubtedly helped define their family lives. To an even greater extent than among white families, each black family constituted an economic partnership among all of its members. While the men worked primarily as sailors and day laborers, women earned wages by cooking, cleaning homes, caring for children, and washing clothes for whites. Some parents, recently freed from slavery, found the task of providing for their offspring extremely difficult.

88. On the migration of blacks from the countryside to the city, see Nash, *Forging Freedom*, 72–73; and White, "'We Dwell in Safety,'" 448–451. While the data about birth rates are limited, it appears that neither the gender ratio nor the age structure among blacks could have accounted for the dramatic change in their rates from the colonial period to the last decades of the century. The burial statistics by gender suggest that males slightly outnumbered females during the 1780s and 1790s. That most blacks during these decades were migrants probably skewed their age structure toward people in their child-producing years. Still, the birth rates of blacks after the Revolution were below those of Catholics, a predominantly white immigrant group. On these topics, see Klepp, "Demographic Characteristics of Philadelphia," 204, 207, 217, 221.

89. I tabulated these percentages from a sample of 60 percent of households on the 1790 federal census and a sample of 50 percent of households on the 1800 federal census. Black women headed 17 percent and 12 percent of households in 1790 and 1800, respectively, compared to 13 percent and 15 percent of households headed by white women in those years. About 33 percent of free blacks lived in white households in New York City in 1790 and 1800; White, "'We Dwell in Safety,'" 451–452.

One common solution, occasionally imposed on them by city authorities, was to bind out their children to other families. Thus, indentured children accounted for 25 percent of the blacks who lived in white households in 1790.[90]

Several examples from the almshouse illustrate the family fragility created by difficult financial circumstances. When their father fell ill and their mother, who worked as a domestic servant, could not care for them, Isaac and Samuel, aged three and five, entered the almshouse. Sarah Boardley and her small daughter, Ann, were freed in Robert Thompson's will, whereupon Sarah moved to Philadelphia and for two years "maintained herself and child in the line or business of a washerwoman." But on December 2, 1800, "much afflicted with pains through her limbs [so] that she cannot labour for her support," Sarah, "in a perishing condition," applied for aid. Ann was indentured a week later and Sarah discharged from the almshouse the following March. Harry Goolin deserted his wife and infant, Jeremiah, in 1798. Two years later, Jeremiah's mother gave him to the almshouse clerk since she was "poor, and not able to support [him] and herself [and] having no other means to live but by hiring herself out at service as a Maid in a family which she could not do with the child." Jeremiah was bound eight months later.[91] Other records reveal the more stable and normal conditions in which most black families existed, for example, the Saviel, Cranshaw, and Duncan families discussed in chapter 1.

90. Nash, *Forging Freedom*, 144–154. Occupations of many blacks are given in Edmund Hogan, *The Prospect of Philadelphia and Check on the Next Directory* (Philadelphia, 1795). See also White, "'We Dwell in Safety,'" 453–457.

91. Isaac and Samuel appear in Almshouse Census, 1807, Guardians of the Poor, PCA; Daily Occurrences: Sarah and Ann entered on Dec. 2, 1800, and Ann was bound on Dec. 8; Jeremiah Goolin entered on Nov. 23, 1800 and was indentured the following August.

Chapter Eight

Conclusion

For history records the patterns of men's lives, they say. . . . But not quite, for actually it is only the known, the seen, the heard and only those events that the recorder regards as important that are put down. . . . What did they ever think of us transitory ones? . . . birds of passage who were too obscure for learned classification, too silent for the most sensitive recorders of sound.

— Ralph Ellison, *Invisible Man*

THIS BOOK HAS ATTEMPTED to recreate the daily lives of laboring Philadelphians during the second half of the eighteenth century. The primary methodological emphasis has been on systematic analysis and precise measurement of various aspects of their lives as described in contemporary records. The observations and descriptions of contemporaries provide additional information about the demographic and material characteristics of the urban lower sort, their advancement opportunities, the composition and character of their families, their migratory patterns, the nature of their housing, and their strategies in coping with financial distress.

Like all of the city's inhabitants, laboring Philadelphians suffered from illness, disease, and premature death. But inadequate diets, shelter, and clothing, the inability to flee the city during epidemics, the high cost of smallpox immunization, and their migratory behavior exposed the lower classes more frequently than their wealthier counterparts to debilitating and fatal ailments. The lower sort still managed to produce numerous children, although at a rate somewhat below the rest of the population.

A detailed examination of the place laboring people occupied within the city's economy and of their material circumstances is necessary to understand and explain the difficulties that many of them encountered. Laborers, mariners, cordwainers, and tailors—as well as the workers they represented— generally led uncertain and spartan physical lives. The opportunities of males to accumulate savings to establish their independence as master craftsmen or as farmers, and their chances to move up the occupational and economic ladders were much more limited than has sometimes been portrayed. The available evidence is too incomplete to evaluate whether a "culture of poverty" existed in which one generation bequeathed their status to the next, although more than a few such examples appear in the records.

Although these bleak findings about the laboring inhabitants of America's wealthiest city are emphasized in the previous chapters, a "gloom and doom" interpretation that all laboring people suffered interminable horrors is not warranted. A good many poor inhabitants earned security, independence, and material rewards. Still, the gloomy conclusions offset and confront the considerably rosier picture portrayed by historians for decades. Reasoning from the supposed scarcity of labor in the New World, scholars have argued that nearly all free white males could, with a modicum of hard work and talent, succeed in material terms. While many, perhaps most, social and labor historians have begun during the past two decades to doubt that assertion, scholars who analyze the early American economy still often present the image of America as the wealthiest nation in the world and a land necessarily filled with opportunity for common people.[1] The paradox remains difficult to resolve.

Understanding the daily lives of the urban lower classes is invaluable to the task of interpreting other aspects of their existence. Lacking diaries, journals, and other traditional historical sources that provide insight into the values and ideas of laboring people, we must use the context of their everyday experiences to derive as much as possible about the felt meaning of their lives. Thus, the nature of their political activity, ideology, consciousness, and community orientation is best understood against the background of daily life.

In political terms, Consensus historians have argued that, unlike the French Revolution, the American Revolution did not involve a reaction to misery or poverty. The debate about the nature of the Revolution in Philadelphia has continued in recent studies. To simplify the controversy, Gary B. Nash, a neo-Progressive historian, linked the evolution of ideology and political activity to structural weaknesses in the urban economy that had severely undercut the position of many laboring folk. Thomas M. Doerflinger, a neo-Whig, minimized the pre-Revolutionary economic structural flaws, at least for the city's merchants, and inferred that the laboring populace most likely benefited in the midst of general prosperity. My own analysis suggests that the city's economy was not as unsound structurally as Nash believed. Yet, not unlike the nation's economy during the 1980s, it operated

---

1. One of the clearest recent statements of this view is Edwin J. Perkins, *The Economy of Colonial America* (New York, 1980).

in ways that were not particularly beneficial for the lower sort during the closing years of the colonial era. None of the major economic sectors expanded swiftly enough to provide additional employment to the rapidly growing population. Moreover, the "high wages" paid American workers burned quickly in the fires of the city's exorbitant living costs. If, as Doerflinger maintained, economic prosperity impelled the city's merchants to adopt a conservative political position at the outbreak of the Revolution, then, by the same token, economic difficulties encouraged much of the more radical opposition of laborers, sailors, and lesser-skilled laborers, which Eric Foner and Stephen Rosswurm discovered.[2]

For many laboring Philadelphians, life was nasty, short, and brutish. To poor men and women who made the rounds among seasonal employment, dependency on outrelief and charity, and institutionalization in the almshouse, workhouse, and jail, participation in political events (especially those focused on a national or international level) would not have appeared to be a viable solution to the problems of their lives. If they were moved to complain or protest, it may have been at a local level about immediately pressing issues—the increase in the assize of bread during the early 1760s, the ending of cost controls on bread during the 1790s, or the monopolizers and engrossers who pushed up food and fuel prices at the city's market. Master cordwainers had the wherewithal to protest to city officials about the high wholesale cost of leather and, later, to petition the state and national governments for protective tariffs on shoes. But their situation differed markedly from the down and out, whose despair would have made any political action ineffectual.

As other scholars have demonstrated, a great many laboring Philadelphians rallied to Tom Paine's call for "republicanism" and "equality." Their commitment to and understanding of those terms are evident when evaluated against the reality of the Quaker City. Historians can measure statistically the growth of inequality in the distribution of taxable wealth and the evolution of residential segregation in the eighteenth-century city. But poor people observed it firsthand as great numbers of opulent carriages rumbled through the streets and the elite vied with one another to construct the most elegant town houses and country mansions. At the same time, inexpensive rental property grew more scarce and cheap units were relegated increasingly to the peripheral blocks or confined to inconspicuous alleys and lanes within

2. Gary B. Nash, *The Urban Crucible: Social Change, Political Consciousness, and the Origins of the American Revolution* (Cambridge, Mass., 1979); Thomas M. Doerflinger, *A Vigorous Spirit of Enterprise: Merchants and Economic Development in Revolutionary Philadelphia* (Chapel Hill, N.C., 1986); Eric Foner, *Tom Paine and Revolutionary America* (New York, 1976); Steven Rosswurm, *Arms, Country, and Class: The Philadelphia Militia and "Lower Sort" during the American Revolution, 1775–1783* (New Brunswick, N.J., 1987).

the city. As the almshouse dockets vividly illustrate, the specter of poverty never disappeared, nor did it haunt merely the old and infirm. The populace did not endure the subsistence crises of European urban dwellers, but throughout the second half of the eighteenth century some Philadelphians begged their lives' needs while others literally starved to death or died from exposure to the elements.

We should resist idealizing the "community life"—one of the favorite themes of new labor historians—led by the lower classes. Many felt alienated from the community as well as physically separated from neighbors, friends, and kin. Their peripatetic existence meant that they relinquished much of their sense of "belonging," a feeling particularly difficult to recapture in a city filled with strangers, migrants, and various ethnic and racial groups. Most laboring people, for example, did not affiliate with any church. Their neighborhoods were in continuous flux as residents moved in and out in a perpetual cycle of subsistence migration. On the more positive side, some enjoyed an atomized existence. Ironically, free blacks managed to construct the most stable and successful community among the city's poor residents after the Revolution.[3]

The findings of this study have implications for our understanding of nineteenth-century industrialization as well. In view of the bleakness of the lives of some urban laboring people, perhaps the negative changes wrought by the factory have been overestimated, the deleterious impact exaggerated. This is not to argue that industrialization was necessarily a "positive" event from which laboring people suffered little. But it is to draw attention to the fact that the preindustrial period was not a golden age. Poverty, unemployment, underemployment, inequality, and exploitation hardly were artifacts of the machine era. Financial difficulties, paternalistic relations that often restricted the lives of workers, large numbers of wage laborers, and the inability of many workers ever to achieve an independent status were all part of life in eighteenth-century Philadelphia.

3. Gary B. Nash, *Forging Freedom: The Formation of Philadelphia's Black Community, 1720–1840* (Cambridge, Mass., 1988).

Limited Prosopography

I RECONSTRUCTED various aspects of the lives of Philadelphians, especially for chapter 1, using the technique of "limited prosopography." That is, with the aid of research assistants and a computer, I collected data on the lives of fifty thousand Philadelphians from a large number of documents and then matched the information on specific people who appeared in various records. The resulting profiles range from a single piece of information, such as a tax assessment, occupation, or house address, to sufficient material to construct a short biography. I pursued a limited rather than a total prosopography because the several hundred thousand people who inhabited the city during the second half of the century made the process of gathering information on all of their lives nearly impossible. Thus, I amassed data primarily, but not exclusively, from those sources most likely to contain information about laboring people.

The types of information and records analyzed to reconstruct the lives of Philadelphians are as follows: house address and occupation are included in Francis White, *The Philadelphia Directory* (Philadelphia, 1785); Clement Biddle, *The Philadelphia Directory* (Philadelphia, 1791); Edmund Hogan, *The Prospect of Philadelphia and Check on the Next Directory* (Philadelphia, 1795); Cornelius William Stafford, *The Philadelphia Directory for 1797* (Philadelphia, 1797); Stafford, *The Philadelphia Directory for 1800* (Philadelphia, 1800); Anon., *The New Trade Directory for Philadelphia Anno 1800* (Philadelphia, 1799); Stafford, *The Philadelphia Directory for 1801* (Philadelphia, 1801); and Jane Aitken, *Census Directory for 1811* (Philadelphia, 1811); all are available at the HSP. The 1772, 1780, 1789, and 1798 Provincial Tax Lists provide data on the possession of taxable wealth and occupations; this material is located in the PCA. The 1756 tax list was published by Hannah Benner Roach, comp., "Taxables in the City of Philadelphia, 1756," *Pennsyl-*

vania Genealogical Magazine, 22 (1961), 3–41. Dwellings are described in detail and their values assessed in the U.S. Direct Tax of 1798: South Ward, 26, Form A; Walnut Ward, 28, Form A; High Street Ward, 4, Form A; East Northern Liberties, 43, Form A; available in the NA. The composition of households are detailed in the U.S. Bureau of the Census, *Heads of Families of the First Census of the United States Taken in the Year 1790: Pennsylvania* (Washington, D.C., 1908); and the U.S. Census Office, *Return of the Whole Number of Persons within the Several Districts of the United States: Second Census* (Washington, D.C., 1800).

Vignettes and biographical information of poor people are contained in the following records of the Guardians of the Poor, located in the PCA: Daily Occurrences Docket (of the Almshouse); Index of Admissions and Discharges (to the Almshouse), 1785–1827; Almshouse Census, 1807–1810; Examination of Paupers, 1822–1844; Register of Relief Recipients, 1814–1815 and 1828–1832; Indentures, 1751–1797; and Indenture Papers and Bonds, 1795–1799.[1] Various characteristics of prisoners and their crimes are contained in the following records, in the PCA: Prisoners for Trial Docket, Philadelphia County Prison; and Prison Sentence Docket, 1794–1810, Philadelphia County Prison.

Data on family life, inheritance, and the property that individuals owned at death were gathered from Records of the Supreme Court, Divorce Papers, 1786–1815, Record Group 33, PHMC; Wills, Philadelphia County Probate Records, 1683–1901, RW; and County Probate Records, Inventories of Estate, 1683–1801, RW. Stories of the lives of Revolutionary War soldiers and their families, as told in their own words, are contained in Petitions for Revolutionary War Pensions, NA. The traits of itinerant people apprehended by the authorities and confined to the workhouse are recorded in the Vagrancy Dockets, 1790–1797 and 1804–1809, PCA.

Data on year of death, age, and religious affiliation of some decedents were obtained from Francis Olcott Allen, comp., "Earliest Records of the Burials in Philadelphia from the Board of Health," *Publications of the Genealogical Society of Pennsylvania* (Philadelphia, 1845), 1:225–250; and Burial Records of the Board of Health of Philadelphia, 1807–1814, GSP. Information about people who were baptized, married, and interred in the cemetery of Gloria Dei church, annotated by the church rector, is contained in Old Swedes Church: Baptism Records, 1789–1822; Marriage Records, 1759–1818; and Burial Records, 1750–1831, GSP.[2]

1. Excerpts of these records have been published by Billy G. Smith and Cynthia Shelton, "The Daily Occurrence Docket of the Philadelphia Almshouse, 1800," *PH*, 52 (1985), 88–116; and Smith and Shelton, "The Daily Occurrence Docket of the Philadelphia Almshouse: Selected Entries, 1800–1804," ibid., 183–205.

2. Excerpts of these records appear in Billy G. Smith and Susan E. Klepp, "The Records of Gloria Dei Church: Burials, 1800–1804," *PH*, 53 (1986), 56–79; and Klepp and Smith, "The

Additional demographic data and information on church affiliation were compiled and families reconstructed from the following sources: First Baptist Church Records, Philadelphia, film 5237; Church Records of the First Reformed Church of Philadelphia, as copied by William J. Hinke, volumes 1–4, film 5232; Second Presbyterian Church, Burials, 1799–1808, film 50042; Second Presbyterian Church, Pew Rent Book, 1779–1781 and 1792–1810, film 505495; Third Presbyterian Church, Church Register, 1768–1839, film 913134; First Presbyterian Church, Register of Marriages, Baptisms, and Communicants, 1760–1806; Journal of Christ Church and St. Peter's Church, Pew Renters, film 49595; all of the above are available from the Genealogical Society of the Church of Latter Day Saints, Salt Lake City, Utah; and the Marriages in St. Michael's and Zion Church, Philadelphia, *Pennsylvania Archives*, 2d Ser., 9:291–458.

Records of Gloria Dei Church: Marriages and 'Remarkable Occurrences,' 1794–1806," ibid., 125–151.

Demographic Conditions
of Philadelphia

A NUMBER OF SCHOLARS have intensely studied Philadelphia's demographic characteristics during the eighteenth century. Calculating reliable population estimates is the initial step in determining the city's vital rates. Since the 1790 federal census was the first conducted in Philadelphia, historians have used various methods to estimate the city's colonial population, resulting in a nearly equal variety of projections.[1] In general, the population of precensus areas is most accurately computed by multiplying the number of houses, taxables, polls, or families by an arithmetic constant. Philadelphia is well suited to this type of analysis since both the number of dwellings and of taxable inhabitants are recorded for many years during the eighteenth century. The crucial problem involves developing proper conversion figures between homes, taxables, and the total population. John K. Alexander initially determined a multiplier to convert the number of houses to population figures, and Gary B. Nash and Billy G. Smith subsequently calculated population estimates based on the total number of taxpayers in the city.[2] Using

1. Carl Bridenbaugh estimated the size of Philadelphia's urban population as 10,000 in 1720, 13,000 in 1743, 23,750 in 1760, and 40,000 in 1775, in *Cities in the Wilderness* (New York, 1955), 143n; and *Cities in Revolt: Urban Life in America, 1743–1776*, rev. ed. (New York, 1971), 224. Sam Bass Warner, Jr., calculated that 23,739 people lived in the city and suburbs in 1775, in *The Private City: Philadelphia in Three Periods of Its Growth* (Philadelphia, 1968), 225. Other figures are offered by Stella H. Sutherland, *Population Distribution in Colonial America* (New York, 1936), 123–124, 128; and Lawrence A. Cremin, *American Education: The Colonial Experience, 1607–1783* (New York, 1970), 573–574.
2. John K. Alexander, "The Philadelphia Numbers Game: An Analysis of Philadelphia's Eighteenth-Century Population," *PMHB*, 98 (1974), 314–324; Gary B. Nash and Billy G. Smith, "The Population of Eighteenth-Century Philadelphia, ibid., 99 (1975), 362–368; and Billy G. Smith, "Death and Life in a Colonial Immigrant City: A Demographic Analysis of Philadelphia," *JEH*, 37 (1977), 863–889.

the 1775 Constables' Returns (a type of census), Sharon V. Salinger and Charles Wetherell established slightly different population figures for the city at the end of the colonial period, but their primary source and some of their assumptions are suspect.[3]

P.M.G. Harris recently produced the best population series by adapting the various estimates to a compelling model of population growth. Those figures form the basis of the population estimates for the pre-1790 period included in Table B.1.[4] The population of Philadelphia for each year during the 1790s is interpolated from the reports of federal census takers in 1790 and 1800.[5] Table B.2 contains the number of houses and taxpayers from which the population estimates are calculated.

The evidence required to establish Philadelphia's death rates are contained primarily in the bills of mortality issued each year by the city's Anglican churches. The bills indicate the number of people buried annually in church cemeteries and in the public grounds for "Negroes" and "Strangers" for many of the years during the second half of the century. Susan E. Klepp has uncovered burial figures from church records and almanacs that are particularly useful for the closing decades of the century.[6]

3. Sharon V. Salinger and Charles Wetherell, "A Note on the Population of Pre-Revolutionary Philadelphia," *PMHB*, 109 (1985), 369–386. Since neither spouses nor relatives of the household heads, other than children, were recorded, the 1775 Constables' Returns undoubtedly missed a considerable number of people. In estimating the city's population, Salinger and Wetherell too readily accepted the tabulations of the constables, thereby arriving at dubious conclusions. They calculated, for instance, that between 22 percent and 36 percent of all households contained only one person, figures that are highly suspect for any eighteenth-century locale. By comparison, only 4 percent of Philadelphia's households contained only one person in 1790, while less than 1 percent of households contained a single person in 1800. These figures are from my counts of 60 percent of the households in the 1790 census and 50 percent of the households in the 1800 census; see U.S. Bureau of the Census, *Heads of Families of the First Census of the United States Taken in the Year 1790: Pennsylvania* (Washington, D.C., 1908), hereafter cited as *First Census*; and U.S. Census Office, *Return of the Whole Number of Persons within the Several Districts of the United States . . .* (Washington, D.C., 1801).

4. P.M.G. Harris, "The Demographic Development of Colonial Philadelphia in Some Comparative Perspective," *Proceedings of the APS*, forthcoming. The entire issue focuses on the city's demographic conditions during the eighteenth century.

5. The federal censuses of 1790 and 1800 provide population data for those years; see *First Census*; and U.S. Census Office, *Return of the Whole Number of Persons*. The annual population estimates are calculated using the geometric method to measure population growth, as explained by George Barclay, *Techniques of Population Analysis* (New York, 1958), 206–207.

6. The Bills of Mortality for 1747 through 1792 (except for 1749, 1750, and 1777 through 1787) are available on microcard, listed from 1750 through 1762 as "An Account of the Births and Burials in Christ-Church Parish," and from 1763 to 1792 as "An Account of the Births and Burials in the United Churches of Christ-Church and St. Peter's," in Charles Evans, *American Bibliography: A Chronological Dictionary of all Books, Pamphlets and Periodical Publications Printed in the United States . . . 1639 . . . 1820* (Chicago, Ill. and Worcester, Mass., 1903–1959), together cited hereafter as Bills of Mortality. The number of deaths in 1750 was computed from information included in the mortality bill of 1751. Burials for the post-Revolutionary period are reported in Thomas Wilson, *Picture of Philadelphia, for 1824, containing the "Picture of Philadelphia, for 1811, by James Mease, M.D." with All Its Improvements Since That Period* (Philadelphia, 1823), 49; Zachariah Poulson, *Poulson's Town and Country Almanac . . .* (Philadelphia,

Table B.1. Estimated population and crude death rates in urban Philadelphia, 1750–1800

Year	Population	Number of burials[a]	Crude death rate (per 1,000 inhabitants)	Five-year moving death rate averages
1750	12,736	716	56	
1751	13,237	926	70	
1752	13,884	673	48	55
1753	14,563	623	43	50
1754	15,084	856	57	50
1755	15,623	502	32	48
1756	16,182	1,104	68	49
1757	16,790	714	42	53
1758	17,422	766	44	57
1759	18,076	1,406	78	51
1760	18,756	957	51	54
1761	19,701	790	40	55
1762	20,694	1,189	57	49
1763	21,737	1,095	50	50
1764	22,832	1,091	48	49
1765	23,982	1,273	53	44
1766	25,191	990	39	40
1767	26,460	809	30	38
1768	27,240	801	29	35
1769	28,042	1,160	41	34
1770	28,802	971	34	36
1771	29,582	1,007	34	39
1772	30,384	1,273	42	36
1773	32,073	1,344	42	37
1774	33,856	1,022	30	
1775	33,290	1,180	35	
1782	38,798	976	25	
1783	39,227	1,536	39	
1784	39,656	1,362	34	31
1785	40,089	1,125	28	31
1786	40,528	1,095	27	28
1787	40,971	1,140	28	26
1788	41,414	998	24	25
1789	41,849	996	24	26
1790	42,520	1,035	24	25
1791	45,049	1,309	29	27
1792	47,578	1,245	26	41
1793	50,107	1,497	30	42
1794	52,636	4,992	95	45
1795	55,165	1,759	32	45
1796	57,694	2,283	40	47
1797	60,223	1,666	28	41
1798	62,752	2,356	38	40
1799	65,281	4,463	68	
1800	67,811	1,762	26	

Source: See text of Appendix B.

Note: Urban Philadelphia includes the city and the suburbs of Southwark and Northern Liberties. Records are unreliable for years not included in sequence, as explained in n. 6.

[a]The number of burials from 1788 through 1790 includes interments for the first eight months of each year and the last four months of the preceding year. From 1791 through 1799 the number of burials comprise interments during the initial seven months of each year and the final five months of the preceding year.

Table B.2. Houses and taxpayers in urban Philadelphia, 1749–1801

Year	Houses (*N*)	Taxpayers (*N*)
1749	2,076	
1751		2,668
1753	2,300	
1756		3,216
1760	2,969	3,318
1767		4,074
1769	4,474	4,185
1772		4,886
1774		5,085
1775		5,609
1777	5,470	
1783	6,000	7,006
1789		7,432
1790	6,784	
1798		11,143
1801	11,200	

Source: John F. Watson reported the contemporary counts of houses in each year before 1777, in *Annals of Philadelphia, and Pennsylvania, in the Olden Time . . .* , 3 vols. (Philadelphia, 1881), 2:404–407; James Mease recorded data for 1783 and 1801 in *The Picture of Philadelphia . . .* (Philadelphia, 1811), 31; 1790 figure from Benjamin Davies, *Some Account of the City of Philadelphia . . .* (Philadelphia, 1794), 17. The numbers of taxpayers before the Revolution are included in Billy G. Smith, "Death and Life in a Colonial Immigrant City: A Demographic Analysis of Philadelphia," *JEH,* 37 (1977), 865. I counted taxpayers in the post-Revolutionary years from the Provincial Tax Lists, PCA.

Note: Records are unavailable for years with missing data and for years not included in sequence.

How reliable are these burial statistics? Scattered evidence suggests that they are dependable, although they may not include all of the deaths in the city. First, independent records of two churches confirm the number of burials attributed to their cemeteries by the bills of mortality.[7] Second, deaths registered by the bills during the final two decades of the century

---

1800), 1; and Mathew Carey, *A Short Account of the Malignant Fever, Lately Prevalent in Philadelphia* (New York, 1970; Philadelphia, 1794), 117. The evidence is easily accessible in Susan E. Klepp, '*The Swift Progress of Population': A Documentary and Bibliographic Study of Philadelphia's Population, 1642–1860* (Philadelphia, 1989); Klepp, "Demography in Early Philadelphia, 1690–1860," *Proceedings of the APS,* forthcoming; and Klepp, "The Demographic Characteristics of Philadelphia, 1788–1801: Zachariah Poulson's Bills of Mortality," *PH,* 53 (1986), 201–221. Because they are the most unreliable, data for the Revolutionary War years have not been included in Table B.1. However, using the church records for the years during the Revolution, Klepp has estimated the following annual death rates per thousand inhabitants for 1777 through 1781: 42, 41, 34, 34, and 32, respectively, in "Demographic Characteristics," *Proceedings of the APS,* forthcoming.

7. The names and ages of decedents interred in two church graveyards are available in Records of Christ Church, vol. 174, and Church Records of the First Reformed Church, vol. 1, 1748–1785, GSP, hereafter cited as Records of Christ Church, and Records of the First Reformed Church.

correspond closely to those recorded by three separate city residents.[8] Third, between 1750 and 1775 the mortality bills annually reported interments in the majority of the cemeteries, including all of the major ones. These sources may have neglected burials in five grounds belonging to smaller denominations, particularly during the late 1760s and 1770s when those churches were first established.[9] However, the overall impact of underregistration of burials in these cemeteries would not have been significant: during the years in which interments are recorded for the five churches, the burials constitute only 5 percent of the city's total deaths.[10]

Other factors contributed to the underregistration of burials. Entombments in family grounds and in graveyards outside the city generally went unrecorded, as did the deaths of Philadelphia's mariners at sea or while in other ports. Because seamen were a large portion of the city's population and worked in a hazardous occupation, the number of their deaths must have been large.[11] The magnitude of these unrecorded burials cannot be estimated accurately. In similar cases, historical demographers often inflate the number of burials by 10 or 15 percent.[12] I have decided not to follow that policy, instead establishing absolute minimum death rates.

The combination of these burial data with the population estimates produces the crude death rates in Table B.1. The column of burials contains the

8. Wilson, *Picture of Philadelphia*, 49; Poulson, *Town and Country Almanac*, 1; and Carey, *Short Account*, 117.

9. The Bills of Mortality recorded burials for each year in thirteen of the nineteen cemeteries in the city between 1750 and 1775. The Third Presbyterian Church, although unfinished, began services in 1768, but its interments appear in the bills only from 1772 to 1775; whether burials occurred before 1772 is unknown. Philadelphians may have been entombed in St. George's Methodist cemetery for ten years after its establishment in 1763, yet the bills note interments there only for 1763 and 1764. The bills indicate burials both for Moravians and Scotch Presbyterians for 1774 and 1775, but the founding dates of their grounds are unknown. Finally, the bills fail to register any burials for the Zion Lutheran Church, even though the church was constructed in 1766. Whether Zion possessed a graveyard of its own or shared one with its sister Lutheran church, St. Michael's, is unknown. The establishment of these churches and cemeteries is detailed in Horace Mather Lippincott, *Early Philadelphia: Its People, Life and Progress* (Philadelphia, 1917), 76–77, 100–101; Norris Stanley Barratt, *Outline of the History of Old St. Paul's Church, Philadelphia, Pennsylvania, 1760–1898* (Lancaster, Pa., 1918), 25–26; Rev. Thomas C. Middleton, "Interments in St. Mary's Burying Ground, Philadelphia, from 1788–1800," *American Catholic Historical Society Records*, 5 (1894), 21–22; and Joseph J. Kelly, Jr., *Life and Times in Colonial Philadelphia* (Harrisburg, Pa., 1973), 145–146.

10. During the years in which burials in their cemeteries were registered, the Third Presbyterian, St. George's, Moravian, and Scotch-Presbyterian churches accounted for approximately 5 percent of Philadelphia's burials. The problem of underregistration of burials is discussed more fully in Smith, "Death and Life," 863–889.

11. To some extent the demise of Philadelphia's mariners while away from home must have been offset by the deaths of transient seamen living temporarily in the city. The significance of mortality among mariners absent from their port of origin is discussed by Maris A. Vinovskis, "Mortality Rates and Trends in Massachusetts before 1860," *JEH*, 32 (1972), 189, 193.

12. See E. A. Wrigley, ed., *An Introduction to English Historical Demography* (London, 1966), 83–84.

Table B.3. Estimated child death rates in select churches, 1751–1775

Period	Anglican infant death rate	Anglican 1-to-3-year-old death rate	Dutch Calvinist 1-to-3-year-old death rate
1751–1752	234		
1753–1755	265	102	
1756–1758	330	145	
1760–1761	202		
1762–1763	145	96	45
1764–1766	138	60	81
1767–1769	98	41	70
1770–1772	112	53	60
1773–1775	106	63	60

Source: See text of Appendix B for data sources (n. 7) and an explanation of methods of calculation.

Note: All death rates are per thousand inhabitants at risk. Records are unavailable for years with missing data and for the year 1759.

"adjusted" number of burials corrected downward from the actual number reported to account for interment in the city's cemeteries of people who had resided outside urban Philadelphia and thus were not part of the population at risk.[13] These adjusted burial figures were used to estimate the death rates.

Christ Church and the Dutch Calvinists maintained records of births and baptisms that permit a measurement, albeit imprecise, of child mortality, an important index of general health conditions. The estimated infant death rates (Table B.3) represent the ratio of the number of burials of children one year of age or younger in each year to the number of infant baptisms in that year. Calculating the death rates of one-to-three-year-old children is slightly more complex. The population at risk of one-to-three-year olds in any single year was computed as the sum of the number of infant baptisms less the burials of children one year of age or younger for the two preceding years. Death rates of children between one and three years old were then estimated as the ratio of their burials to their population at risk.

While this means of estimation is tentative, the accuracy is sufficient to indicate a marked improvement in the death rates of young children in the city at the close of the colonial era. Qualitative evidence reinforces the

13. The annual number of burials in Philadelphia before the Revolution was corrected downward by 7 percent to account for people entombed in the city who had resided in the area surrounding the Pennsylvania capital. I determined this correctional factor by checking the names of people buried both in the Christ Church and in the First Reformed Church cemeteries in 1775 against the Provincial Tax List of Philadelphia county for 1774. Of the deceased taxpayers, 7 percent resided outside of the urban center.

quantitative measurement, since various physicians claimed remarkable progress in child welfare throughout the colonies. Dr. David Ramsay of Charleston, South Carolina, argued that "a great reformation" in infant mortality rates occurred during the second half of the century, while Dr. Benjamin Rush felt that the mortality of Philadelphia's newborns and mothers dropped sharply after 1760. During the early 1790s Dr. William Currie calculated that one of every five babies died before the age of two, a statistic that supports the figures in Table B.3.[14]

Although every church in the city did not keep a record of its baptisms, birth rates can, with some caution, be estimated (see Table B.4). The primary difficulty in establishing these estimates involves calculating the number of baptisms for those denominations that failed to keep records or did not christen infants. To compute that figure, I assumed that the ratio of burials to baptisms in the churches without records matched the ratio in churches that did register interments and baptisms.[15] Susan E. Klepp has used the extant

14. As quoted in Richard Shryock, *Medicine and Society in America, 1660–1860* (Ithaca, 1960), 99. Shryock found fragmentary statistical evidence that pointed in the direction of improved infant mortality in the colonies during this period. Rush's views are noted in Shryock, "A Century of Medical Progress in Philadelphia: 1750–1850," *PH*, 8 (1941), 11. See also William Currie, *An Historical Account of the Climates and Diseases of the United States . . .* (Philadelphia, 1792), 112.

15. For example, six churches recorded 829 baptisms and 481 burials in 1766, making the ratio of burials to baptisms in those churches equal to .58 (see ratio column in Table B.4). The remaining church grounds accounted for 164 burials. Assuming the ratio of burials to baptisms is identical for both groups of churches, I compute that 283 children were born to the members of denominations that did not register infant baptisms. The total number of baptisms in the city is thus calculated as 1,112. This method of estimating births is somewhat hazardous since birth, death, and recording rates for the two groups of churches might vary. However, the potential extent of that variation is minimized by the size and heterogeneity of the sample of churches with recorded infant baptisms. Those churches accounted for approximately 60 percent of the interments in church burial grounds throughout the colonial period and included diverse social and economic groups, as represented by the Anglican, Dutch Lutheran, Old Swedes, Catholic, Dutch Calvinist, and Presbyterian churches.

Scattered evidence supports these computed birth rates. First, the rates of the early 1760s (the most questionable estimates because of their extremely high level) would still be substantial even if only the number of infant baptisms actually recorded was used to calculate the city's birth rates. The total numbers of baptisms registered by the six churches that kept records produce birth rates per thousand inhabitants of 41, 46, 44, and 45 for 1761 through 1764, respectively. Second, the estimated birth rates match those calculated from the 1762 and 1775 Constables' Returns for Walnut ward, PCA. These records contain the number of people and the age of the youngest and oldest child in each household in Philadelphia's Walnut ward during those two years. Of 411 people residing in the ward in 1762, 20 were children younger than one year of age, indicating a minimum birth rate of 49 per thousand. Applying the Anglican infant mortality rate of 152 per thousand for 1762 (Table B.3) yields a birth rate estimate of 57 per thousand. Based on the same analysis, the 1775 Constables' Returns imply a minimum birth rate of 45 per thousand and, using the Anglican infant mortality rate of 100 per thousand for 1775, a birth rate estimate of 50 per thousand. These figures compare closely with the average of the 1761–1762 and the 1774–1775 birth rate estimates in Table B.4, which are 60 and 42, respectively.

Table B.4. Estimated birth rates in urban Philadelphia, 1750–1800

Year	Ratio of burials to births[a]	Number of births	Crude birth rate (per 1,000 inhabitants)	Five-year moving birth rate averages
1750	.57	674	53	
1751	.77	652	49	
1752	.62	563	40	47
1753	.61	573	39	45
1754	.47	784	52	45
1755	.51	684	44	47
1756	.93	781	48	50
1757	.50	892	53	51
1758	.54	907	52	53
1759	.88	1,065	59	55
1760	.64	1,014	54	57
1761	.46	1,146	58	58
1762	.69	1,261	61	59
1763	.65	1,274	59	60
1764	.45	1,408	62	57
1765	.61	1,380	58	55
1766	.58	1,112	44	53
1767	.40	1,364	52	49
1768	.40	1,287	47	46
1769	.70	1,274	45	46
1770	.48	1,263	44	44
1771	.45	1,310	44	45
1772	.63	1,284	42	45
1773	.60	1,555	48	44
1774	.50	1,545	46	
1775	.61	1,301	39	
1782		1,898	49	
1783		1,844	47	
1784		2,047	52	52
1785		2,152	54	54
1786		2,294	57	56
1787		2,520	62	55
1788		2,192	53	54
1789		2,019	48	52
1790		2,094	49	50
1791		2,256	50	49
1792		2,407	50	49
1793		2,511	50	47
1794		2,379	45	47
1795		2,324	42	46
1796		2,847	49	45
1797		2,694	45	44
1798		2,755	44	43
1799		2,648	40	
1800		2,657	39	

Source: See text of Appendix B for data sources (n. 16) and an explanation of methods of calculation.

Note: Records are unreliable for years not included in sequence, as explained in n. 16.

[a]For the following churches that registered infant baptisms: Christ Church, Dutch Lutheran, Old Swedes, Catholic, Dutch Calvinist, and First Presbyterian.

church records to estimate annual birth rates for the 1782–1787 period, while contemporary almanacs recorded baptisms in every church in the city during the final thirteen years of the century.[16]

16. Baptisms during the colonial era are registered in Records of Christ Church; Records of the First Reformed Church; and Bills of Mortality. Birth rate estimates for 1782 through 1787 are in Klepp, "Demographic Characteristics." In that same paper, Klepp calculates from the extant church records the following birth rates during the war years, which have not been included here in Table B.4 because of their unreliability: 31 births per thousand inhabitants for 1777, 29 for 1778, 42 for 1779, 47 for 1780, and 43 for 1781. The annual numbers of baptisms for many years in the post-Revolutionary period are contained in Poulson, *Town and Country Almanac*, 1; and Klepp, "Demographic Characteristics of Philadelphia."

Occupational Structure
of Philadelphia

THE OCCUPATIONAL structure of Philadelphia presented in Table C.1 is reconstructed from various tax lists.[1] Assigning the occupations to distinct groups is difficult since men performing the same jobs often functioned in somewhat different capacities. Shoemakers, for example, manufactured shoes for domestic consumption before the Revolution, but made some footwear for export during the 1790s. And while butchers and bakers served the local market primarily, they also cut meat and baked bread for overseas shipment. For the sake of consistency with other historical studies, I used categories established by Jacob M. Price and by Gary B. Nash.[2] I modified these classifications slightly by shifting cordwainers and hatters from the industrial to the service sector (since they produced goods primarily for the local market); moving porters from the "other service" category (where they were identified with servants) to "travel and transport"; and placing laborers in a separate category.

The statistics in Table C.1 are biased toward wealthy and stable occupational groups since tax assessors sometimes excused potential taxpayers from paying taxes because of their poverty and frequently missed others who were mobile. This tax assessment problem was particularly acute for mariners. If calculated solely from tax lists, mariners accounted for about 5 percent of the

1. The 1756 tax list is in Hannah Benner Roach, comp., "Taxables in the City of Philadelphia, 1756," *Pennsylvania Genealogical Magazine*, 22 (1961), 3–41. The 1774 data were compiled from figures in Jacob M. Price, "Economic Function and Growth of American Port Towns in the Eighteenth Century," *Perspectives in American History*, 8 (1974), 177–183. The 1772, 1780, 1789, and 1798 Provincial Tax Lists are in the PCA.
2. Price, "Economic Function," 177–183; and Gary B. Nash, *The Urban Crucible: Social Change, Political Consciousness, and the Origins of the American Revolution* (Cambridge, Mass., 1979), 387–391.

Table C.1. Occupational structure of Philadelphia taxpayers, 1756–1798

Economic sector	1756 (%)	1772 (%)	1774 (%)	1780[a] (%)	1789[b] (%)	1798[a] (%)
Government	1.2	1.1	1.3	2.4	.5	1.7
Service/manufactures	51.5	49.6	48.2	54.3	59.4	53.3
Professional	4.1	3.6	2.9	2.6	3.9	5.0
Retail and local wholesale	6.4	6.0	6.8	10.3	11.8	10.9
Retail crafts	19.9	17.0	17.4	23.4	23.1	17.9
Building crafts	9.7	11.2	9.7	7.1	9.7	11.3
Travel and transport	9.5	10.0	10.3	9.4	8.2	6.0
Other services	1.9	1.8	1.1	1.4	2.7	2.2
Industrial	16.3	15.8	17.0	17.8	16.4	12.7
Textile	1.5	1.3	2.5	2.4	1.2	.2
Leather and fur using	2.4	1.9	2.6	3.2	2.6	1.8
Food and drink processing	1.8	1.3	1.3	1.2	1.7	.9
Shipbuilding and fitting	2.3	4.1	4.2	1.9	1.1	1.6
Metal crafts	3.4	2.9	2.3	4.0	3.6	3.4
Furniture	1.2	1.4	.8	1.6	1.5	1.8
Miscellaneous trades	3.6	3.0	3.2	3.4	4.8	3.0
Commerce	25.8	25.9	20.0	18.1	16.7	27.1
Mariners	8.4	10.6	7.5	5.1	2.0	5.2
Merchants and assistants	17.4	15.3	12.0	13.0	14.7	21.9
Laborers	5.1	7.6	13.9	7.4	7.0	5.1

Source: See text of Appendix C for data sources (n. 1) and an explanation of the occupational structure.

[a]Based on a sample of 60 percent of the tax list.

[b]Based on a sample of 80 percent of the tax list.

male work force in late eighteenth-century Philadelphia. However, in all likelihood, mariners were the largest occupational group in the city, accounting for as much as 20 percent of the free male work force on the eve of the Revolutionary War.[3] The poverty and mobility of seamen caused the majority of them to be excluded from the tax lists. Only 164 seamen appear on the 1772 Provincial Tax List, for example, but other sources indicate a much greater number of sailors in the city. During the 1770s, about two hundred ship captains belonged to Philadelphia's Society for the Relief of Poor and

3. Eric Foner, *Tom Paine and Revolutionary America* (New York, 1976), 45. The minutes of the Philadelphia County Commissioners record the citizens too poor to pay taxes. Three volumes (1718–1766) are in the PCA, another volume (1771–1774) is in the HSP, and a final volume (1774–1776) is in the Tax and Exoneration Records, PHMC. Gary B. Nash found that 471 adult males were excused from taxation in 1772 because of their poverty, in "Poverty and Poor Relief in Pre-Revolutionary Philadelphia," *WMQ*, 3d Ser., 33 (1976), 22–23. See also Sharon V. Salinger and Charles Wetherell, "A Note on the Population of Pre-Revolutionary Philadelphia," *PMHB*, 109 (1985), 372–373.

Distressed Masters of Ships, Their Widows and Children.[4] Since vessels averaged approximately six crew members, the city probably contained roughly 1,200 merchant seamen in the early years of the decade. Between July 1, 1770, and July 1, 1771, custom officials collected a tax of 71,164*d*. from Philadelphia sailors at the rate of 6*d*. for each month they drew wages.[5] This suggests a total of 1,186 seamen in the city, assuming each mariner worked ten months during the year, and a larger number if they worked less than that. Corroborating this estimate is a remark by the customs house officer in 1770 that "there are not less than a thousand Seamen here at this time."[6]

4. Society for the Relief of Poor and Distressed Masters of Ships, Their Widows and Children, Quarterly Payments, 1768–1776, HSP.

5. By an act of Parliament in 1696, this tax, which supported the Greenwich Hospital for disabled seamen, was paid by sailors who served on ships owned by citizens of the British Empire. The collections from Philadelphia mariners during 1770–1771 are recorded in the Customs House Papers, vol. 11, 1409, HSP.

6. Ibid., vol. 10 (not paginated).

Maritime Economy of Philadelphia

Ship entrances rather than clearances from the port are used in Table D.1 to assess the maritime activity of Philadelphia because data on the former are more accurate than those for the latter. By most counts, arrivals generally exceeded departures each year.[1] Some craft docking at the wharves must have been worn and not fit to make another voyage, thereby accounting for part of the difference between entrances and exits. But the number of vessels making their final journey should have been offset by the clearances of newly constructed ships setting sail for the first time. The difference between entrances and departures probably resulted from the greater vigilance of customs house officials in counting and reporting the arrivals. They had a greater incentive to keep track of incoming vessels than outgoing since they collected duties on their cargoes and Greenwich Hospital taxes from their crews.

The annual number of ship entrances in Table D.1 during most of the third quarter of the eighteenth century were tabulated by Walter Winningham from weekly reports in Philadelphia newspapers.[2] Customs house officials recorded the 1760–1762 and 1769–1772 figures.[3] Thomas M.

---

1. Walter Gaines Winningham, "The Commerce of Colonial Philadelphia" (Ph.D. diss., Yale University, 1933), 426–427. See also the U.S. Bureau of the Census, *Historical Statistics of the United States: Colonial Times to 1970*, 2 vols. (Washington, D.C., 1975), 2:1181, hereafter cited as *Historical Statistics*.

2. Winningham, "Commerce of Colonial Philadelphia," 426–427.

3. The 1760–1762 data are from An Account of the Number of Ships and Vessels Entering Inwards and Outwards in the British Plantation and the Continent of North America . . . , Manuscript Large Collection, Massachusetts Historical Society, hereafter cited as An Account of the Number of Ships. The 1769–1772 data are from *Historical Statistics*, 2:1181. Using a register of tonnage duties, Thomas M. Doerflinger tallied slightly different figures for the number of annual ship entrances between 1766 and 1775, in *A Vigorous Spirit of Enterprise: Merchants and Economic Development in Revolutionary Philadelphia* (Chapel Hill, N.C., 1986), 373.

Table D.1. Number and registered tonnage of vessels entering the port of Philadelphia, 1750–1800

Year	Number of vessels	Registered tonnage of vessels	Number of vessels per inhabitant	Registered tonnage per inhabitant
1750	317	17,964	.025	1.4
1751	365	20,754	.028	1.6
1752	472	26,932	.034	1.9
1753	484	27,699	.033	1.9
1754	470	26,950	.031	1.8
1755	385	21,244	.025	1.4
1756	388	21,437	.024	1.3
1757	381	21,065	.023	1.2
1758	483	26,406	.028	1.5
1759	566	30,949	.031	1.7
1760	522	29,375	.028	1.6
1761	552	28,018	.028	1.4
1762	645	33,329	.031	1.6
1763	601	31,054	.028	1.4
1764	637	35,678	.028	1.6
1765	611	36,872	.025	1.5
1766	703	42,456	.028	1.7
1767	667	40,280	.025	1.5
1768	621	37,862	.023	1.4
1769	698	42,333	.025	1.5
1770	750	47,489	.026	1.6
1771	719	41,740	.024	1.4
1772	730	42,300	.024	1.4
1773	761	46,398	.024	1.4
1774	882	53,776	.026	1.6
1775	809	49,325	.024	1.5
1781	192		.005	
1782	308		.008	
1784	1,087	74,839	.027	1.9
1785	1,068		.027	
1786	1,074		.026	
1787	986		.024	
1788	901		.022	
1789	1,261		.030	
1790	1,354		.032	
1791	1,448	47,000	.032	1.0
1792	1,161		.024	
1793	1,420		.028	
1794	1,868		.036	
1795	2,007		.036	
1796	1,869		.032	
1797	1,540		.026	
1798	1,461		.023	
1799	1,268		.019	
1800	1,587		.023	

Source: See text of Appendix D.
Note: Records are unavailable for years with missing data and for years not included in sequence.

Doerflinger counted the number of vessels docking at the wharves in 1781 and 1782 from a register of duties paid on imports.[4] Statistics for annual ship arrivals from 1784 through 1800, with the exception of 1789, were recorded by the port officials of Philadelphia, as reported by E. P. Cheyney.[5] Since Cheyney indicated that these records were incomplete in 1789, the figure noted by James Mease is used instead.[6]

The data on registered tonnage of ships entering the port in 1760, 1761, 1762, 1764, 1765, 1769 through 1772, and 1784 in Table D.1 are contained in records of the customs house, while the figure for 1791 was determined and adjusted by James F. Shepherd.[7] I calculated the total tonnage of docking vessels in other years by the following method: The size of ships arriving from different ports varied; transatlantic vessels, for example, were considerably larger than coastal craft. By determining the average tonnage of ships from various trading areas, weighting each of these mean tonnages by the proportion of vessels from each port, and then summing the products, I computed an average tonnage of ships entering Philadelphia annually. Multiplying this figure by the number of ship arrivals per year yielded the total tonnage.[8]

The number and tonnage of vessels are, of course, an imperfect measure of

4. Doerflinger, *Vigorous Spirit of Enterprise*, 208.

5. E. P. Cheyney, "Annual Report of the Secretary of Internal Affairs of the Commonwealth of Pennsylvania, Part 3," in *Industrial Statistics*, vol. 19.1891 (Harrisburg, Pa., 1892), 22c, 32c, hereafter cited as *Industrial Statistics*.

6. James Mease, *The Picture of Philadelphia* . . . (New York, 1970; Philadelphia, 1811), 52–53.

7. Figures for 1760–1762 are from An Account of the Number of Ships; data for the other pre-Revolutionary years are in *Historical Statistics*, 2:1181; and the 1784 statistic is in *Industrial Statistics*, 22c. James Shepherd calculated that an average of forty-seven thousand registered tons of ships entered the port annually between 1790 and 1792, in "British America and the Atlantic Economy," in Ronald Hoffman et al., eds., *The Economy of Early America: The Revolutionary Period, 1763–1790* (Charlottesville, Va., 1988), 42–43. Economic historians have used somewhat different statistics for tonnage docking at Philadelphia during these years. Shepherd used lower figures for the 1760–1762 and 1768–1772 periods, in "British America," 42. Thomas M. Doerflinger employed considerably higher figures for the years 1766–1769, in "Enterprise on the Delaware: Merchants and Economic Development in Philadelphia, 1750–1791" (Ph.D. diss., Harvard University, 1980), 145.

8. John J. McCusker records the mean size of ships in 1741, 1742, and 1768 through 1772 that cleared for Great Britain and Ireland, Southern Europe, the West Indies, and the American coast, in "Sources of Investment Capital in the Colonial Philadelphia Shipping Industry," *JEH*, 32 (1972), 146. Using the growth rate in the mean tonnage of ships between the early 1740s and the late 1760s, I computed the average tonnage of vessels arriving from each of the four areas. From my tabulations of the weekly reports of harbor activity in the *Pennsylvania Gazette* (Philadelphia), I determined the proportion of ships entering from each of the four areas during the period 1756–1762. I used these proportions to weight the average size of vessels from each area in order to compute the mean tonnage of all ships entering Philadelphia. Other relevant studies include McCusker, "The Tonnage of Ships Engaged in British Colonial Trade during the Eighteenth Century," *Research in Economic History*, 6 (1981), 73–105; and Christopher J. French, "Eighteenth-Century Shipping Tonnage Measurements," *JEH*, 33 (1973), 434–443.

the physical volume of trade. Ships did not always sail with full cargoes, and advances in packaging and stowing probably increased the quantity of goods shipped per ton during this period. These data, however, are the best available continuous series of the dimensions of the city's maritime activity, and their indication of changes in commerce should be sufficiently accurate to support the arguments presented.

The official value of Pennsylvania's trade with England (Table D.2), bread and flour exports from Philadelphia (Table D.3), and the ships entering the port from various geographic areas (Table D.4) also describe the maritime economy. Several problems are inherent in the data about the magnitude of trade in Tables D.1, D.2, D.3, and D.4. The figures measure transactions that occurred at the "port of Philadelphia," a customs district that stretched fifty-five miles along the Pennsylvania side of the Delaware River. Ships docking at any point along that shoreline were recorded as entering the port of Philadelphia, and the vast majority of vessels undoubtedly did arrive in the city itself. But if the proportion of ships landing outside the city yet within the customs district decreased (and the proportion docking in the city increased correspondingly), then the per capita volume of trade actually passing through Philadelphia could have expanded slightly rather than declined during the third quarter of the century. However, a very large shift in the area where ships landed would have been required to produce such a change in the trend in the per capita volume of trade. It is more likely that the number of ships docking outside the city grew during the second half of the century with the construction of new wharves immediately north and south of the city. A comparison of the number and tonnage of ship entrances, the official volume of trade with England, and the exports of bread and flour with the population of Philadelphia thus probably maximizes the physical dimension of the city's commerce per capita between 1750 and 1775.[9] When the volume of trade is matched with the population of the entire area (represented by the number of inhabitants in Pennsylvania), a similar pattern of decline in the volume of trade per capita emerges.[10]

Simon J. Crowther tabulated the data for shipbuilding during the colonial period that appear in Table D.5.[11] The number and tonnage of vessels calculated by John J. McCusker for those years are slightly lower than the figures computed by Crowther, but the trends of both series are similar.[12]

9. For the definition of the "port of Philadelphia," see John J. McCusker, "The Pennsylvania Shipping Industry in the Eighteenth Century," MS, 1973, HSP, 22–23.

10. Population figures for Pennsylvania are available in *Historical Statistics*, 1:33, 2:1168.

11. Simon J. Crowther, "The Shipbuilding Industry and the Economic Development of the Delaware Valley, 1681–1776" (Ph.D. diss., University of Pennsylvania, 1970), 91–92; and Crowther, "The Shipbuilding Output of the Delaware Valley, 1722–1776," *Proceedings of the APS*, 117 (1973), 93.

12. McCusker, "Pennsylvania Shipping Industry," 148–149.

Table D.2. Official value of Pennsylvania's exports to and imports from England, 1750–1791

Year	Value of imports	Value of exports	Value of imports per Philadelphia inhabitant	Value of exports per Philadelphia inhabitant
1750	218	28	17	2.2
1751	191	24	14	1.8
1752	202	30	14	2.2
1753	246	39	17	2.7
1754	245	31	16	2.0
1755	144	32	9	2.0
1756	200	20	12	1.2
1757	268	14	16	.8
1758	261	21	15	1.2
1759	498	22	28	1.2
1760	708	23	38	1.2
1761	204	39	10	2.0
1762	206	38	10	1.8
1763	284	38	13	1.7
1764	435	36	19	1.6
1765	363	25	15	1.0
1766	327	27	13	1.1
1767	372	38	14	1.4
1768	432	59	16	2.2
1769	200	26	7	.9
1770	135	28	5	1.0
1771	729	32	25	1.1
1772	508	29	17	.9
1773	426	37	13	1.2
1774	626	70	18	2.1
1784	654	69	16	1.7
1785	345	56	9	1.4
1786	204	23	5	.6
1787	206	35	5	.8
1788	203	30	5	.7
1789	350	36	8	.9
1790	728	51	17	1.2
1791	697	54	16	1.2

Source: The official values of imports and exports are from the U.S. Bureau of the Census, *Historical Statistics of the United States: Colonial Times to 1970,* 2 vols. (Washington, D.C., 1975), 2:1176.

Note: Values of imports and exports are in thousands of pounds sterling; values of imports and exports per inhabitant are in pounds sterling. Records are unavailable for years not included in sequence.

Table D.3. Bread and flour exports from Philadelphia, 1752–1792

Year	Tons of bread and flour exported	Tons exported per inhabitant of Philadelphia
1752	14,963	1.08
1759	20,516	1.13
1760	20,681	1.10
1761	20,532	1.04
1762	20,035	.97
1763	16,080	.74
1765	18,714	.78
1768	18,378	.67
1769	34,151	1.22
1770	32,696	1.14
1771	29,564	1.00
1772	30,159	.99
1773	29,608	.92
1774	31,125	.92
1784	21,831	.55
1785	21,769	.54
1786	15,347	.38
1787	19,372	.48
1788	21,796	.53
1789	36,900	.88
1791	28,363	.63
1792	34,401	.72

Source: Figures for 1752, 1773, 1774, 1791, and 1792 in Helen Louise Klopfer, "Statistics of Foreign Trade of Philadelphia, 1700–1860," MS, 1936, Eleutherian Mills-Hagley Library, Wilmington, Del., 173, 247; data for 1759 through 1765 in Customs House Papers, vol. 2, HSP; statistics for 1768 through 1772 from Public Record Office, Customs 16/1, as noted in Arthur L. Jensen, *The Maritime Commerce of Colonial Philadelphia* (Madison, Wis., 1963), 292; figures for 1784 through 1789 in C. Bjork, *Stagnation and Growth in the American Economy, 1784–1792* (New York, 1985), 56–57. Tons are equal to 2,240 pounds, as measured at the time. Barrels of flour were converted at 224 pounds each for 1759–1763 and 196 pounds each for 1784–1792; barrels of bread were converted at 140 pounds and 95 pounds each during the two periods, respectively. These weights are based on information in Klopfer, "Statistics of Foreign Trade," 40, 45.

Note: Records are unavailable for years not included in sequence.

Table D.4. Ships entering Philadelphia from select geographic areas, select years 1750–1787

	Percentages						
Port of departure	1750–1754	1756–1762	1769	1770–1774	1781–1782	1784–1785	1786–1787
British Isles	12.8	6.3	11.2	9.5	0	11.1	5.9
Southern Europe	9.7	4.6	15.5	13.2	6.0	3.5	6.0
West Indies	33.3	38.7	30.7	34.4	28.4	27.1	25.1
American coast	44.3	50.3	42.7	42.9	65.6	58.3	62.9

Source: Figures for 1750–1754 and 1770–1774 in Arthur L. Jensen, *The Maritime Commerce of Colonial Philadelphia* (Madison, Wis., 1963), 290; data for 1756–1762 based on my count of weekly reports in the *Pennsylvania Gazette* (Philadelphia); proportions for 1769 calculated from statistics in U.S. Bureau of the Census, *Historical Statistics of the United States: Colonial Times to 1970,* 2 vols. (Washington, D.C., 1976), 2:1181; percentages for 1781 and 1782 in Thomas M. Doerflinger, *A Vigorous Spirit of Enterprise: Merchants and Economic Development in Revolutionary Philadelphia* (Chapel Hill, N.C., 1986), 208; and figures for the remaining years of the 1780s computed from Customs House Records, Inward Entries, Mar. 15, 1784 to Apr. 30, 1785, and June 1, 1786 to Dec. 29, 1787, HSP.

Statistics for the years after 1780 are from E. P. Cheyney and Andrew Burnaby.[13] Since the figures for the 1780s were based on the "registered" tonnage of ships built, they were adjusted upward by 40 percent to transform them into "measured" tonnage.[14] Cheyney's data for the 1790s were not modified because registered and measured tonnage became equivalent after 1789.

These shipbuilding statistics are marred by a problem similar to the one related to commerce, as discussed above. The district to which the data apply included all of the Delaware Valley, making it impossible to distinguish the vessels constructed in the city from those fashioned in shipyards in neighboring areas. The vast majority of shipyards in the district were located in Philadelphia and its suburbs, but during the second half of the century shipyards in other areas increased in number and prominence. Because they include ships constructed outside the city, the statistics in Table D.5 and Figure 10 exaggerate the actual level of production, a distortion greater at the end of the period than at its beginning.[15]

13. *Industrial Statistics*, 53–54c, 74c; and Andrew Burnaby, *Burnaby's Travels through North America*, ed. Rufus Rockwell Wilson (New York, 1904), 188.

14. The basis of this adjustment is explained by McCusker, "Sources of Investment Capital," 148; and Shepherd, "British America," 43. Doerflinger apparently failed to make these necessary adjustments when he used shipbuilding statistics, in *Vigorous Spirit of Enterprise*, 265.

15. For a further discussion of this problem, see McCusker, "Pennsylvania Shipping Industry," 27–28.

Table D.5. Shipbuilding in Philadelphia, 1750–1796

Year	Number of vessels constructed	Total measured tonnage of vessels constructed	Mean measured tonnage per vessel	Total measured tonnage per inhabitant of Philadelphia
1750	39	2,580	66	.20
1751	30	1,803	60	.14
1752	31	2,029	65	.15
1753	16	1,180	74	.08
1754	20	1,640	82	.11
1755	17	1,051	62	.07
1756	20	1,058	53	.06
1757	21	1,636	78	.10
1758	18	1,402	78	.08
1759	28	1,711	61	.09
1760	30	2,191	73	.12
1761	26	1,969	76	.10
1765	31	2,114	68	.09
1766	21	1,555	74	.06
1767	21	1,810	86	.07
1768	17	1,096	64	.04
1769	18	1,335	74	.05
1770	18	1,880	104	.06
1771	20	1,913	96	.06
1772	21	2,220	106	.07
1773	31	3,438	111	.11
1774	29	3,397	117	.10
1775	19	2,910	153	.09
1781	7	1,867	267	.05
1782	22	3,577	162	.09
1783	40	7,412	185	.19
1784	44	8,838	201	.22
1785	20	4,020	201	.10
1786	13	1,508	116	.04
1787	16	2,740	171	.07
1789	19	2,966	211	.07
1793	46	8,145	177	.16
1794	23	4,118	179	.08
1795	31	5,506	178	.10
1796	22	3,907	178	.07

Source: See text of Appendix D.
Note: Records are unavailable for years not included in sequence.

Distribution of Taxable
Wealth in Philadelphia

VARIOUS PROBLEMS in tax assessment mean that tax lists must be used with considerable care to measure the nature and changes in the wealth structure: First, Philadelphia's tax assessments significantly understate the actual degree of economic inequality among residents. Because many important assets such as mortgages, land owned outside the city, bonds, specie, shop inventories, book debts, and ships were excluded from taxation, much of the wealth in the city, particularly that of the richest Philadelphians, was missed by assessors. A few figures indicate the magnitude to which tax data underestimate actual inequality. The total assessed value of taxable items in the city in 1772 amounted to approximately eighty thousand Pennsylvania pounds. At that time, according to John J. McCusker's estimates, Pennsylvanians had invested over ten times that amount in ships alone. If, as is probable, wealthy Philadelphians invested a large part of that untaxed capital, then the extent of actual inequality was much greater than that indicated by the tax data. Furthermore, the assessors excused a large number of people who could not afford to pay taxes, while they often missed a great many mariners and other transients among the mobile poor (as discussed in Appendix C). The real concentration of wealth thus very significantly exceeded that measured from tax data.[1]

1. John J. McCusker's calculations are in "Sources of Investment Capital in the Colonial Philadelphia Shipping Industry," *JEH*, 32 (1972), 154. Gary B. Nash discusses this type of bias in Philadelphia's tax lists, in "Urban Wealth and Poverty in Pre-Revolutionary Philadelphia," *Journal of Interdisciplinary History*, 6 (1976), 547–548. For tax lists in Connecticut, Jackson Turner Main reaches a similar conclusion that the "tax system was regressive in that the property which escaped taxation belonged mostly to the rich," in "The Distribution of Property in Colonial Connecticut," in James Kirby Martin, ed., *The Human Dimensions of Nation Making: Essays on Colonial and Revolutionary America* (Madison, Wis., 1976), 55.

Second, it is essential to avoid confusing actual transformations in the wealth structure with spurious changes created by varying assessment procedures. Methods of taxation were identical for all of the pre-Revolutionary years except 1756 in Table 2. As calculated from the 1756 tax list, the five tax brackets (from poorest to wealthiest) in Table 2 owned 11.4, 16.4, 32.6, 14.2, and 25.4 percent of the taxable wealth, respectively. But two factors distorted this measured wealth distribution, resulting in overstatement of existing equality when compared to other colonial wealth profiles. In 1756, tax assessors excluded single men from taxation and set the minimum assessment substantially higher than in any other year before 1775. Table 2 thus presents an adjusted wealth distribution for 1756, as calculated by Gary B. Nash.[2] He added 11 percent of propertyless taxpayers to compensate for the absence of unmarried taxpayers and lowered the minimum assessment to equal that of the other years before the end of the colonial era. This adjusted wealth structure is more inequitable than the unadjusted one: the Schutz coefficient of inequality (where 0 denotes perfect equality and 1 denotes total inequality) is .45 for the former and only .35 for the latter.

One other change in the assessment procedure, however, means that the 1756 adjusted wealth structure may artificially inflate inequality in comparison to other pre-Revolutionary wealth distributions. After 1764, tax laws directed assessors to impose a "personal" or "occupation" assessment—based on their evaluations of the "worth" of each taxpayer's job—in addition to specific assessments on each item of real property, such as horses, cows, slaves, indentured servants, and real estate.[3] This assessment of occupations, for reasons explained below, skewed the wealth structure toward equality. Thus, the 1756 adjusted wealth profile, which does not include assessments on occupations, distorts the distribution of taxable resources toward inequality when compared to other pre-Revolutionary wealth structures in Table 2. As a result, the intensification of inequality between 1756 and 1767 is even greater than it appears in Table 2.

The statistics in Table 2 indicate that taxable resources grew less concentrated in the hands of the rich both in 1780 and 1798, but these impressions are primarily artifacts resulting from shifting methods of assessment. In reality, the wealth structure in 1780 was only slightly more equal than in 1774, and the wealth profile was actually less equal in 1798 than in 1789. Larger assessments on occupations and smaller valuations on real property exaggerated the 1780 and 1798 wealth structures toward greater equality. A

2. Nash, "Urban Wealth and Poverty," 551–552.

3. Between 1725 and 1764 taxes were assessed only on real property, as specified in the tax law of 1725. A new tax law in 1764 indicated that in addition to an assessment on realty, "all trades, occupations and professions shall be rated at the discretion of the assessor"; James T. Mitchell and Henry Flanders, comps. *The Statutes at Large of Pennsylvania from 1682 to 1801*, 18 vols. (Philadelphia and Harrisburg, Pa., 1896–1911), 4:10–26, 5:201–212, 6:357 (quotation), 344–360, hereafter cited as *Statutes at Large*.

detailed examination of changing assessment procedures and the distribution of taxable wealth in one city ward, Chestnut, should clarify the way in which the city's measured wealth structure was distorted during the final decades of the century.

The primary components of the total tax assessment consisted of the tax assessors' evaluations of the worth of occupations, real estate, and merchandise (Table E.1), and the relative weight of these three strongly influenced the distribution of total assessments. Because the range of assessments on occupations was much narrower than the variation of assessments on either real estate or merchandise, the distribution of assessments on the former (Table E.2) was more equal than the distribution of assessments on either of the latter (Table E.3).[4] Hence, the greater the value of occupational assessments relative to assessments on real estate and merchandise, the more the distribution of total assessments was skewed toward greater equality. Occupational assessments comprised an abnormally large component of total assessments in both 1780 and 1798. In Chestnut ward during those two years, assessments on occupations accounted for approximately 45 percent of the total tax assessments, whereas in 1779 and 1789 they comprised only 17 percent and 25 percent, respectively, of total assessments (Table E.1). Nearly all of the greater equality in the distribution of total tax assessment in Chestnut ward in 1780 and 1798 (Table E.4) thus can be attributed to the increased worth accorded by the tax assessors to occupations.

The change in the wealth structure of Chestnut ward between 1795 and 1796 illustrates the dramatic impact that an increased emphasis on occupational assessments could have on the distribution of total assessments. The 1796 tax law set upper and lower limits on assessments of various occupational categories for the first time.[5] As a result, the proportion of total assessments constituted by occupational assessments rose from 19 percent in 1795 to 56 percent in 1796. The distribution of total assessments correspondingly was distorted toward greater equality, as the Schutz coefficient dropped from .72 to .53 within one year (Table E.4). Changes in the procedure of assessing occupations in 1780 affected the wealth structure of Chestnut ward between 1779 and 1780 in a similar, if less significant, fashion. The 1780 tax law stipulated that occupations were to be rated by the commissioners rather than by assessors, as had been customary.[6] The net effect was that occupational assessments in 1780 comprised a much larger proportion of total assessments than they had in 1779 (Table E.1). Thus,

4. This distributional difference meant that taxpayers in the low-income brackets were hit hardest by taxes on occupations and affected least by assessments on real estate and merchandise. Similarly, wealthier taxpayers paid relatively more in realty taxes and less in occupational taxes.

5. *Statutes at Large*, 15:324–325.

6. Ibid., 10:205–214.

Table E.1. Components of tax assessments in Chestnut ward, select years 1779–1798

	Proportion of assessments			
Items assessed	1779 (%)	1780 (%)	1789 (%)	1798 (%)
Occupation (personal)	17.2	43.3	25.0	46.5
Wrought plate	2.9	0.8	1.7	a
Riding chairs	0.8	0.6	1.1	a
Horses	0.7	0.4	1.4	1.5
Cows	2.0	0.2	0.3	0.1
Slaves	2.3	1.4	1.4	0.1
Indentured servants	0.0	0.0	.3	0.0
Real estate	31.3	42.6	68.8	51.9
Merchandise	42.7	10.7	a	a

Source: Provincial Tax Lists, PCA.
ᵃNot taxed.

Table E.2. Distribution of assessments on occupations in Chestnut ward, select years 1779–1798

Tax bracket (%)	1779 (%)	1780 (%)	1789 (%)	1795 (%)	1796 (%)	1798 (%)
0–10	1.9	1.1	2.3	2.2	2.2	2.4
11–20	4.2	2.2	3.9	3.2	2.4	3.7
21–30	5.9	3.1	4.3	3.8	3.4	4.4
31–40	8.2	3.8	5.3	6.0	5.0	4.4
41–50	8.6	6.2	6.9	8.1	6.6	5.8
51–60	9.8	6.7	8.7	9.8	8.7	8.8
61–70	11.9	10.2	9.4	11.9	10.4	9.1
71–80	12.8	11.7	13.2	14.4	16.3	15.4
81–90	15.3	17.5	15.1	14.4	17.8	18.6
91–100	21.3	37.5	30.9	26.2	27.2	27.4
Schutz coeff.	.21	.37	.29	.22	.32	.31

Source: Provincial Tax Lists, PCA.

even though the distribution of assessments on real estate remained essentially the same and the distribution of assessments on merchandise and occupations actually grew more unequal between 1779 and 1780, the distribution of total assessments in those two years became more equal merely because of the relative increase in the value of assessments on occupations. What appears at first glance to be a substantial leveling of wealth in a one-year period (with the top 10 percent holding 43.9 percent instead of 47.4 percent of the wealth) was actually created by an alteration in the assessment procedures.

Table E.3. Distribution of assessments on real estate and merchandise in Chestnut ward, select years 1779–1798

	Real estate				Merchandise	
Tax bracket (%)	1779 (%)	1780 (%)	1789 (%)	1798 (%)	1779 (%)	1780 (%)
0–10	0.0	0.0	0.0	0.0	0.0	0.0
11–20	0.0	0.0	0.0	0.0	0.0	0.0
21–30	0.0	0.0	0.0	0.0	0.0	0.0
31–40	0.0	0.0	0.0	0.0	0.0	0.0
41–50	0.0	0.0	0.0	0.0	0.2	0.0
51–60	0.0	0.0	0.0	0.0	1.7	0.0
61–70	0.0	0.0	0.0	0.0	4.0	0.4
71–80	0.0	0.0	0.0	0.0	9.1	3.5
81–90	20.1	23.7	11.5	2.3	15.9	12.8
91–100	79.9	76.3	88.5	97.7	69.1	83.3
Schutz coeff.	.80	.80	.80	.88	.65	.76

Source: Provincial Tax Lists, PCA.

Table E.4. Distribution of total assessed wealth in Chestnut ward, select years 1779–1798

Tax bracket (%)	1779 (%)	1780 (%)	1789 (%)	1795 (%)	1796 (%)	1798 (%)
0–10	0.1	0.0	0.0	0.0	0.0	1.4
11–20	0.4	0.8	0.0	0.0	0.0	2.1
21–30	1.2	1.5	0.3	0.0	0.0	2.5
31–40	2.2	2.2	1.2	0.0	0.0	2.5
41–50	3.2	3.7	1.7	0.7	3.4	2.9
51–60	5.1	6.0	2.4	1.2	5.4	4.7
61–70	6.6	8.8	3.7	2.5	7.8	5.6
71–80	12.7	13.3	6.2	4.7	10.9	9.4
81–90	21.2	20.0	17.6	9.2	16.8	14.8
91–100	47.4	43.9	67.0	81.7	55.8	54.2
Schutz coeff.	.51	.47	.65	.72	.53	.49

Source: Provincial Tax Lists, PCA.

The effect of changes in the items taxed also requires brief consideration. Merchandise, wrought plate, and riding chairs were assessed in 1780, but the first was exempted from taxation in 1789, and all three were excluded from assessment in 1798.[7] Assessments on plate and riding chairs accounted for a very small proportion of total assessments, less than 3 percent in 1780 and

7. Ibid., 10:205–214, 11:454–486, 15:324–325.

1789, and the failure to tax these items in 1798 consequently affected the distribution of total assessments only minimally. The value of merchandise was more significant, constituting nearly 11 percent of total assessments in 1780. The bulk of the tax that would have been levied on merchandise in 1789 and 1798 was instead assessed on real estate, representing a partial transfer of the tax burden from merchants and shopkeepers to a broad assortment of property owners. Because the distribution of assessments on real estate approximated the distribution of assessments on merchandise, at least in 1779 and 1780, the exemption of merchandise from taxation in 1789 and 1798 probably had little impact on the distribution of total assessments in those years.

One technical difficulty in handling Philadelphia's post-Revolutionary tax lists should be noted. The primary tax entry for each person included only the property located at the taxpayer's place of residence. Taxable property owned in other city wards was listed by the assessors of those wards under the renter's name, although the owner was identified. Thus, assessments on properties not associated with a taxpayer's primary residence had to be reassigned to the actual property owner in order to obtain his or her correct total assessment. An accurate depiction of the total assessment of each taxpayer was therefore possible only if a tax list for the entire city existed. Such lists are extant for only a few years after 1776, and it was the completeness of the lists in 1780, 1789, and 1798 that at least partially dictated their use in establishing the city's wealth distributions, even though the results were not easily comparable because of the factors discussed above.[8]

8. Thomas M. Doerflinger decided not to include property listed under the renter's name with the assets of the owner, meaning that many of the merchants he studied owned considerably more valuable taxable assets than what he examined; see *A Vigorous Spirit of Enterprise: Merchants and Economic Development in Revolutionary Philadelphia* (Chapel Hill, N.C., 1986), 385–386.

Wages and Prices

THE FOLLOWING NOTES correspond to the sources of laborers' wages in Table 5. The location of all records is the HSP unless otherwise indicated:

a. Bills and Receipts, 1751–1754 and 1755–1767, Coates and Reynell Papers.
b. Matron and Steward's Cash Books, Pennsylvania Hospital Records, APS.
c. Minutes of the County Commissioners.
d. Ledger of Isaac Zane, 1748–1759.
e. Clifford Papers, Correspondence, vol. 2, 1760–1762.
f. Account Book, Folder: Brigantine *Elizabeth* Accounts, Richard Waln Collection.
g. Dutilh and Wachsmuth Papers, Miscellaneous Box 1704–1800, folder 32.
h. Isaac Norris Cash Book.
i. Norris Fairhill Papers (accounts of the addition to the statehouse in the early 1750s).
j. Minutes of the Friendship Carpenters' Company, 1768–1776.
k. Minutes of the Commissioners for Paving Streets.
l. U.S. Department of Labor, "Wages and Hours of Labor," *Bulletin of the United States Bureau of Labor Statistics*, 128 (Washington, D.C., 1913), 21.
m. Bills, Receipts, and Accounts, Shippen Family Papers, vols. 28–30, 1754–1822.
n. Incoming Correspondence: Bills and Receipts of John Cadwalader, Cadwalader Collection, Boxes 1–6, 12–14.
o. Ledgers of Joshua Humphreys, 1766–1777, 1772–1773, 1784–1805, Joshua Humphreys Papers.
p. Ledger of Mifflin and Massey, 1760–1763.
q. Journal of John and Peter Chevalier.
r. Ledger of Joseph Wharton, Wharton Papers.
s. Business Papers of Levy Hollingsworth, Hollingsworth Collection, sec. 7: Bills, 1751–1789, and sec. 3: Invoices, 1764–1789.

t. Samuel Morris's Day Book, 1755–1767, and Ledgers, 1755–1772, 1761–1763.

u. Thomas A. Biddle Shipbook, 1784–1792.

v. Forde and Reed Papers.

w. Account of Richard Meadow, Ball Papers.

x. Business Records of Stephen Girard, APS.

y. Philip Benezet's Account with Sloop *Sally*, Dreer Collection.

z. *Minutes of the Supreme Executive Council of Pennsylvania: Colonial Records of Pennsylvania* (Harrisburg, Pa., 1852).

z1. Donald R. Adams, Jr., "Wage Rates in Philadelphia, 1790–1830" (Ph.D. diss., University of Pennsylvania, 1967).

The actual prices and the price relatives of each of twenty-seven food items purchased by the Pennsylvania Hospital are available in Billy G. Smith, "'The Best Poor Man's Country': Living Standards of the 'Lower Sort' in Late Eighteenth-Century Philadelphia," in Glenn Porter and William H. Mulligan, Jr., eds., *Working Papers from the Regional Economic History Research Center*, vol. 2 (Greenville, Del., 1979), 50, 64–68. Table F.1 contains weighted indices for the twenty-seven foodstuffs and the nineteen items that constituted the Philadelphia laborers' diet in Table 3. Table F.2 presents the prices and wages in 1762, the base year for all of the indices constructed in chapter 4. Tables F.3, F.4, F.5, and F.6 include indices of the cost of twenty-seven different food items.

Table F.1. Diet cost indices (base year = 1762), 1754–1800

Year	Food price index: 27 items evenly weighted	Food budget index: 19 items weighted by diet[a]
1754	97	94
1755	90	89
1756	99	99
1757	98[b]	98[b]
1758	88[b]	80[b]
1759	98	89
1760	98	95
1761	92	86
1762	100	100
1763	110	115
1764	98	101
1765	97	91
1766	94	90
1767	90	94
1768	81	86
1769	77	81
1770	91	90
1771	94	96
1772	102	99
1773	89	90
1774	94	100
1775	97	89
1776	123	97
1783	168	154
1784	134	147
1785	117	123
1786	116	124
1787	112	119
1788	92	99
1789	94	107
1790	109	134
1791	114	130
1792	114	131
1793	131	143
1794	142	161
1795	173	207
1796	185	227
1797	183	192
1798	150	183
1799	181	188
1800	156	201

Source: See chapter 4.

Note: Records are unreliable for years not included in sequence.

[a]Estimated Diet in Table 3.

[b]Interpolated from the wholesale cost of 9 food items in Anne Bezanson, Robert D. Gray, and Miriam Hussey, *Prices in Colonial Philadelphia* (Philadelphia, 1935), 422–423.

Table F.2. Bases of indices: Prices and wages in 1762

Item	Estimated average price or wage rate[a]
Food cost for family of four	£30.66 per year
Rent of laborers	£9.0 per year
Rent of mariners	£10.58 per year
Rent of cordwainers	£19.63 per year
Rent of tailors	£20.37 per year
Firewood cost	£5.6 per year
Clothing cost for family of four	£8.5 per year
Wages of laborer	3.8s. per day
Wages of seamen	£4.12 per month
Wages of mate	£5.38 per month
Wages of ship captain	£7.50 per month
Beef	3.54d. per pound
Mutton	3.36d. per pound
Pork	3.59d. per pound
Veal	3.41d. per pound
Meat	3.48d. per pound
Oysters	3.23s. per bushel
Chicken	.78s. each
Milk	.89s. per gallon
Chocolate	1.83s. per pound
Coffee	.92s. per pound
Bohea tea	8.65s. per pound
Philadelphia rum	3.82s. per gallon
Wine	6.57s. per gallon
Molasses	2.83s. per gallon
Butter	.98s. per pound
Fine salt	4.37s. per bushel
Pepper	2.50s. per pound
Muscovado sugar	.56s. per pound
Vinegar	1.11s. per gallon
Rice	2.05d. per pound
Potatoes	4.79s. per bushel
Turnips	2.50s. per bushel
Corn	3.62s. per bushel
"Indian" meal	3.86s. per bushel
Bran	1.97s. per bushel
Common flour	1.83d. per pound
Middling flour	1.76d. per pound

Source: See chapter 4.

[a] Pennsylvania currency.

Table F.3. Cost indices of food items, turnips–middling flour (base year = 1762), 1754–1800

Year	Turnips	Corn	Cornmeal	Bran	Common flour	Middling flour
1754						
1755					88	88
1756						
1757						
1758						
1759	60				95	85
1760						
1761						
1762	100	100	100	100	100	100
1763	129		130	116	105	104
1764	70		97	95	74	73
1765	105		130		78	
1766	166	138	78		88	97
1767	130	101	127		100	97
1768		88	97		101	93
1769		87			81	82
1770	47	101	91	76	84	89
1771	50	111	91	85	103	100
1772		101	119	93	117	
1773		98	123	90	93	
1774		83	114	80	100	102
1775	50	94		102	82	80
1776	107				73	
1783	115	180	194	83	105	122
1784	80	110	146		131	128
1785	50	119	134		131	131
1786	50	122	130	118	119	
1787		110	128		122	118
1788	40	76	92		103	91
1789	70	78	91		128	112
1790		97	136		175	162
1791		104	115		126	
1792	75	134	125		116	106
1793	80		146		143	
1794			161		165	129
1795			194		283	241
1796			240		314	
1797		160	212		212	
1798	100	101	188		195	
1799		108	196		189	
1800	60		169		240	

Source: Matron and Steward's Cash Books, Pennsylvania Hospital Records, APS.
Note: Records are unreliable for years not included in sequence.

Table F.4. Cost indices of food items, butter–potatoes (base year = 1762), 1754–1800

Year	Butter	Fine salt	Pepper	Muscovado sugar	Vinegar	Rice	Potatoes
1754	70			89		147	
1755	63			88		130	
1756				89		122	
1757							
1758							
1759	74			89		131	
1760	87			120			
1761	90			96			
1762	100	100	100	100	100	100	100
1763	117	87	107	97	102	98	111
1764	105	100	116		75	95	
1765	88	96	113	104	95	94	73
1766	90	114		96	105	105	42
1767	87	67	60	104	90	105	42
1768	68			93		102	37
1769	69			93			31
1770	99	55	201	99	90	86	36
1771	98	51	150	104	100	92	40
1772	98	51	147	89	86	115	63
1773	99	71	100	89	90	101	25
1774	100	57		193	68	91	
1775	94	100	150	96	86	84	35
1776	121	135	280	197	83		79
1783	176	163	177	139		193	209
1784	173	86	140	143		157	107
1785	142	84		120		147	77
1786	119	60	140	127	90	137	78
1787	108	69		113	90	154	50
1788	85	47		107		127	78
1789	101	47	120	110	60	118	34
1790	122	59		129	60	122	43
1791	121	61	160	123	49		
1792	137	69	150	183	62	114	64
1793	153	117	153	175	126	157	77
1794	172	132	150	161		118	104
1795	183	134	150	166	135	261	98
1796	175	152	166	166			106
1797	196	138				238	
1798	187	141					63
1799	181	149		268			
1800	194	143				135	65

Source: Matron and Steward's Cash Books, Pennsylvania Hospital Records, APS.
Note: Records are unreliable for years not included in sequence.

Table F.5. Cost indices of food items, milk–molasses (base year = 1762), 1754–1800

Year	Milk	Chocolate	Coffee	Bohea tea	Philadelphia rum	Wine	Molasses
1754	112						
1755	103	66					
1756	103						
1757							
1758							
1759	93				170		
1760	93						
1761					105		100
1762	100	100	100	100	100	100	100
1763	133	105	102	83	105	123	100
1764	131	91	138	85	94	112	59
1765		85	54	85	98	107	68
1766	75	100	54	69	81	84	
1767	75	91	54	67	96	84	65
1768	75				94		65
1769	75				79		62
1770	75	80	145	72	105	76	92
1771	75	75	154	61	105		
1772	75	71	147	53	131	183	68
1773	75	64	117	81		107	59
1774	75	73	93	63	107	93	
1775	75	114	106		193	99	
1776	75	137	146			99	
1783	188	129	199	80	220	304	230
1784	188	85	124	52	119	107	82
1785	112	91	138	35	124	112	63
1786	150	70	151	35	112	97	68
1787		66	168	35		114	78
1788	112	59	155	31	100	118	66
1789		60	173	25	131	118	75
1790		58	143	25	144	114	89
1791	169	59	127	33	157		102
1792	169	69	164	35			132
1793	149	75	145	35	196		118
1794		80	157	32			186
1795	169	100	172	40			190
1796		101	214				179
1797		111	236				142
1798							
1799							222
1800		125	209				

Source: Matron and Steward's Cash Books, Pennsylvania Hospital Records, APS.
Note: Records are unreliable for years not included in sequence.

Table F.6. Cost indices of food items, beef–chicken (base year = 1762), 1754–1800

Year	Beef	Mutton	Pork	Veal	Meat[a]	Oysters	Chicken
1754	106	82	84	88			
1755	102	89	63	81			
1756	108	94	95	83			
1757							
1758							
1759	99	86	89	101			
1760	116	94	84	90			
1761	85			73			
1762	100	100	100	100	100	100	100
1763	132	118	131	113		104	96
1764	131	111	133	119		83	
1765	115	113	107	99			
1766	99	102	97	94			
1767	106				112	114	
1768					93		
1769					93		
1770			111		93		
1771			111		101	117	
1772			111		103	113	
1773					103		100
1774					103		
1775					103		
1776		104			103		
1783	146	149	160	169	166	178	192
1784	149		153	136	172	201	249
1785	131		153	117	147	182	160
1786	138	126	171	132	131	155	182
1787	132	138	162	148	129		
1788	103	110	109	110	108	85	
1789	107	104	111	90	101	93	
1790	111	119	135	105	115	124	
1791	117	132	143	125	128	139	
1792	115		145	115			
1793	124	149	169	130	144		
1794	154	161	153	167	172		
1795	184	171	243	178	167		
1796	169	192	179	174	223		
1797	169	201	178	180			
1798		184	181	161			
1799		189	163	148			
1800		187	185	162			

Source: Matron and Steward's Cash Books, Pennsylvania Hospital Records, APS.
Note: Records are unreliable for years not included in sequence.
[a]Includes beef, mutton, pork, and veal.

Appendix G. Residential Segregation in Philadelphia

Table G.1. Residential segregation in each city ward, select years 1772–1798

Tax bracket (%)	Index of dissimilarity for each ward									
	Mulberry	Walnut	South	Upper Delaware	North	Middle	High Street	Dock	Chestnut	Lower Delaware
					1772					
1–20	−10.0	+.9	+2.3	+.4	+.1	+2.4	+.8	+1.6	+1.3	+.2
21–40	+14.7	−1.8	−1.0	−1.8	−3.4	−.1	−1.3	−.9	−.9	−3.4
41–60	+10.2	−1.6	−.6	0.0	−3.1	−2.9	−.9	+.4	−1.2	−.3
61–80	−2.4	+1.4	−1.3	+.9	+2.3	−2.4	+.2	−.3	+.5	+1.1
81–100	−10.5	+.6	+.9	−.1	+3.3	+4.0	+1.0	−.7	+.3	+1.2
					1789					
1–20	−16.3	+1.4	+.9	+3.7	−3.9	+8.4	+1.3	−.9	+1.2	+4.2
21–40	+15.5	−2.2	−3.2	−1.2	−4.5	−3.8	−2.1	+5.8	−2.5	−1.7
41–60	+6.2	+.6	−1.6	+3.3	+2.6	−6.0	−.4	−3.3	+.6	−2.0
61–80	+1.8	+.3	+1.5	−1.5	+4.9	−1.2	−2.7	−2.1	+.2	−1.1
81–100	−7.1	−.1	+2.3	−4.3	+.9	+2.7	+4.0	+.5	+.4	+.7
					1798					
1–20	+10.7	−1.5	+6.2	+3.2	−15.5	−3.1	+4.8	−2.9	−.6	−1.2
21–40	+16.0	−1.4	−1.8	+4.6	−6.4	−9.0	−2.4	+6.4	−2.4	−3.6
41–60	−2.5	−1.1	−4.4	−4.2	−7.0	+5.6	+1.5	+7.0	+3.0	+2.1
61–80	−13.3	+3.3	−2.8	−2.0	+13.7	+5.1	−3.5	−1.1	−2.0	+2.8
81–100	−10.9	+.9	+2.8	−1.6	+15.3	+1.5	−.4	−9.5	+1.9	+.1

Source: 1772, 1789, and 1798 Provincial Tax Lists, PCA.
Note: The index of dissimilarity measures the degree to which a group of people clustered in each ward in higher or lower proportions than their proportion of the city's total population. Larger index numbers indicate greater segregation.

Index

Library of Congress Cataloging-in-Publication Data

Smith, Billy Gordon.
  The "lower sort": Philadelphia's laboring people, 1750–1800   /   Billy G. Smith
    p.   cm.
  ISBN 0-8014-2242-6 (alk. paper)
  1. Working class—Pennsylvania—Philadelphia—History—18th century. I. Title.
HD8085.P53S65   1990
305.5′62′0974811—dc20   89-46174